Eliot Freidson, Editor

THE
PROFESSIONS
AND THEIR PROSPECTS

THE PROFESSIONS

AND THEIR PROSPECTS

THE PROFESSIONS
AND THEIR PROSPECTS

Eliot Freidson, *Editor*

HT
687
.F73

SAGE PUBLICATIONS   Beverly Hills / London

Portions of this volume appeared in the March-April, 1971 issue of The American Behavioral Scientist *(Volume 14, Number 4), published by Sage Publications, Inc.*

For information address:

SAGE PUBLICATIONS, INC.
275 South Beverly Drive
Beverly Hills, California 90212

SAGE PUBLICATIONS LTD
St George's House / 44 Hatton Garden
London EC1N 8ER

Printed in the United States of America
ISBN 0-8039-0174-7 (cloth)
ISBN 0-8039-0937-3 (paper)
Library of Congress Catalog Card No. 72-84048

SECOND PRINTING

For
EVERETT CHERRINGTON HUGHES

FOREWORD

Much of what we feel is true of professions in general tends to be derived from our knowledge of one profession in particular. This is so in part because it is difficult for any one person to know much about more than one profession in any great and secure detail, and in part because we really have rather little systematic, empirical information about most of the professions. This book is an attempt to contribute to a remedy by bringing together sixteen original papers (seven composing an issue of *America Behavioral Scientist* 14 [1971] 475-597) reporting work on a rather varied collection of occupations which have been loosely called professions.

The papers were not selected to represent a single conceptual orientation, but rather the variety of orientations and questions present in sociology today. Furthermore, the emphasis of the papers is largely on evaluating the role of the professions in society today, and assessing their likely roles in the future. While each author had a particular problem in mind, and was not attempting to review all that is known about the profession with which he was concerned, he was encouraged to provide references to what he believed to be a fair selection of some of the basic works on that profession. In this sense, while each paper should stand on its own feet, it is hoped that it can also serve the student as both stimulus and point of entry into the study of a particular analytical issue or of a particular profession.

Any collection of papers can be arranged in a variety of ways, each way a function of the purpose one has in mind. Because it is not possible to anticipate the variety of purposes which a reader or an instructor may have, I have chosen to use a very broad and general arrangement. Thus, the collection is loosely divided into three parts, the first being addressed to comparatively general issues without concentration on any particular profession, the second devoted to particular professions, and the third to a brief look at the equipment of sociology itself for the study of professions.

GENERAL ISSUES

In the first chapter of Part One, I try to sketch out the analytical framework within which the study of professions might be placed, a framework devoted to analyzing the organization of control over work. I suggest that professions are an instance of a particular principle of organization which is both logically and substantively in contrast with the principle generally employed by sociologists. This occupational principle inheres in the worker's authority over his own work, and may be contrasted to the administrative principle, whereby tasks are created and assigned to workers by a managerial hierarchy making use of the authority of office. The increasing professionalization of this century, I suggest, may be moving us toward a serious challenge to the preeminence of managerial and bureaucratic authority in the future.

If professions are defined primarily by the way in which they control their own work, then the critical question for evaluating their performance lies in the effectiveness of the way they control their work in the public interest. Daniels evaluates the extent to which professions generate their own responsible modes of self-regulation through effective ethical codes, systems of recruitment and training, and review of performance subsequent to training and credentialling. Her conclusions do not favor leaving the professions alone to control themselves without lay interference.

Daniels' analysis deals with the way professional organization controls the work performed by individual members of the profession. Implicit in that analysis is a conceptual distinction explored self-consciously by Ritzer—how an occupational organization can be "professional" and how an individual member of an occupation can be "professional." Once the distinction is recognized, we can see how the phrases, "professional nonprofessionals" and "unprofessional professionals" are not contradictory. And by the same token, we are led to avoid definitions of professions which include within themselves definitions of the characteristics of individuals, which do not necessarily follow from organizations.

The remaining papers in Part One are concerned with assessing the social significance of the professions and their prospects in the society of the future. Engel and Hall show how the organized circumstances surrounding the work of traditionally free professionals are changing. They are less and less likely to be able to operate as self-employed entrepreneurs in a lucrative, protected market, and they are less and less likely to be able to work alone, unobserved by others. They are becoming increasingly dependent on the skills of other occupations in an increasingly complex division of labor. The authors see a new kind of profession emerging in the future, one which is in some ways less autonomous and dominant, but in other ways freed from circumstances which have in the past prevented its members from performing effectively the functions for which they possess true expertise.

Engel and Hall are concerned largely with the circumstances surrounding professional role-performance. Role-performance, however, is in some sense structured by the organization of the occupation to which the performer belongs. Haug and Sussman are concerned primarily with how and why workers choose one mode of occupational organization rather than another. They focus on the new service occupations of the present day which claim but which have not gained professional status. Such occupations are faced with problems of organizing themselves so as to gain both economic security and social recognition. The choice they make, as well as the choices traditional professionals face once they are primarily employees, will have great significance for their position in the society of the future and for the public interest. Traditional forms of unionism and professionalism may be adopted, but it is also possible that quite new forms of occupational organization may be invented for these new purposes.

In conclusion to Part One, Mok reviews what many writers believe to be the critical role of the professional man of knowledge in the society of the future. Such a society is thought to depend on the innovative activities of professionals in general and scientists in particular. But given the social trend which is reducing the traditional autonomy of the professions, Mok believes that the conditions under which truly creative innovation can take place are disappearing at the same time as which the importance of innovation to the viability of society is increasing.

PARTICULAR PROFESSIONS

In the context of prophecies of a technocracy emerging in the postindustrial society, Perrucci examines a profession often granted technocratic prospects—engineering. He suggests that the profession today is organized so poorly that it cannot generate the power necessary to serve a truly technocratic role. Fragmented into specialties without a common core, its members heterogeneous in their training and professionalism, engineering is seen to be in a position only to implement goals dictated by industry and government. To assert and implement an independent mission it must be organized otherwise.

Montagna discusses another occupation with technocratic potential—public accountancy. He describes the source and substance of its strength and the changes taking place in its core tasks. Organized far more coherently than engineering, it is a far more likely candidate for the role of technical advisor to the directors of the major institutions of our society. In assessing the likely substance of the profession's advice, Montagna points to the implicit ideology, or "domain assumption" of the profession; it is oriented toward improving the efficiency of society as it is presently constituted rather than changing basic structural sources of difficulty.

With the paper of Zola and Miller we turn to look at the prototypical profession, medicine. They see the increasing specialization of knowledge and technique, conflicting orientations to social policy and other internal factors splitting the "community" of medicine to the point where its coherence as an organized profession is eroding. Furthermore, from outside the profession challenge comes from new occupations claiming professional mandate and from the increasingly sophisticated demands of the consumer, whose voice is being in some sense strengthened and organized by new modes of financing health care. These, and other forces, could convert the organization of medicine in the future into something resembling engineering today.

Ference, Goldner, and Ritti discuss the changes occurring in the oldest established profession—the priesthood of the Roman Church. In the course of doing so, they delineate a taxonomically unusual form of occupational organization whereby the profession is an essentially self-contained organization, recruiting, training, employing, coordinating and supervising the work of its own members through its own professionally staffed administrative hierarchy composed of colleague-superiors. Occupationally based as the structure of the Church may be, however, structural differences between those performing the everyday work of the priesthood and those engaged in ordering and coordinating their efforts have led to attempts at collective organization of the practicing professionals, the priests. The thrust of that attempt lies in reducing the power of members of the hierarchy and strengthening the occupational principle of collegiality, thereby "reprofessionalizing" the organized profession. Whatever the outcome of this movement, its context represents a provocative challenge to our concepts of professional and administrative organization.

The priest, like the engineer and the accountant, is an employee. A persistent theme running through the contemporary literature of the professions, including a number of papers in this volume, is the compatibility of professional status and performance with employment in a complex organization. On balance, most writers seem to believe that employment in some way reduces professional autonomy. However, their data come from reports by employed individuals, and neglect the larger dimension of occupational organization. In his paper, Marcus discusses how the weak, traditionally salaried occupation of schoolteaching, which has never gained full professional status in the United States, is organizing itself in such a fashion as to erase many of the past consequences of employment, and even gain new strength. Interestingly enough, contrary to conventional expectations, he sees increased organizational size, complexity, administrative centralization and even specialization to have encouraged the development of a strong occupational organization. The organization is called a union but it seeks "professional" working conditions as well as economic security. The former are designed to give the workers far more control over what work they do and how, as well as over who may legitimately observe and evaluate their work. Such "unionism" in effect strengthens professionalization. Of course, as Marcus points out, both public expectations and changes in the labor market can operate as countervailing forces to long-term success.

In Ruzek's paper, we are confronted with an occupation similar in prestige to schoolteaching, and similar in its traditional employee status, but different in its task and organization. Working in a variety of institutions with great differences in goals and tasks, wishing to serve a therapeutic advice role but often obliged to serve as an agent of social control, the social worker is seen to be a captive professional with a mixed mandate. Occupational organization is weak, without the support of state licensing. Employed by lay-controlled agencies, social workers cannot determine the character of the services they provide, and while their supervisors tend to be fellow social workers, agency goals and policies seem to be dominant in specifying what work is done and how. When the social worker feels that the welfare of the client would benefit by violating agency rules, only arbitrary individual action which may or may not benefit the client seems to be possible. Responsible professional control of discretionary acts does not seem to be a presently viable alternative to administrative control of agency work.

In the next paper, Etheridge addresses herself to what might be called the mentality of the profession—the characteristic way it thinks and talks about a problem of work. Like all professions, law claims to be committed to the ethical ideal of service, service equally to the poor and the rich. Recently pushed by the requirement imposed on the profession by the Supreme Court to provide counsel for the indigent, lawyers have been engaged in a revealing debate over which of two alternative modes of providing counsel should be instituted. As Etheridge notes, it is characteristically taken for granted in the debate that so long as it is lawyers who serve them, indigent defendants will get good service. The debate is thus preoccupied with which lawyers will serve them from the public purse, and how they will get paid. The debate has not reflected the fact that both public defender and assigned counsel systems have about the same consequences for the indigent in comparison with the nonindigent. Indeed, it may be that the characteristic claim of service to mankind which professions make is as much an unquestioned assertion that everything and anything a professional does is *by definition* service to humanity as it is an assertion that professionals are obliged to determine what it is that does serve humanity and how they might better strive to do so.

Finally, it must be pointed out that defects in the effective self-regulation of the quality of work are not restricted to one or two odd cases. They also seem to lie in the professions of those who write papers for this volume. Lewis' paper brings us into that domain, asking whether the "universalistic" criterion of competent performance is used when recommending individuals for jobs in academe. Analyzing letters of recommendation, he finds that more is known and discussed about the individual's capacity to get along with his colleagues than about his skill at teaching or doing research. That the former is important in what is essentially a social enterprise cannot be denied: that the latter is so little emphasized in face of the claim that competence is the essential criterion by which choice of colleagues is justified is something else again.

THE STUDENTS OF PROFESSIONS

The last part of this volume constitutes an unfortunately brief hint of the issues involved in the way the questions asked of other professions may also be asked of the professional who studies other professions—the sociologist. Paul Halmos, concerned with the importance of the personal service professions in present-day society, examines the values underlying the way sociologists have reacted to the phenomenon. He suggests that there is a hidden bias toward pessimism in sociological analysis, a bias which concentrates on "threatening catastrophes, manifest wrongs, and blatant failures." (Of course, others have accused sociology of precisely the reverse—glossing over waste, corruption and inhumanity.) He points out that the personal service professions need the knowledge and disciplined modes of analysis of sociology to help them work effectively, but that in order to be motivated to work they also need a hopeful, optimistic view of the nature of man and his possibilities, and of the value of their work to the improvement of the human situation. Since the sociological stance Halmos describes obviously fails to satisfy that need, the relations between the two are problematic.

Finally, there is the issue of the adequacy of the knowledge claimed by a profession—in the case of sociology, the basis on which it claims its status as a science which deserves recognition and a regular seat at policy-making councils. Phillips reviews the evidence available on the amount of variance which sociological explanations have accounted for, and on the reliability and validity of what are taken as the facts to be explained or as the explanation of the facts. The picture he draws is dark indeed, particularly when one takes into account the consequences of taking error as truth and establishing harmful courses of action on that basis. But even if it does contain a large proportion of "objective fact" and secure generalization, the knowledge of sociology, like the knowledge of engineering, medicine, social work and other professions, both can and should be examined from the outside, rather than being taken for granted. Indeed, here as elsewhere in this volume, the point is less to provide definitive statements about professions than to display some of the stances toward analysis which can enhance our understanding of professions and their position in our society both today and tomorrow.

—*Eliot Freidson*

CONTENTS

PART I

GENERAL
ISSUES

Chapter 1

PROFESSIONS AND THE
OCCUPATIONAL PRINCIPLE

ELIOT FREIDSON

For countries presently in an advanced stage of industrialization, the professions have come to assume an importance which has been of increasing interest to scholars and practical men alike. While the usage of the word is highly confused, and its definition for purposes both of scholarship and social accounting a matter of wearisome debate, the phenomena addressed are of very special theoretical and practical importance (cf. Parsons, 1968). The growth of the professions in the twentieth century represents the rebirth of a principle for organizing work which has been virtually dormant since the Industrial Revolution. It might be called the occupational principle, one which is implied, though almost completely undeveloped, in Durkheim's vision of society as a division of labor. It is logically and substantively in contrast to what might be called the administrative principle, which figures prominently in Max Weber's view of the rationalization of society. Let us examine the two.

Author's Note: *I wish to acknowledge with thanks the useful critical comments on an earlier version of this paper by Arnold Arluke, Arlene Kaplan Daniels, William A. Form, Mary E. W. Goss, and Charles Perrow.*

THE ADMINISTRATIVE PRINCIPLE

The theory of formal or complex organization is one of the most highly developed fields in sociology today. Its essential strategy of analysis may be seen to be derived from a choice to follow out the ramifications of an administrative principle of organization. That principle is implied by emphasis on such things as "bureaucracy," "management," hierarchy," "administration" and the like. The source of authority for the organization of work is found in the administrator or manager—i.e., in the authority of the incumbents in formal offices in a hierarchy. The worker who produces the essential goods or services which justify the existence of the organization is ordered by his superiors in the hierarchy. As Max Weber analyzed the phenomenon, it consists in the imperative coordination of work on the basis of the legitimate authority of office.

Emphasis on the administrative principle has sound empirical justification in history, for it was the owner-entrepreneur and his administrative and technical staff who were responsible for the radical transformation of work during the course of the Industrial Revolution. Everyone knows how products which were once created by craftsmen came to be created by machines which were tended by men hired as mere unskilled hands. In this revolution in the organization of work, the machine-tending task was a creation of management, and management instructed the worker about what he should do and how he should do it. The worker was defined by his general skill level, and by his administratively created job title in the organization. As such, he had no definite occupational identity and in fact could not be said to belong to a particular occupation except in the loosest of terms. Such rationalization in essence destroyed occupation as an organization of men committed to a particular kind of work independently of the institution in which they happened to perform it: occupation was dissolved and reconstituted into general skill class and particular job titles.

THE EMPIRICAL WEAKENING OF
THE ADMINISTRATIVE PRINCIPLE

The administrative principle of organizing and controlling work is of course a conceptual construct designed to point to important elements of the world of empirical experience. Like any concept, it does not describe the world completely and faithfully so much as highlight particular elements in it. Its usefulness is evaluated partly by its "fit" with that world. Up until this century, it has been quite faithful to the essential facts of the organization of work in manufacturing enterprises. But when governmental regulation imposed standards of employment, safety and hygiene on management, and when the workers themselves organized into stable collective bargaining units, the character of the authority of management over the organization of work became considerably less direct and straightforward. From that point in history on, models of work organizations which presuppose a truly mono-cratic administration or management could only be literally inaccurate even if still analytically useful.

Apart from governmental regulation of work organizations, which may be seen as a higher level of rationalization and application of the administrative principle than the actions of management, the rise of industrial trade unionism represents a weakening of management's capacity to control and organize work and as an assertion of worker control. But it is a rather incomplete form of control over work, an important but nonetheless highly "impure" empirical instance of the occupational principle. The industrial union represents a source of the organization of work which largely influences economic and other terms and conditions of work, but generally it does not influence the content of work itself. What the job should be, how it should be performed, and who should perform it pretty much remain matters to be determined by management, and management remains fairly, even if not entirely, free to continue to fragment, mechanize and rationalize tasks in the same way it did at the outset of the Industrial Revolution. However, yet another source of control over work has developed in the twentieth century which, unlike unionization, removes or withholds from the hands of management the authority to create and direct the substance, performance and even the goals of the work itself. That source of organization stems from the professionalization of occupations.

PROFESSIONALIZATION AND ADMINISTRATION

Professionalization might be defined as a process by which an organized occupation, usually but not always by virtue of making a claim to special esoteric competence and to concern for the quality of its work and its benefits to society, obtains the exclusive right to perform a particular kind of work, control training for and access to it, and control the right of determining and evaluating the way the work is performed (cf. Vollmer and Mills, 1966). It represents a basis for organizing jobs and work in a division of labor which is entirely different from the administrative principle. It is not a historically new form of organization, since it was manifested in earlier days primarily in the guilds and the crafts. But by the middle of the twentieth century its renewed vigor established it as a source of control which may well rival that of management.

Part of its recent vigor might stem from the strength it gains from the growing number of workers obtaining or aspiring to professional status, and from the class position of their leaders—educated members of the upper-middle class who have become committed to careers of performing productive or substantive rather than entrepreneurial or managerial labor. The contemporary professions might be regarded as an educated, middle-class variant of the occupational principle of organization already represented by the working-class crafts, the difference between the two being that the claim for autonomy and self-control among professions is usually based on formal "higher" education rather than on trade school or long apprenticeship in practicing some manual skill said to require complex judgment.

In any case, when an occupation has become fully professionalized, even if its work characteristically goes on in an organization, management can control the resources connected with work, but cannot control most of what the workers do and how they do it. Indeed, the position of management in such a situation is so far removed from the kind of administrative authority sketched out by Max Weber that it could be argued that the use of a model predicated on the administrative principle obscures more than it illuminates. This is not to say that one must deny the empirical fact that there is an administration: rather, one questions only its capacity for imperative coordination. If one were to use instead an occupational model, one could conceive of the work organization as being composed of an administrative framework organized monocratically, but without authority over work, and a set of jobs whose performance is determined and organized by the external occupational groups to which the workers belong, with workers possessing the basic authority over work. Jobs become opportunity points in occupational careers extending across organizations and created and organized by occupations; they are not, as they are in conventional industrial organizations, mere isolated task positions in individual plants created by management for its own purposes, and having no independent existence.

It would be one thing if professionals constituted only one isolated set of workers in a plant, all others subject to administrative and industrial union control. This is largely the case with contemporary manufacturing organizations where, while we do read of the problems posed to and by management in the research and development departments manned by scientists and engineers within the organization, the issues raised do not pervade the entire organization (cf. Marcson, 1960; Kornhauser, 1962). In such cases, the central tasks of production remain the duty of line workers whose jobs, as I have already noted, remain formulated, evaluated and controlled by management. It is quite another thing in professionalized service organizations like law firms, hospitals, correctional agencies, social agencies, schools, accounting firms and research organizations. There, the central task around which all others swing is performed or controlled by professional or would-be professional workers, not by semi-skilled workers without singular occupational identity or aspiration. And it escapes or at least strongly resists the exercise of administrative authority over the work.

When the central, strategic task of an organization is formulated, controlled and evaluated primarily by the workers, as it is in the case of the established professions, management does perform logistic functions, but is essentially stripped of what Weber considered to be the prime characteristic of administrative authority—the legitimate right to exercise imperative coordination. Management may control the terms and conditions of work by virtue of a buyer's labor market, but the professional worker controls the work itself, and the work itself is the key to production. In unionized industrial settings, the situation is usually precisely reversed: the organized worker controls many of the terms and conditions of his work through his union, and can stop the work by walking out, but management controls the work that is done.

THE ORGANIZATION OF THE
DIVISION OF LABOR

In discussing the control of work, it is important to differentiate the work of a particular job, and the relationship of one job to others. The latter, of course, is addressed by the concept of the division of labor, a concept which presupposes some kind of mechanism or set of mechanisms ordering and coordinating the interrelationships of jobs. While he emphasized the division of labor, Durkheim did not really discuss its mechanisms, more or less assuming an automatic, functional interdependence of various kinds of tasks and workers. Weber, on the other hand, did not dwell on the idea of the division of labor, but he specified administrative authority, or the authority of office, as the major mechanism of "imperative coordination." Administrative authority is not, however, the only possible coordinating mechanism. There is also the authority implied by the occupational principle— the authority of imputed expertise. A worker can get to control his own work because he has managed to persuade others that he and only he is competent to do so. A worker can get to control the work of others when belief in their functional interdependence exists to link their work with his, and when there is belief in the greater salience of his work as well as the superiority of his knowledge and skill compared to the others in the division of labor. "Objective" functional interdependence independent of historically established social meanings need not be assumed, and in fact is not assumed here. Nor need it be assumed that there are objective rather than historical and social criteria by which differential salience and superior knowledge and skill are determined. Indeed, it seems most wise to assume that the authority of expertise is as much established by a social and political process as is the authority of administrative office. There is very great intellectual danger in falsely objectifying social variables as "hard" technology, "scientific" knowledge and "complex" skill.

Predicated on the authority of expertise, professionalization includes the establishment of authority to coordinate a division of labor. Its growth has thus radically changed the position of management in yet another way: management loses much of the authority to control and coordinate the functioning of the division of labor. Unlike research and development in manufacturing organizations, which is but one of many departments, each of which operates more or less separately from the other but which is coordinated around production by upper-level management, professional services in organizations like schools and hospitals are the most salient activities in the organization-wide division of labor. This means that the work of many other occupations in the organization is coordinated around the professionalized service. Coordination, however, does not take place by orders of management so much as by orders from the professional worker who is dominant in the division of labor. Insofar as it both performs and controls the focal service, the profession must also control the supportive tasks around that service. Thus, not management but the profession coordinates the division of labor in the organization. A hierarchical structure of authority is often found, but it is professional and not administrative, based on the authority of imputed expertise rather than on the authority of administrative office (cf. Freidson, 1970a). An administrative structure does exist, but it is largely restricted to authority over supportive economic, clerical and maintenance services.

Furthermore, in such a highly professionalized domain as health, the interrelations of many of the workers are specified by licensing legislation which exists outside and independently of the organizations in which work takes place. The labor force in the health services, for example, is not only an aggregation of unskilled, semi-skilled, semi-professional and professional workers as labor force and occupational mobility analysis are prone to treat it, but also an imperatively coordinated social organization of occupations. The structural relations among occupations, and what they do, are not established by the management of work organizations, but by the occupational principle—exercise of authority over work by occupations themselves, often with the support of the state which approves exclusive licensing and jurisdiction.

Workers entering the organization enter with their work defined in advance by their training outside, and as part of that work there is the obligation to take orders from some, cooperate with others, and order members of still other occupations. Management does not usually create or control either the work or the jobs, as it does in industry. It merely sets up the organization of occupationally ordained positions and tasks and administers the financial, clerical and other supportive resources necessary to maintain it. In industry a job title is a creation of management and need not imply an occupation: such is not the case in a professionalized work setting. What work is done, and how, becomes a function of a socially organized division of labor which is largely independent of any particular organization, established by occupational associations and legislatures which form the environment of the organization. This is a radically different mode of organizing work than that which followed the Industrial Revolution in manufacturing. It is in fact a central manifestation of what is being called the post-Industrial Revolution, where services take precedence over goods, where factory hands are replaced by machines, and where much of what human work is left must be performed by highly trained occupations. That the worker may be employed in a bureaucratically organized institution rather than be a free professional or craftsman is considerably less important to the occupational principle than his position in the labor market. Self-employment in a glutted labor market allows little self-determination of task, while a scarce labor market strengthens enormously the position of the employee. What is of direct analytical importance to the occupational principle is the fact of autonomy from direction at work, autonomy which can be lost when one is an employee but equally when one is self-employed. Under some circumstances, including that of a well-controlled labor market, one may work in the service of management, but how he works may remain his own right to determine.

KNOWLEDGE AND THE OCCUPATIONAL PRINCIPLE

Thus far I have emphasized history and change, and in that light the strategic value of attending to a comparatively neglected dimension of human affairs rather than to remain fixed on what may very well be at the present time an overused dimension. I emphasize this not only in light of the past, but also in the light of what seems to be coming in our future. Virtually all prophets—or as they are now called, futurologists—seem agreed that the future will see ever-increasing reliance on specialized knowledge and skill, and on applying that knowledge to the solution of practical problems by specially trained men (e.g., Bell, 1968). Political leaders need their staffs of experts to provide them with briefings before they can make intelligent decisions (Wilensky, 1967). And once political decisions are made, the programs by which they are put into effect need to be formulated and carried out by a growing army of trained personnel thought to have the knowledge and skill required for practical success. Writers fearful of the consequences of this growing dependence on experts use the word, "technocracy." Writers more neutral or positive have used words like "the knowledgeable society" (Lane, 1966) and "the active society" (Etzioni, 1968).

However, while many of these writers have stressed the increased importance of specialized knowledge in the emerging society of the future, none has addressed himself seriously to the question of where the knowledge comes from, how it gets established as recognized knowledge, and how its development and utilization become organized, evaluated and controlled. Knowledge, after all, is not disembodied spirit. It is expressed in the activities of men. And knowledgeable men are not mere individuals. Those engaged in the process of creating, communicating and applying knowledge are identified and identify themselves with recognizable, increasingly organized occupational groups. Scholars, scientists and engineers are all members of occupations. The production, dissemination and application of knowledge must be seen as a set of industries (Machlup, 1962) and many of the men working in those industries must be seen as performing definite social roles embedded in particular social circles. (Znaniecki, 1968). The occupational organization of the workers in those industries is obviously important to understanding the way knowledge is produced and used in the post-industrial society. Such occupational organization has consequences which the class position of the professional (Ben-David, 1964) by itself does not allow us to predict.

Once we turn to examine how knowledge is related to human activities, we are drawn into the traditional but newly revived field of the sociology of knowledge (especially Holzner, 1968). And in that field, we cannot avoid examining special occupations, and particularly professions, for their role in organizing the activities surrounding knowledge. It is the concept of occupation, and particularly profession, which provides us with the sociological link between knowledge as such and its organized role in present-day society. It is not, after all, the fact of specialized knowledge which has the practical potential for developing a technocracy, but rather the fact of organized occupations and/or agencies, leaders and classes which have exclusive access to such knowledge. Knowledge itself does not give special power: only *exclusive* knowledge gives power to its possessors. And it is precisely in the occupational principle of organization, by which recruitment, training and the performance of the work of creating, disseminating and applying knowledge are controlled by the "knowledge occupations" that such power is obtained.

PROFESSIONS AND POLITICS

I noted earlier in this essay that both the crafts and the established professions are the purest empirical matches of the concept of the occupational principle. They are differentiated largely by the locus of their training and the substance of their claims to exclusive knowledge and skill. But the professions are especially important because they have much more control over the full range of their work than the crafts, and they exercise much greater, wide-ranging control over human affairs. Furthermore, the knowledge of the professions, learned in formal institutions of higher education and phrased in abstract terms, is far more likely to be able to successfully claim privilege on the basis of its esoteric character.

Insofar as privilege is deliberately organized on a legal basis, it has a political foundation. It is the power of government which grants the profession the exclusive right to use or evaluate a certain body of knowledge and skill. Granted the exclusive right to use knowledge, the profession gains power. It is in this sense that the professions are intimately connected with formal political processes. Such connection has generally been implied in many of the sketches of the process of professionalization, in the course of which occupations organize into associations (Millerson, 1964), sometimes change their names, and press both for public recognition and formal political recognition in the form of exclusive registration, licensing and the like. Quite apart from the *development* of a profession, however, the *maintenance* and *improvement* of the profession's position in the marketplace, and in the division of labor surrounding it, requires continuous political activity. No matter how disinterested its concern for knowledge, humanity, art, or whatever, the profession must become an interest group to at once advance its aims and to protect itself from those with competing aims. On the formal associational level, professions are inextricably and deeply involved in politics. The general analysis of Gilb (1966) and the particular studies of such analysts as Jamous and Peloille (1970) are examples of work which is needed to illuminate this almost ignored area of the sociology of professions.

PROFESSIONS AND IDEOLOGY

Perhaps the political context in which professions operate has been underexamined by sociologists because, like most scholars, scientists and intellectuals, they are not prone to question the status of the knowledge and skill involved. Indeed, special knowledge and skill is used to *define* professions (Goode, 1969) and aspiring occupations have been excluded from consideration as professions on the basis of the sociologist's judgment that they do not possess "basic" knowledge and skill. Once an occupation is accepted as a profession, then by definition it is knowledgeable. When seen as part of a political process, however, knowledge and skill are claimed by a group to advance its interests. True or false the knowledge, disinterested or interested the motive, claims of knowledge function as ideologies, and can be evaluated independently of their validity for their part in gaining public and legislative support for an organized occupation. Indeed, it seems likely that insofar as claims to knowledge and skill are essential elements in a political process which takes place in an arena of conflicting or competing claims from other interest groups, occupational or otherwise, it is highly unlikely that they can remain neutrally descriptive. Patently, they require close attention.

There has been little study of the substance of professional ideology, and even less of the substance of professional "knowledge" as ideology. Dibble's brief but provocative paper (1962) is one of the few to address the question of the analytical differentiation of occupational ideology. In a concrete way, Mills (1942) has shown how an ideology in one professional area can be analyzed, as has Layton (1971) recently for turn-of-the-century engineering, and Halmos (1966, 1970) for those engaged in personal counseling. My own (Freidson, 1970b) analysis of the "clinical mentality" argues that a special way of looking at self and others arises out of the work of consultants who must intervene in everyday practical affairs. And in another context (Freidson, 1970a) I have argued that professional ideologies are intrinsically imperialistic, claiming more for the profession's knowledge and skill, and a broader jurisdiction, than can in fact be justified by demonstrable effectiveness. Such imperialism can of course be a function of crude self-interest, but it can as well be seen as a natural outcome of the deep commitment to the value of his work developed by the thoroughly socialized professional who has devoted his entire adult life to it.

Embedded in the claims of each of the professions is what Thomas Kuhn (1962) called a "paradigm," a taken-for-granted conception of what the issue is, and how it is solvable. Each tends to see the world in terms of its own characteristic conception of problems and solutions, and in the political arena each tries to argue for more resources as a way of advancing the general good. Each has its own eloquent spokesmen testifying for more support of pure science, for the capacity of engineering to solve contemporary problems, on the huge cost to the nation of working days lost due to illness, on the essential role of education in training informed citizenry and capable labor force, and so on. Much of the political activity of the professions may be characterized by appeals to the superior importance and relevance of one paradigm over another. Thus the competition between professions for jurisdiction over a particular area may be analyzed as conflicting definitions of the nature of the problem or activity each is seeking to control, and claims about the way they can best be solved or carried out. In a technocracy, the outcome of such competition establishes who is to be the technocrat and who not.

PROFESSIONALS AT WORK

Thus far, I have devoted myself to a discussion of professions as complex organizations, consonant with my concern with professions as manifestations of the occupational principle of organizing work. In particular, I have addressed myself to the issue of the way professions gain the political power to in fact control and organize their work. Such power provides the framework for formal organization and control, the character for what, in his seminal work, Hughes (1958) called "license and mandate." It sets up the legal authority for the profession to recruit, train, examine, license and review performance, and establishes the formal limits of its exclusive jurisdiction.

It has largely been within a given framework of formal occupational organization that sociologists have studied professionals. (For a recent review by a well-known analyst, along with an extensive bibliography of the American literature, see Moore, 1970. For a recent collection of original papers, primarily British, see Jackson, 1970. For three recent American textbooks, see Hall, 1969, Krause, 1971, and Pavalko, 1971.) Indeed, it seems that most studies have paid rather little attention to the larger political and economic characteristics of the profession which place formal limits on the performance of work by professionals, and on their interaction with colleagues, clients, and members of other occupations.

Nonetheless, studies of individual professionals in particular settings do perform the essential function of building up a comprehensive picture of the way concrete institutions contribute to the development and maintenance of commitments to a particular profession both as a lifelong career and as a special perspective on self and others. Studies of the process of professional education try to show how one's conception of self-as-professional develops, as well as how one learns the knowledge, skill and perspective which teachers in professional schools expect of their students. Both the substance of the process of choice of profession and of the process of formal socialization in professional school obviously play a great part in explaining the behavior of individuals in work settings.

But while formal education establishes qualifications for work, it does not explain enough of the actual behavior of individuals at work to be satisfactory by itself. Every work setting contains its own special source of influence over the work of individual professionals. For obvious reasons of accessibility and convenience, bureaucratically organized elite settings like large law firms, teaching hospitals and universities have been studied considerably more often than the more modest and ubiquitous settings of individual or small practices in community or otherwise ordinary locales. More and more professionals are coming to work in bureaucratically organized settings but as long as study goes on without comparative examination of work in other settings, it will be difficult if not impossible to tell how significant is its influence on the professional worker's work, or on the character of his relationships with other workers. In the latter case, as I have already noted, where a number of occupations in a particular institution's division of labor are registered or more particularly licensed, their interrelationships at work are in part limited and defined irrespective of administrative authority or their members' negotiative relationships.

PROFESSIONAL CONTROL OVER WORK

The crucial issue for the evaluation of any kind of work is its outcome in quantity and quality. For professional workers the issue is whether they are able to exercise control over their work and its outcome, and what methods of control they use. Control over work performance is of course the basic prize over which occupation and administration contend in particular work settings. The strongest professions have thus far managed to preserve much of the right to be the arbiters of their own work performance, justified by the claim that they are the only ones who know enough to be able to evaluate it properly, and that they are also actively committed to ensuring that performance lives up to basic standards. How responsibly that control is exercised constitutes an essential problem for both theoretical and practical analysis.

It is probably impossible to say whether or not professions in general are any more or less conscientious in maintaining their own work performance standards than, say, a similarly organized set of occupations, the crafts. But it is possible to suggest the *vice d'estime* of professions, which is to say, the typical form taken by their failure to maintain formal standards of work performance, when the failure does occur. When professionals fail to control work so as to have it conform to their own academic standards, they seem to do so because they have chosen to avoid the institution and enforcement of any formal rules or standards. They seem to do so because their members tend to believe that their work is of such a complex character, requiring so much judgment, that formal standards or rules are too arbitrary to be applicable. Typically, they insist on individual discretion, denying the possibility and propriety of formal rules. It is quite the opposite for the typical form failure takes in bureaucracy, for there the administrative organization of work characteristically cripples its capacity for controlling the standards of work performance by proliferating so many formal rules designed to minimize discretion that none can be enforced. Professional failure is marked by dissolution into pure discretion, while administrative failure is marked by petrification of forms.

THE PROSPECTS FOR PROFESSIONS

Clearly, the logics of the occupational principle and the administrative principle are distinctly different, and are in a sense opposed to each other. What, then, is the fate of each to be in the developing post-industrial society of our future? There is evidence for the strengthening of both principles. On the one hand, work organizations have gotten larger and larger, absorbing once small and independently organized units of production into rationalized national corporations. Even the personal services, many of which are new to this century, are being organized on a large scale by both private and public management, and traditionally independent professions like physicians have more and more been drawn into bureaucratically administered practices. Bureaucratization seems never stronger. But on the other hand the established professions have reached a position of wealth, prestige and influence in the twentieth century higher than ever before in past history. And many other occupations have begun to struggle for the same position to such a degree and with such energy that it may not be inappropriate to consider professionalization to be a major social movement of the twentieth century. While there are distinct limits to the occupations likely to become professions (Goode, 1969), the occupations composing a division of labor can be organized around professional authority.

Obviously, predicting outcomes is treacherous. Much has been made of the fact that by coming to work as employees in bureaucratic organizations professions become vulnerable to administrative direction and the loss of autonomy, and that the new, aspiring occupations which developed in administratively organized work settings may be incapable of attaining true professional autonomy simply because they are employees. It may very well be that professions reached the peak of their autonomy in the first half of this century and will, in the second half, lose control over their work and become mere "technical workers," merely a special category of skilled labor in the organizational charts of management.

To evaluate this possibility, however, seems to require taking two factors into careful account. First, it would seem that the likelihood of the further extension of the administrative principle of organization hinges in no small part on the likelihood that management can do for professional work what it did earlier for manual work—break it down into a series of discrete, simple operations which those with minimal training can perform and which, when coordinated and reconstituted by management, together produce the same whole outcome or product as was previously produced by the professional worker. If the work of scientists, professors, lawyers, and doctors can be so rationalized, then the post-Industrial Revolution need not be seen as something very new so much as a natural continuation of the Industrial Revolution, an extension of the rationalization of work from manufacturing to services. Only such administrative rationalization can support the exercise of managerial authority.

But since more and more formal education is being required for work in our time, it is hard to see any trend in the direction of weakening the occupational principle. Quite the contrary, we could see the twentieth century as a point when a particular principle of authority rose and flourished as a challenging alternative to the authority of office, a principle inherent in a truly "knowledgeable" society. I refer to the authority of expertise or skill, institutionalized as the special ground for particular kinds of occupational organization. Such authority, in theory if not in practice once institutionalized, rests upon special knowledge and ability rather than incumbency in office, rests upon productive, even creative craftsmanship rather than upon the management of working men. And its assertion is motivated by the worker's commitment to what he sees as his work and his special capacity to evaluate it because he is the one who does it.

The autonomy connected with skill should not be confused, as it often is in the literature, with the economic autonomy of the traditional self-employed professional. It is something quite different. It is related more to the informal attempts of all workers, even those on assembly lines, to do their work as they see fit on the basis of their own sense of knowing how to do it. That he has been an employee for centuries has not left the professor without important freedom. Control over the terms and conditions of work is certainly weakened by being an employee rather than an entrepreneur in a favorable marketplace. Nonetheless, control over the *content* of work is not at all necessarily so weakened. If esoteric knowledge and skill are really necessary to perform most of the work of the future, the grounds for administrative rationalization of work seem likely to become increasingly tenuous and, employee or not, the possibility for the occupational principle to take precedence over the administrative principle becomes greater.

Finally, it must be noted that in assessing the prospects for increasing the strength of the professions, one must assess not only the status of their knowledge and skill but also the status of their occupational organization, which is an independent and necessary, though perhaps not sufficient, variable. After all, the crafts have managed to resist industrialization far more than our evaluation of their knowledge and skill could lead us to predict. It is by their organization that this has been accomplished. There is no reason to assume that present-day professional associations will continue their present tactics and strategies without change, particularly when their members have become employees, or otherwise economically dependent on some central administrative body. What may happen?

No doubt professional associations will continue to be devoted to influencing legislation which preserves a favorable market for their members, but in order to survive they will also have to develop techniques for collective bargaining. From what has already occurred in Western Europe and North America, the strike seems likely to be such a technique. And the strike is likely to revolve around issues of autonomy at work as much as it will revolve around compensation. In the course of such collective actions, there is no doubt that the rhetoric will justify demands by reference to special knowledge and skill and to the terms and conditions (i.e., professional or academic freedom) which are required for their proper exercise, but the action of the strike itself must be a function of occupational organization. Thus, while the future forms of occupational organization and action among the professional workers of tomorrow are only developing now, and so are inconspicuous, they cannot be assigned less weight than knowledge and skill in assessing how far it is reasonable to assume that managerial control of work will continue to grow. At the least, they will constitute a counterforce to the extension of the administrative principle to the control of professional work. Possibly they will so far sustain the continued growth of the occupational principle that the post-industrial society will be the professional society.

REFERENCES

BELL, D. (1968) "The measurement of knowledge and technology," in E. B. Sheldon and W. E. Moore (eds.) Indicators of Social Change. New York: Russell Sage Foundation.

BEN-DAVID, J. (1964) "Professions in the class system of present-day societies." Current Sociology 12: 247-330.

DIBBLE, V. K. (1962) "Occupations and ideologies." Amer. J. Sociology 68 (Sept.): 229-241.

ETZIONI, A. (1968) The Active Society. New York: Free Press.

FREIDSON, E. (1970a) Professional Dominance. New York: Atherton.

——— (1970b) Profession of Medicine. New York: Dodd, Mead.

GILB, C. L. (1966) Hidden Hierarchies. New York: Harper & Row.

GOODE, W. J. (1969) "The theoretical limits of professionalization," pp. 266-313 in A. Etzioni (ed.) The Semi-Professions and their Organization. New York: Free Press.

HALL, R. H. (1969) Occupations and the Social Structure. Englewood Cliffs, N.J.: Prentice-Hall.

HALMOS, P. (1970) The Personal Service Society. New York: Schocken.

——— (1966) The Faith of the Counsellors. New York: Schocken.

HOLZNER, B. (1968) Reality Construction in Society. Cambridge: Schenkman.

HUGHES, E. C. (1958) Men and Their Work. New York: Free Press.

JACKSON, J. A. [ed.] (1970) Professions and Professionalization. Cambridge: Cambridge University Press.

JAMOUS, H. and B. PELOILLE (1970) "Changes in the French university-hospital system," pp. 111-152 in J. A. Jackson (ed.) Professions and Professionalization. Cambridge: Cambridge University Press.

KORNHAUSER, W. (1962) Scientists in Industry. Berkeley: University of California Press.

KRAUSE, E. (1971) The Sociology of Occupations. Boston: Little, Brown.

KUHN, T. S. (1962) The Structure of Scientific Revolutions. Chicago: University of Chicago Press.

LANE, R. E. (1966) "The decline of politics and ideology in a knowledgeable society." Amer. Soc. Rev. 31 (Oct.): 649-662.

LAYTON, E. T. (1971) The Revolt of the Engineers. Cleveland: Case Western Reserve University Press.

MACHLUP, F. (1962) The Production and Distribution of Knowledge in the United States. Princeton: Princeton University Press.

MARCSON, S. (1960) The Scientist in American Industry. Princeton: Industrial Relations Section, Princeton University.

MILLERSON, G. (1964) The Qualifying Associations. London: Routledge & Kegan Paul.

MILLS, C. W. (1942) "The professional ideology of social pathologists." Amer. J. Sociology 49 (Sept.): 165-180.

MOORE, W. E. (1970) The Professions: Roles and Rules. New York: Russell Sage Foundation.

PARSONS, T. (1968) "Professions," International Encyclopedia of the Social Sciences, Vol. 12: 536-547.

PAVALKO, R. M. (1971) Sociology of Occupations and Professions. Itasca, Ill.: F. E. Peacock.

VOLLMER, H. M. and D. L. MILLS [eds.] (1966) Professionalization. Englewood Cliffs, N.J.: Prentice-Hall.

WILENSKY, H. L. (1967) Organizational Intelligence. New York: Basic Books.

ZNANIECKI, F. (1968) The Social Role of the Man of Knowledge. New York: Harper Torchbooks.

Chapter 2

HOW FREE SHOULD
PROFESSIONS BE?

ARLENE KAPLAN DANIELS

It is generally argued that one of the crucial characteristics of a profession is its autonomy: the professional organization rather than the society or the client defines the nature of the expected service and the manner of its transmittal because the profession claims to be the only legitimate arbiter of improper performance of service. Every profession has a professional ideology which explains why professional autonomy is not desired out of self-interest, but is a requirement for offering the best possible service in the public interest. In practice, autonomy exists when the leaders of a profession define or regulate the nature of the service offered in the following ways: they control recruitment and certification of members, and set the standards of adequate practice.

Author's Note: *This paper was written while the author was principal investigator of a grant from the National Institutes of Health (HD-02776) to study Problems of Social Change and Control in Professions. I am especially grateful to Professor Morris J. Daniels, who was the co-investigator in this research and who made extremely important contributions to the ideas and scope of this paper. I would also like to thank the good friends and colleagues who advised me on editing and organizing this paper. First and foremost, thanks are owed to my long-term associate, Rachel Kahn-Hut. Additionally, I am grateful to Howard Becker, Eliot Freidson, Edwin Lemert, Erwin Linn, Dorothy Miller, Julius Roth, and Sheryl Ruzek.*

THE QUESTION OF PROFESSIONAL AUTONOMY
AND SOCIAL CONTROL

The supporting ideology rests upon certain assumptions about what a professional relation to a client means. The ideal image of the relationship which has influenced the development of emerging professions is that of the free professional in a fee-for-service relationship with his client. This image is modeled upon the profession of medicine, particularly as that profession has developed in the United States (see Freidson, 1970a). So strong is this image that professions which never resembled this model (as the military, or teaching) have been influenced by it and share much of the ideology developed in its history. One consequence of this focus upon the individual practitioner in a fee-for-service relation with his client is that no adequate supervision of the practitioner is built into the system. And this structure of practice becomes support for the ideology that the professional group should supervise or police its own members. It is argued that a professional group must have this power because peers or colleagues are the only persons qualified to judge professional performance; they alone have the necessary background knowledge and technical training. Obviously, much technical and theoretical expertise is involved in reaching professional decisions. And professionals believe that only persons with proper training and experience can evaluate how this expertise should be used. An *educated* evaluation requires a professional education.

All professionals use this same basic argument, though they have different types of esoteric knowledge on which to base their claims for autonomy. Scientific knowledge is the most respected knowledge in our society, and some professions present as "evidence" to support the contention that they possess professional expertise the fact that they use knowledge which rests on a scientific base. Medicine, and occupations such as medical technology and nursing, lay claim to portions of biological and physical sciences in assertion of professional status. Engineering rests its claim for professional status on its foundations in the physical sciences and mathematics. Other groups, such as computer programmers, also attempt to claim affiliation with science in their efforts to raise the status of their work to that of a profession. Teachers claim a scientific knowledge of methods for inculcating knowledge as well as their expertise in traditional academic disciplines.

But association with scientific knowledge is only one way to claim an expertise which justifies professional status. Professions such as the law rest their claim upon their knowledge of an arbitrarily constructed model of social organization. The knowledge is not scientific, but it is complex and critical for circumventing or overcoming certain problems which arise in modern society. Astrologers, in another arbitrarily constructed field of knowledge, claim expertise over a highly esoteric subject matter. Great training, skill, and mastery of detail are required to chart horoscopes and read astrological signs properly.

Still other professions present a religious base for their claims to expertise. Only persons who have mastered the theory and rites of the faith are suitably trained to practice the profession. Thus, even in religious sects which require little "formal" education, there are requisite skills built upon an esoteric body of knowledge which must be developed, such as speaking in tongues, exorcising the devil, and laying on of hands.

However, it is not just the question of technical adequacy of a practitioner's knowledge which must be evaluated by professional colleagues; competence includes judgment about quality of service. The nature of professional practice is such that the practitioner must make many unique and special decisions based on the singularity of any particular client-practitioner transaction. Professional ideology suggests that the particular practitioner involved must make judgments on the spot. Afterward, should any question arise, only another professional can determine if the decisions were appropriate for conditions at that time.

This problem is complicated by the fact that the professional service is said to require not only special skills from the practitioner, but also a particular kind of relationship between professional and client. Some aspects of the professional-client relation may require an intuitive ability akin to art (i.e., a combination of training, experience, and the ability to make creative extrapolations or follow hunches on the basis of some collection of evidence). And these aspects of decisions cannot be specified sufficiently for any nonprofessional to evaluate them adequately.

And so the construction and development of this practitioner-client relationship is also a phenomenon which can only be supervised or evaluated by appropriate professional authorities. Though lawyers, for example, may behave differently with clients coming to the public defender's office than they do with clients who purchase their services in private practice, no layman is able to judge whether these differences are *professionally* appropriate and required by the exigencies of the law rather than for the convenience and benefit of the individual lawyer. Any questionable practice would have to be considered by a professional review.

Let us now examine the rationale for these claims that professional autonomy is necessary. When we look at the rationale we will see how professional groups expect to provide the control which they have demanded or assumed over the behavior of individual practitioners. Finally we shall critically evaluate this rationale.

The literature emanating from individual professions as well as the literature in the sociology of professions suggests that the following three characteristics of professions are basic to the justification for professional control over members: (1) the assumed power of ethical codes; (2) the consequences of control over recruitment and certification; and (3) the professional review boards and their assumed control over individual practitioners.

THE POWER OF ETHICAL CODES

Fortunately, it is argued, the need for evaluation by others or by peers rarely arises in professions. First, the very idea of professional *callings,* what Weber (Gerth and Mills, 1946) called a *beruf,* suggests that individuals who enter professions are called by inner promptings to provide some service to humanity, their country, or God. (In the introduction and title of his book Freidson [1970a] suggests that the significance of the very term "profession" is suggested by the statement of commitment found in the use of the term, to profess faith.) Members of professions wish to behave appropriately in order to attain such noble aims. The necessary inhibitions on unbridled self-interest will be self-imposed because the notion of service is uppermost in the mind of the budding practitioners.

The fact that professional myths of an idealistic type are expected to attract recruits indicates a belief in the high level of idealism of those entering professional service. Young men and women may enter a training program because their enthusiasm has been captured by the stories of Florence Nightingale, Clarence Darrow, Jane Addams, Ignatz Semmelweiss, Ernie Pyle, and other dramatic figures, innovators, or founders of professions (Smith, 1958: 413).

While such committed recruits are expected, it is recognized that idealism is not sufficient. One must be trained to turn vague idealistic notions into appropriate practice. In professional training, aspiring practitioners internalize appropriate attitudes and values toward clients along with their technical training. In this way, appropriate behavior becomes "natural," so that an elaborate system of social controls will not be required later. The professional is taught to monitor himself. If there should be cases of dereliction, colleagues can manage erring members through informal pressures. A formal structure of review and sanction becomes virtually unnecessary. For professional groups, to borrow a concept from Durkheim, are like the corporation in classic antiquity: i.e., a guild or occupational group with many ethical and quasi-religious ties between members. Participation in occupations with such ties and with high service ideals is thought to create a sense of brotherhood—a community of interests and shared values which provides the interpersonal incentives to appropriate behavior found in the family; members care very much about each other's good opinion. The corporation provides the moral force and incentive to subordinate particular interests to the general interest (Durkheim, 1965: 1-32). Thus this type of association provides interest in ethical concerns and the desire to meet ethical standards.

Furthermore, it is believed that ethics are based not only on idealism but also on practicality. A reputation for honesty and competence enhances the desirability of a practitioner to his clients and thus the rewards available to him in his professional career. For when students emerge from training and enter practice, they will discover that altruism is good business (Parsons, 1951: 473).

Central to all these assumptions is the existence of an ethical code. While it is difficult to make generalizations about what such codes contain, a few observations seem to apply to any professional code. All professional codes contain some general statements about the service offered to humanity or to some special public. They contain exhortations to the practitioner to maintain standards of conduct appropriate to a professional. And they suggest the relevant publics to which these standards will apply: the client, the public at large, fellow professionals, professionals in related or neighboring fields.

But codes show more variety than similarity. They vary in the specificity or detail in instructions by which they direct or guide practitioners. Some codes, as in the more established professions, have developed slowly over time; others have been developed by professional commissions with relative speed.

When one begins to consider this diversity between codes, and the differing emphases on responsibilities to the various publics which these codes contain, serious questions are raised about their usefulness, at least in the specification of standards of service to the client. Why is there so much variety? If some ethical codes spell out in detail what is appropriate and inappropriate behavior for the individual practitioner, why do not others?

The care with which some professional groups have created and revised codes to keep them current compared to the indifference of others to such effort raises serious questions. Are some professions more ethical than others?

Psychologists, for example, have expended considerable effort to describe and give advice about ethical problems to their members who engage in clinical practice and do psychotherapy. Their efforts in this regard have been consolidated in a code of ethics. Psychiatrists with many parallel functions surely have similar problems. Yet they have never developed any code of ethics applicable to the problems of their speciality. Psychiatrists must depend upon the code provided by the principles of medical ethics—and applicable to all physicians. Medicine has been slow to revise and prepare ethical principles in other areas as well. In 1964, Gross, a layman, complained that the medical profession did not have an adequate code to guide practitioners in research and experimentation with human subjects (Gross, 1966: 312-312). He suggested a code and formulated its main principles; however, the profession has ignored this set of specific, practical suggestions and instead formulated a much more diffuse and ambiguous set of principles in 1969 (see Revised Section 2, Principles of Medical Ethics, in Opinions and Reports of the Judicial Council, AMA, pp. 9-12).

Where new professions emerge—or old occupations become upwardly mobile—ethical codes seem to be constructed as much to serve as evidence of professional intentions and ideals as they are to provide behavioral guidelines to practitioners concerned with providing ethical service. Greenwood (1957), in his analysis of the elements of a profession, may have unwittingly contributed to the proliferation of ethical codes. Since he states that the possession of an ethical code is an important requirement of every profession, any upwardly mobile occupation need only construct one, point to it, and proclaim itself a profession according to Greenwood's criterion. For example, a professor of accountancy writes the following, commenting upon ethics in Certified Public Accounting (Mautz, 1964):

> An established code of ethics is an indication that a given occupation is on the way to becoming an established profession.

Thus, the very statement of ethical codes stands as the sign of the type of self-policing the professional group offers when justifying its desire for autonomy. The spokesmen for the profession may then argue that this written document may *stand for* assurance that professionals will police themselves. In consequence, every established and rising profession has such a code to which it can point. The membership anticipates that the ethical code is the equivalent of folding money, so to speak, or a certified check cashable into confidence that a client may feel when he puts himself into the hands of a practitioner. For the newer professions, formation of professional codes may be viewed as part of a defensive strategy. The occupation "proves" that it is a profession by presenting its credentials (i.e., the code of ethics).

The use of codes—or portions of them—for defensive strategies is illustrated when professions under fire revise or amend codes to take account of criticisms. For example, changes in the development of the CPA code of ethics reflect public and governmental pressure to assure independence of the audit. The adoption of a new rule 1.01 in 1964 enabled the profession to state more clearly and specifically what kinds of activity would be considered unethical (because they compromise the professional's ability to perform the audit properly). This new rule replaced a more ambiguously worded statement which left each practitioner considerable freedom to decide how far he might ethically involve himself in the business affairs of a firm whose books he audited. When it appeared that the Security Exchange Commission (SEC) would set regulations governing the conduct of the CPA, the American Institute of Certified Public Accounting (AICPA) took the initiative and amended the professional code to give warning to practitioners that more rigorous standards for independence must now be expected.

The history of such changes in the AICPA code suggests that outside pressures aid the professional leaders to galvanize the membership to espouse higher standards (Casler, 1964). The codes and actions of other professions which are affected by external regulation, as engineering and architecture, have similar patterns in their historical development (Gilb, 1966). In the mid-sixties, the professional hospital administrators showed responsiveness to these types of pressure in a reversal of an earlier stand against socialized medicine—or any form of governmental health insurance. It could be argued that one of the reasons for this reversal was a fear that government would intervene and take over the regulation of hospital management if they proved recalcitrant. And this fear may have influenced the American Hospital Association when it repudiated the position that it would be unethical for professional administrators to cooperate with governmental planning in medical care.

Such responsiveness to external conditions through changes in ethical codes or professional stands provides an interesting comparisons to medicine where changes in the code and the formal stands of the profession are slow and infrequent. But this immobility in the principles of ethics for medicine is not too surprising if one remembers that medicine is the most prestigious of the professions and has been able to transform its prestige into power. While less secure professions have had to show how they plan to adapt to changing circumstances—at the very least through new ethical guidelines—medicine has not. (Other professions may have to fight with or adjust to competitors in neighboring jurisdictions; but medicine has a clear monopoly and need only worry about regulating internal competition. As a matter of fact, such regulation is given considerable attention in their code. This observation leads to another dimension of analysis for ethical codes.

A second way to gauge the intent of ethical codes is through content analysis of their focus. As Taeusch (1926) notes, for example, the code of medical ethics announces that the key responsibility of a physician is disinterested service to patients. Yet the largest number of sections in the code are devoted to regulation of fees and the proper regulation of relations with colleagues: i.e., the regulation of competition between practitioners. One may also question the rationale for the emphasis placed upon describing or differentiating the proper practitioner from others which appears in many codes. Some of the exhortations in the principles of medical ethics which urge physicians to denounce quacks and to fight charlatans may be viewed as a preoccupation with preventing undesired competitors from encroaching upon the professional territory. These adjurations can also be read as a warning to accredited professionals in bordering jurisdictions to stay clear (see "The relation between psychiatrists and psychologists," Section 6, 9 of the 1969 revision of the AMA Principles of Medical Ethics). Alternatively, codes may imply that professionals should never encroach upon the territory of more powerful groups. In the code of ethics adopted by psychology, clinical practitioners are warned against trying to treat cases which should be referred to a medical specialist. Since the area between psychology and psychiatry is not always clear, the code may be read to suggest that the final decision in these matters belongs to the medical practitioner. Finally, ethical codes may caution members to stand firm against a more powerful profession, if necessary. In the Principles of Conduct for Hospital Administrators, for example, the seventh principle reads:

> In his relationships with the medical staff of the hospital he will support that which is constructive, sound and in the interests of good hospital professional practice. *He will resist and oppose that which is, in his judgment, harmful, destructive and unwise* [italics added] .

Perhaps an analysis of the variations in codes indicates the different concerns professions possess. In all codes, some attention is focused upon the direct responsibility to the individual client. But in medicine, as noted, the greatest attention is upon responsibilities to colleagues and related professionals. In social work, considerable emphasis is given to appropriate relations with employers; engineering devotes much space to the responsibility of the practitioner to the public at large in its code. But is seems reasonable to argue that occupations attempting to secure professional status for members (as psychologists, purchasing agents) show the greatest concern about any or all of these matters and urge their membership to adopt stringent ethical codes. Occupations with secure professional status, like medicine, may not worry so much about the matter. It may require a number of systematic exposures and a rash of dramatic scandals before the profession takes action (Gross, 1966, and Michelfelder, 1961, are among the many who have presented very sharp criticisms of medicine without as yet causing any substantial alterations in the ethical codes).

These observations all suggest that codes do not simply fulfill the functions suggested by the professional ideology. Rather, they are part of the ideology, designed for public relations and justification for the status and prestige which professions assume vis-à-vis more lowly occupations. Roth (1969) sums up this position in a rather sharp letter at the onset of a movement to produce an ethical code for sociologists.

> I want to register my protest against the latest effort to push through a code of ethics for sociologists. It seems to me that sociologists' own studies of occupational spheres, including the use of codes of ethics by various professional and business groups, should have convinced them that this is a fruitless undertaking. But apparently this is not the case. When we examine the codes of ethics of medicine, real estate, psychology, and a variety of other spheres of activities, we find that such codes are primarily designed to do the following:
>
> 1. Reduce the conflict among members of a professional or business fraternity (or at least the public manifestations of such conflict).
>
> 2. Maintain a monopoly of lucrative professional tasks.
>
> 3. Ward off criticism from outside the fraternity. Insofar as codes of ethics make a claim to protecting the public against improper professional or business practices, the codes are a fraud. The way in which they are actually used tends to protect the fraternity against the public rather than the other way around.

CONTROL OVER RECRUITMENT AND CERTIFICATION

Whatever the expectations of idealism in the aspirants to a profession, training is still necessary; the right behavior must be learned. It is argued that appropriate service can only be assured if the values and methods are learned properly. Further it is argued that training in the appropriate values and techniques can only be acquired from other members of the profession. All professionals strive to control recruitment and certification of their membership. It is assumed (as an examination of most catalogues for professional schools will indicate) that professional teachers are also the most capable of any to survey the crop of trainees and to weed out those who seem inappropriately motivated as well as technically inadequate. At the same time, it is assumed that these teachers are drawn from among the leaders in the field—in both technical skills and professional judgment, they can provide the models for appropriate professional conduct to those who are being trained (Hughes, 1959). Idealistic youngsters, originally attracted to the profession by some personally known or famous figure, can be further inspired and strengthened by contacts with such teachers. Where students do not respond well to this type of instruction, they are expected to leave. Generally, such systems depend upon attrition through self-selection. It is believed that those who leave are the "wrong kind" for that field in the first place.

In the most advanced, accepted, and powerful professions, this concern with proper education culminates in complete control of the flow of practitioners into practice. Professional associations set the standards for entrants, control admission, education, and examination requirements and the state certification process by which practitioners are officially licensed to practice. The profession has the power to state just what a practitioner is, how he is identified, and where he may be found in society. Prospective practitioners who have not met the conditions set by the profession may not encroach on this territory.

Medicine is the best example (though others—for example, dentistry, engineering, architecture—have many of the same characteristics) of a profession which controls all avenues of entry into professional schools, reaching down into college curricula to specify or delimit appropriate areas of study for preprofessional training. Boards of medical professionals also set the standards for student training and performance. The students must take exams after completion of professional training which are provided by these boards in order to license those who will have permission to practice.

All other professions and semi-professions strive to attain this ideal state of affairs. The American Bar Association, for example, has control over certification and setting entrance requirements for accredited law schools. But Bar spokesmen continually decry the fact that persons who have not attended accredited schools may practice by virtue of passing the Bar examination. The ABA is particularly harsh in its denunciations of the "mail order" law school programs which do not require any college education for enrollment, and which do not, of course, provide association with established professionals as role models.

But how reasonable is this argument that professional socialization assures competent practitioners? If we examine some of the studies of medical education—the system of professional education with the tightest control over the aspirants to a career in the field—we find many serious questions raised. First, the system of education into which the prospective doctors are thrown does not tend to enforce idealism. Instead, many studies (Merton et al., 1957; Eron, 1955; Becker et al., 1961) indicate that students become more cynical as they progress through their professional education. Neither the professional models and the message they impart, nor the conditions of training enforce an idealistic commitment to the service of humanity. In addition, some studies (Bloom, 1963; Harris, 1964) indicate that many students, from the very first, enter medicine with the primary goal of making money and acquiring prestige rather than that of offering service. Using these observations one might just as easily argue that the tendency toward increasing cynicism as one progresses through professional training in medicine discourages the most idealistic, rather than the least, working to the disadvantage rather than the advantage of the patients waiting for the doctor at the end of this training.

Second, the tight control which medicine holds over professional education has not been a guarantee of uniformly high standards of clinical practice. Gross, in his sharp criticisms of the medical profession, complains that the status of research is so overriding in the "best" medical schools that careful, thorough teaching of clinical medicine is neglected and downgraded. Further, students are allowed to proceed at their own pace and according to their own inclination, learning as much or little as they choose. Once the first two difficult years of medical school have been passed, very few students are ever dropped from the program. And so poor students develop bad habits and remain ignorant when permitted to continue unchecked. Finally, it is widely recognized that medical schools, as well as internship and residency programs, do not approach a standardized level of competence and vary widely in the quality of teaching and experience which they provide.

Such criticisms raise serious doubts about the substance behind the professional argument that professional control over education is all that is essential (both necessary and sufficient) in the production of competent practitioners. But, whatever the advantages of such control in training and licensing professionals, the right to control training creates a monopoly for a given credential or type of education which, in the absence of uniform professional control, encourages abuses and laxness within the system.

PROFESSIONAL REVIEW BOARDS

The core of professional autonomy is for professional representatives to have sole power to police the membership once they are practicing in the field. Professions which possess this autonomy receive it from the state. That is, society delegates legal power to a profession to give, suspend, and revoke the license to practice. And this power is supported by the power of the state—the profession can point to imposters or discredited professionals and have them fined or jailed for practicing without the proper license and consent of the professional board. Generally, this power is entrusted to state boards of examiners who are responsible for certifying entrants and sanctioning practitioners for any improper performance called to their attention.

Each board is generally composed of practitioners in the field who are appointed by an elected official—usually the governor of the state. The boards review cases of poor or unethical practice arising among those who are licensed (Gilb, 1966). In medicine, for instance, the state board may deprive a practitioner of his license or suspend it for a stated interval; the state board is the only formal body with any real power to sanction professional members for derelictions in their work performance. (Hospital medical staffs may refuse hospital privileges to practitioners who do not meet expectations or standards set by the medical staff; but they not have the power to interfere with the practice of the physician—their powers are limited to physicians who require the use of that hospital to practice.) But other professions do not have such a centralized authority over members. In law and accounting, for example, the state board is supplemented by professional organizations with power to supervise and sanction colleagues (see Mayer, 1966; Casler, 1964). And these professions are also vulnerable to external regulatory agencies which may or may not contain professional peers in the review structure. In addition to legislative review (Friedman, 1965), the Internal Revenue Service and the Security Exchange Commission, for example, may review practices and initiate proceedings against unethical practitioners of law or certified public accounting in the courts as well as by asking professional associates to review the behavior of questionable members.

These forms of supplemental review and sanction suggest that professional review systems are often recognized as insufficient to provide necessary regulation. First, professions make the assumption that all members are practicing properly. Therefore, no regular or routine pattern of supervision and review is established in order to check this assumption. In other words, there is no system similar to the regularly recurring driver's license examination required for motorists, who are expected to vary or lapse in their driving ability over time. Thus, incompetent or unethical performance may remain undetected by the autonomous professional surveillance system unless a client brings it forward. It is curious to find such complete dependence on the client when the ideology of professionalism has stressed that no client can ever properly judge professional practice. Clearly, it is not sufficient for a profession to depend upon its clients, for they are often cowed or awed by professional prestige, authority and knowledge. Accordingly, they may not use what judgment they do have to complain as often or as determinedly as they might otherwise. Furthermore, unless they are persistent in pressing complaints through formal channels, clients may be ignored. The authority of colleagues, and the belief in their ability, also influences professional review; in consequence the importance of a client's complaint may not be sufficiently recognized.

Apparently, the assumption discussed earlier, that members of a profession should cooperate within a guild structure, has some unfortunate consequences for the effectiveness of colleague control. Loyalty to one's colleagues may outweigh responsibility to clients. Professionals vary in how explicitly they set standards of behavior toward clients, but every profession states quite explicitly that professionals should not criticize one another before nonprofessionals. While codes state that criticism of a colleague to an outsider is unethical—as well as a gross breach of professional etiquette—they do not offer another clear alternative when discovering incompetence in a colleague. The codes suggest that violations of professional conduct should be reported; but they are rather vague. They never explain exactly what responsibilities a professional does have in those cases where he detects or suspects a breach in the proper professional conduct of a colleague. As a result, only the grossest misbehavior, or the most severe pressures from external sources, move professionals to discipline their own members. In law, for example, Carlin (1962) suggests that only highly unfavorable publicity assures action against erring attorneys by the profession.

AUTONOMY AND SELF-CONTROL

The point of the preceding discussion is to suggest that there is really no reason to accept the contention that professional autonomy best meets the requirement for maintaining standards of professional service. For, whatever the rhetoric of professionalism, all the evidence seems to indicate that autonomy does not encourage the development of practical or workable systems of control. In medicine, for example, the ideal typical model of solo practice in a fee-for-service structure actively precludes the possibility of professional review (Freidson, 1970a). As a consequence, this profession with the greatest autonomy of any has a most fragmented system of professional control, while professions such as law and certified public accounting, which are not so independent and which must render account to extra-professional reviews, also possess more well-developed professional review systems.

One of the problems is that great professional autonomy precludes any check on the quality of service. Powerful professions cannot even provide systematic data on incidents of poor service so that practitioners might be warned or advised about pitfalls before they unwittingly fall into them. Since no data are available, professionals simply assume that the system for the transmittal of proper professional service is working when they are personally satisfied with their own level of service. Systems of periodic review—and systems which provide external supervision—may not guarantee high professional standards in performance but they may guarantee a minimal standard of service for protection of the client—something that emphasis on professional autonomy does not do.

Such observations raise the serious question of whether or not autonomy is indeed vital for the performance of high-level professional service. And they also suggest a negative answer. Comparisons in transmittal of health care services where physicians are supervised and where they are not provide some suggestive evidence. Some successes in utilization indicate that controlled surveillance and supervision by peers and *also* by other health care practitioners and by consumers can result in a better quality of medicine, more economically practiced. Paradoxically, we may some day find higher standards of performance in professions which *are* closely regulated than those which are not. (Experiments and trial programs illustrating these possibilities for medicine are reported in the Carnegie Quarterly, 1970.)

The history of professions and professionalism does not really seem to support the contention that professional autonomy contributes to high standards of professional service. Instead, we find the more powerful the profession, the more serious the charges of laxness in concern for public service and zealousness in promoting the individual interests of the practitioners (Hall, 1968).

Those of us interested in the sociology of occupations and professions might do well to consider this apparent anomaly very seriously. If we were critically to reexamine the literature on professions from the early efforts of Carr-Saunders and Wilson (1936) to the present we might find much of this literature entirely too uncritical of the professional perspective. That is, the sociological analyses have tended to confuse statements about the ideal pattern of practice with statements of empirically observable activity. As a result, we often simply report as *fact* what the professionals we study *believe* to be the case. In the light of this discussion (and many other recent analyses of professions— notably those of Freidson, 1970b), we may have been making a serious mistake. What professions say about themselves in justification of their privileged status above ordinary occupations might better be studied as political ideology than as an indication of intrinsic differences between professions and other types of occupations.

REFERENCES

American Medical Association (1969) Opinions and Reports of the Judicial Council. Chicago: American Medical Association.

BECKER, H., B. GEER, E. HUGHES and A. STRAUSS (1961) Boys in White. Chicago: University of Chicago Press.

BLOOM, S. (1963) "The process of becoming a physician." Annals of the American Academy of Political and Social Science 346 (March): 77-87.

CARLIN, J. E. (1962) Lawyers on Their Own. New Jersey: Rutgers University Press.

Carnegie Quarterly (1970) 18 (Summer): Carnegie Corporation of New York.

CARR-SAUNDERS, E. M. and P. A. WILSON (1936) The Professions. Cambridge: Clarendon Press.

CASLER, D. J. (1964) The Evolution of CPA Ethics. Occasional Paper No. 12. East Lansing: Michigan State University.

DURKHEIM, E. (1965) Division of Labor in Society. New York: Free Press.

ERON, L. (1955) "Effect of medical education on medical students' attitudes." J. of Medical Education 30 (October): 559-566.

FREIDSON, E. (1970a) Profession of Medicine. New York: Dodd, Mead.

——— (1970b) Professional Dominance. New York: Atherton.

FRIEDMAN, L. (1965) "Freedom of contract and occupational licensing 1890-1910: a legal and social study." California Law Review 53.

GERTH, H. H. and C. W. MILLS (1946) From Max Weber: Essays in Sociology. New York: Oxford University Press.

GILB, C. (1966) Hidden Hierarchies. New York: Harper & Row.

GREENWOOD, E. (1957) "Attributes of a profession." Social Work 2 (July): 45-55.

GROSS, M. (1966) The Doctors. New York: Random House.

HALL, R. (1968) "Professionalization and bureaucratization." Amer. Soc. Rev. 33 (February): 92-104.

HARRIS, S. (1964) The Economics of American Medicine. New York. Macmillan.

HUGHES, E. (1959) "Stress and strain in professional education." Harvard Ed. Rev. 29 (Fall): 319-329.

MAUTZ, R. K. (1964) in Foreword to D. J. Casler The Evolution of CPA Ethics. East Lansing: Michigan State University.

MAYER, M. (1966) The Lawyers. New York: Dell.

MERTON, R., G. READER and P. L. KENDALL (1957) The Student Physician. Cambridge: Harvard University Press.

MICHELFELDER, W. (1961) It's Cheaper to Die. Derby, Conn.: Monarch Books.

PARSONS, T. (1951) The Social System. New York: Free Press.

ROTH, J. (1969) Letter to The American Sociologist 4 (May): 159.

SMITH, H. (1958) "Contingencies of professional differentiation." Amer. J. of Sociology 63 (January): 413.

TAEUSCH, C. (1926) Professional and Business Ethics. New York: Henry Holt.

Chapter 3

PROFESSIONALISM AND THE INDIVIDUAL

GEORGE RITZER

The sociology of occupations has been dominated by studies of the professions. In the period 1946-1952 Smigel (1954) reports that 58% of the studies of occupations dealt with the professions. In a later period (1953-1959) studied by Smigel et al. (1963) a decline in interest is reported with 48% of the studies focusing on the professions. Despite this decline, studies of the professions continued to be dominant, with its nearest rival being studies of proprietors, managers, and officials (22% of the occupational studies in the period 1953-1959). A large proportion of the studies of the professions have been concerned with the problem of defining exactly what is a profession. Yet in surveying the literature one finds considerable variation in the definition of a profession. To some "professionalism is merely a label used by occupations to win power and prestige," while to others, "Professions are conceptualized as occupations with . . . core characteristics" (Haug and Sussman, 1968: 57). Among those who contend that professions are defined by their core characteristics, there is also considerable disagreement. Caplow (1964: 139-140) feels that there are four steps in the process of an occupation

Author's Note: *This is a revised version of a paper presented at the meetings of the American Sociological Association, Washington, D.C., September, 1970.*

becoming a profession, while Wilensky (1964) sees it as a five-step process. Most, however, do not look at the process, but are concerned with defining the static characteristics which differentiate professions from all other occupations. Greenwood (1957) lists five such characteristics, Strauss (1963) and Barber (1967) outline four, while Goode (1961) feels that there are only two basic characteristics which differentiate professions from other occupations.

Despite the differences between these perspectives they all have one thing in common: a concern with what differentiates professional occupations from nonprofessional occupations. In the process an equally important question has been virtually ignored by occupational sociologists: what differentiates professional individuals from nonprofessional individuals? This paper constitutes an effort to rectify this imbalance by focusing on the question of individual professionalism.

The omission of the individual level in the study of the professions was first pointed out by Cogan (1955): "Very little attention has been given to problems of individual . . . professionalism. Is professionalism inevitably a group phenomenon or may it be achieved individually?" In many of Everett Hughes' essays on occupations there is a dual emphasis on structural and social-psychological factors in the work world. Specifically, in discussing professions, Hughes contends that the "culture and technique, the etiquette and skill of the profession, appear in the individual as personal traits. . . . In general we may say that the longer and more rigorous the period of initiation into an occupation, the more culture and technique are associated with it, and the more deeply impressed are its attitudes upon the person" (Hughes, 1958: 36). There is the clear implication that there is an occupational level of concern composed of culture, technique, etiquette and skill and an individual level to which these are transmitted in the initiation period. There is the additional implication that the degree of inculcation of these factors at the individual level is highly variable. Hughes points out that it varies with the length and rigor of the training period, but individual adoption of professional skills, norms and values may also be affected by a number of other factors. In another essay, Hughes—in discussing the process of becoming professionalized—says of the term professionalized that it is "here used to mean what happens to an occupation, but lately used to refer to what happens to an individual in the course of training for his occupation" (Hughes, 1967: 4). The differentiation between the individual and occupational level of professionalism has recently been made by Richard Hall (1968). Hall contends that the professional model consists of both structural and attitudinal dimensions. The combining of both of these into one professional model obscures the issue. The two levels are conceptually and empirically distinct as Hall discovers: "Among the major findings of this research is the fact that the structural and attitudinal aspects of professionalism do not necessarily vary together. Some 'established' professions have rather weakly developed professional attitudes, while some of the less professional groups have very strong attitudes in this regard" (Hall, 1968: 103). There is not one professional model, but two, and occupational sociologists must keep them distinct.

Despite these exceptions, the question of individual professionalism has been generally ignored by occupational sociologists. In studying the question of professionalism there are, in reality, two continua; an occupational continuum and an individual continuum. All occupations may be placed on a continuum ranging from the nonprofessions on one end to the established professions on the other. But once you pinpoint the position of an occupation on this continuum, the question remains of the degree of professionalism of the individuals in the occupation. Medicine falls on the professional end of the continuum, but individual doctors are likely to vary in their degree of professionalism. Although most doctors are individually professional, some are quacks, others are inept, and still others violate the profession's code of ethics. Thus while medicine is a profession, individual doctors are likely to vary in their degree of professionalism. The same notion applies at the nonprofessional end of the occupational continuum. As an occupation, taxi driving is clearly a nonprofession. However, some individual taxi drivers may be regarded as professionals because of their knowledge of cars and the city, or their commitment to helping people. There is a relationship between occupational and individual professionalism, but the relationship is not perfect. Because medicine is an established profession most doctors are individually professional, but some may be relatively nonprofessional. Similarly, because taxi driving is a nonprofession, most taxi drivers will be individually nonprofessional. Nevertheless, some taxi drivers may be viewed as professional on the individual level. By raising the issue of individual professionalism a new empirical question comes to the fore: what is the relationship between the occupational and individual levels of professionalism? Although a portion of this paper will be devoted to this question, it is not our focal concern. Nevertheless, it certainly deserves considerable attention from occupational sociologists. In fact, it goes right to the heart of sociology. It is concerned with the relationship between social structure (in this case the structure of an occupation) and individual attitudes and behavior.

The focus in this paper will be on the heretofore ignored individual level of professionalism. In the following pages six dimensions of individual professionalism will be discussed and ways of operationalizing these dimensions will be suggested. In addition, some of the reasons why the individual and occupational levels of professionalism may or may not be congruent will be outlined. Finally, an analysis of some of the implications of the individual level of professionalism for the study of occupations, will round out this exploratory paper.

The dimensions of individual professionalism to be discussed below are drawn from generally agreed upon characteristics which have been used to differentiate occupations on their degree of professionalization. We have simply translated these from structural to individual characteristics. Where a person lies on the individual professional continuum depends on how many of the following attitudinal and experiential characteristics he possesses and to what degree he possesses each:

(a) general, systematic knowledge
(b) authority over clients

(c) community rather than self-interest which is related to an emphasis on symbolic rather than monetary rewards

(d) membership in occupational associations, training in occupational schools, and existence of a sponsor

(e) recognition by the public that he is a professional

(f) involvement in the occupational culture

(a) Individuals in many occupations vary in the amount of general systematic knowledge they possess. It is clear, however, that the amount of such knowledge an individual possesses is related to the amount possessed by the occupation. Thus any given doctor is likely to have more general systematic knowledge than a particular plumber. However, not all doctors have the same amount of general systematic knowledge. There is a good deal of variation *within* the medical profession. Some doctors are more expert in general medicine, or in their specialty, than other doctors. Similarly, not all plumbers are completely lacking in general systematic knowledge concerning the theoretical aspects of plumbing.

In order to operationalize this dimension of individual professionalism it is necessary to ascertain the amount of job-related training an individual has had. There is a more direct way, of course, and that is devising tests to determine how knowledgeable he is about his work. This, however, is impossible for several reasons. For one, it would require a separate test for each of the 30,000 or so occupations in the United States. For another, it would be extremely difficult to construct viable tests for each of these occupations. Finally, the test giver would face insurmountable barriers. It is inconceivable that many physicians would submit to the indignity of taking an examination aimed at ascertaining how much knowledge of medicine they possess. Because it cannot be measured directly, the following questions are suggested as indirect ways of determining how much general systematic knowledge an individual has about his area of expertise:

(1) How much job-related education and/or training has the individual had? What was the quality of the school attended or the training program completed?

(2) Where did the individual rank in his graduating class?

(3) Did the individual receive any honors while in training?

(4) How do clients or customers evaluate the individual in terms of his job-related knowledge?

(5) How do peers evaluate the individual in terms of his job-related knowledge? (How do fellow janitors or lawyers evaluate the janitor or lawyer in question?)

(b) Individuals in any occupation also vary in the amount of authority they have over clients. Some doctors have more authority over their patients than others. Freidson (1960) indicates that, in general, specialists have more authority over their clients than general practitioners. The Freidson findings can be extended so that it might be hypothesized that even within specialties of medicine there is individual variation in terms of authority over clients. Some general practitioners clearly have more authority over their patients than others. By the same token individuals in relatively low-status occupations also vary in their amount of authority over clients. For example, we allow some barbers to determine how our hair should be cut while with others we insist that they follow our directions.

In operationalizing this aspect of individual professionalism we might ask the following questions:

(1) Does the individual feel he has authority over his customer/clients on a number of job-related factors?

(2) Do customer/clients question his judgment on issues relating to his job?

(3) Do the customer/clients themselves feel that they can leave important judgments relating to them in the hands of the individual? (e.g., Does a passenger in a taxi leave the route to be taken up to the driver? Does a patient trust in the diagnosis of a single physician or does he get other opinions?)

(c) Individuals in any occupation vary in their emphasis on community and symbolic rewards over self- and monetary rewards. While this variable, and every other one discussed in this section, is highly related to occupational variation, there is much internal differentiation. Many doctors emphasize community and symbolic rewards, but it is not a rarity to find a self-interested doctor who is focally concerned with money. Similarly, most taxi drivers are interested in self- and monetary rewards, but some do have a community interest and are concerned with symbolic rewards (e.g., a citation from the police department for helping apprehend a criminal).

We might ask the individual to rank the following series of rewards in order of importance to him:

(1) money

(2) respect of colleagues

(3) respect of client/customers

(4) helping others

(5) occupational honors (e.g., election to officership in union or professional association, promotions)

(6) community recognition

(d) Self-control, at the occupational level, is exerted through professional associations, training schools and sponsorship patterns. Although self-control is an occupational variable, individuals vary in experience in the means through which it is exerted. One might ask the following questions about individual involvement in the occupational means of self-control:

(1) Is the individual a member of the occupational association? How active is he in these associations? Is he an officer?

(2) How much occupational training has he had?

(3) Did he have a sponsor? What position did the sponsor hold? How active was the sponsor in his behalf? How did the sponsor help him?

(e) Individuals in any occupation vary in how much recognition they receive from the public as a professional. Some doctors are viewed as more professional than others. Conversely, we may consider some taxi drivers more professional than others. Operationalization of this variable would require the study of client/ customers or co-workers. They would be asked how "professional" they regarded a given college professor, accountant, or prostitute.

(f) Individuals in any occupation vary in their degree of involvement in their occupational culture. At the occupational level professions are likely to have a culture which is distinctive. However, all occupations have a culture of some sort and involvement in that culture is an index into individual professionalism. Involvement in an occupational culture has two aspects: activity and attitude. On the one hand we can ask how active an individual is in the formal and informal culture of the occupation or we can ascertain how many of his friends are in his occupation. On the other we can determine how committed an individual is to his occupation. The individual who is active and committed is highly professional on this variable.

A technique previously used by Ritzer and Trice (1969) is useful in ascertaining the commitment of an individual to his occupation and employing organization. The professional is an individual who has a high degree of commitment to his occupation and a low degree of commitment to his employing organization. The respondent would be asked if he would leave, would not leave, or is undecided about leaving his occupation or organization for the following reasons:

(1) with (a) no, (b) a slight, or (c) a large increase in pay

(2) with (a) no more, (b) a little more, or (c) much more freedom

(3) with (a) no more, (b) a little more, or (c) much more status

(4) with (a) no more, (b) a little more, or (c) much more responsibility

(5) with (a) no more, (b) a little more, or (c) much more opportunity to get ahead

The occupational and organizational commitment scores could range from 5 to 25, with the higher score representing a higher degree of commitment. For each of the five groups of factors an individual could get a score from 1 to 5. For example, on the pay factor an individual would be scored as follows:

(1) if he would definitely change with no increase in pay

(2) if he would definitely change with a slight increase in pay

(3) if he would definitely change with a large increase in pay

(4) if he is undecided with a large increase in pay

(5) if he would definitely not change with a large increase in pay

These then are the six dimensions of individual professionalism. There are almost certainly others which could be developed, but these seem at least to be the major dimensions. In using these dimensions empirically the researcher must be careful to use all six and not just one or two. Clearly an individual could be nonprofessional on one or two dimensions, while being highly professional on the others. What is needed is a composite score of individual professionalism based on the operationalization of each of the six dimensions. What we may find through empirical research is that these dimensions form a Guttman scale. A reasonable guess at this point, and it is only a guess, is that if an individual has a high degree of general systematic knowledge he is also likely to score high on the other dimensions of individual professionalism. But this is pure conjecture and the answers lie in the field.

Although it is clear that there is a conceptual difference between the occupational and individual levels of professionalism, it is necessary to pinpoint some of the reasons why, empirically, we find some cases in which there is a discrepancy between the two levels and others in which the two levels are congruent. That is, why do we find some nonprofessional individuals in professional occupations and, conversely, why do we find some professional individuals in nonprofessional occupations? Whether the two levels are congruent or discrepant in a particular case depends on three basic factors—individual, organizational and occupational.

INDIVIDUAL

A starting point here is the psychological makeup of the individual, which may either contribute to a congruence or discrepancy between individual and occupational professionalism. The intelligence of a given individual is important since general systematic knowledge is a component of individual professionalism. The individual in a professional occupation may be considered nonprofessional at the individual level if he does not have the intelligence to understand the theory which underlies his occupation. On the other hand, an intelligent individual in a nonprofessional occupation may be viewed as a professional individual because of his mastery of the technical aspects of the job or its theoretical underpinnings. Personality would also be an important variable here. Need achievement would certainly be a relevant personality characteristic. A physician with low-need achievement might not make the effort necessary to master the knowledge base of medicine and therefore not be considered individually professional. Conversely, a taxi driver with high-need achievement may be motivated to go to school at night and master the theory of the automobile engine or the psychology of the passenger, thereby winning for himself professional recognition. Or consider the need to dominate others. A passive lawyer with a low need to dominate might not have authority over his clients and would be viewed as individually nonprofessional on that dimension. On the other hand, the janitor with high need to dominate might be able to gain authority over his tenants and be individually professional at least in terms of authority over clients. Needless to say there are a huge number of personality characteristics which might affect the degree of congruence between individual and occupational professionalism.

Another reason for the discrepancy between individual and occupational professionalism lies in the degree of involvement of the individual in the occupational culture. In the case of those in professional occupations we might hypothesize that the greater the involvement in the profession, the more professional the individual. Thus an individual in a professional occupation is more likely to be nonprofessional at the individual level if:

(1) he does not come from a family in which one or both parents were professionals

(2) he was not involved in the formal and informal activities of his professional school

(3) he is not involved in his professional associations and has little contact with his colleagues

When we turn to nonprofessional occupations many of the same points hold. A nonprofessional individual in a nonprofessional occupation is one who was not involved in the activities of training schools associated with the occupation, who is not involved in the occupational associations, whose parents were not involved in that occupation, and whose friends do not come from within the occupation. The obverse would also seem to be true, individuals who did have the above experiences would be considered professional individuals in a nonprofessional occupation.

ORGANIZATIONAL

The structure of the organization in which an individual is employed also contributes to the discrepancy or congruence between occupational and individual professionalism. Some types of organizations are more likely to pull an individual in a professional occupation away from professional behavior. For example, professionals in industry frequently experience a pull away from the cosmopolitan behavior of the professional and toward the local behavior of a bureaucrat. When such an individual is employed in a separate research organization the tug is less, but it is still there. On the other hand universities are structured in such a way that the pull away from professional behavior is minimized. For individuals in nonprofessional occupations there are organizations which allow them to behave professionally, that is in accord with occupational norms, not organizational norms. Individuals who are closely supervised are the least likely to be allowed to behave professionally. They must do what the boss asks, even if it is contrary to how they want to do it, or how occupational norms say it should be done. On the other hand, individuals in such occupations as taxi driving, or mailman are relatively free of organizational control and therefore have a greater opportunity to behave professionally and determine for themselves, or with peers, how a given task should be accomplished.

OCCUPATIONAL

Just as there are certain individual and organizational characteristics which increase or decrease the discrepancy between individual and occupational professionalism, the same is true of certain occupational characteristics. First, and most obviously, the more professional the occupation, the more likely the individuals in that occupation are to be professional at the individual level. Most proprietors would find it difficult to behave professionally because of the strong pull toward businesslike behavior which in many ways is antithetical to professional behavior. In some proprietorships the conflict between professional and businesslike behavior is even greater. An example is pharmacy, but even here it is difficult for the pharmacist who is trained in a professional school to behave professionally. Managers and officials, because of their position in their employing organization, would find it most difficult to behave professionally. They must almost always be locals rather than cosmopolitans who place the interests of the organization above those of client, occupation, and the like. The skilled crafts offer their members the greatest likelihood of any nonprofession to behave professionally—perhaps because as an occupation it has many points in common with the professions. The strength of the union, the rigor of the apprenticeship period, and the norms of autonomy make it likely that a large percentage of skilled craftsmen would be considered professional at the individual level. To take one final example, some blue-collar jobs offer more opportunity for individual professionalism than others. Those that are totally independent of control from the top are likely to create an environment in which at least some individuals can behave professionally. On the other hand, occupations which are directly responsible to the organization are least likely to allow an individual to behave in a professional manner.

IMPLICATIONS

The differentiation of the two levels of professionalism does more than suggest a new series of empirical questions to the occupational sociologist. It also does much to clarify some things about the sociology of the professions. For example, it places the question of professional socialization into its proper perspectives. Those who have focused on professional socialization have, in reality, been concerned with individual professionalism. Professional schools are concerned with communicating the skills, knowledge, norms and values which are needed for the individual to be considered, and consider himself, a professional. Medical schools are concerned with training students to view themselves, and be viewed, as physicians. Thus, manifestly, professional socialization has nothing to do with the degree of professionalization of the occupation. The occupation is already considered a profession and some failures in professional socialization are unlikely to jeopardize the standing of the occupation. However, should the occupation continually fail to adequately socialize its new members the professional standing of the occupation will ultimately be jeopardized. Thus professional socialization is focally concerned with the individual level, although it ultimately is also likely to have an impact on the occupational level. The massive amount of literature on professional socialization is theoretically far more understandable when the individual level of professionalism is recognized.

The existence of an individual level also has methodological implications for the sociology of the professions. Assessing the degree of professionalization of an occupation is impossible if the researcher seeks to interview individuals in the occupation.

Finding out how much general systematic knowledge, or community interest an individual has, tells us little about the occupational level. Assessing the degree of professionalization of an occupation requires a more macroscopic approach. We must ascertain, for example, how much general, systematic knowledge the occupation *as a whole* possesses. A more macroscopic approach is necessary in assessing individual professionalism. Attitudes, knowledge, and actions must be measured in an effort to determine how professional are particular individuals.

The differentiation of the two levels of professionalism also serves to clarify some theoretical issues in the sociology of occupations. For example, we might consider the debate on professionalism between Nelson Foote and Harold Wilensky. The debate began with an article by Foote (1953). Foote's major conclusion is that "labor itself is becoming professionalized." Wilensky (1964: 156), in a response to the Foote article, concludes that "this notion of the professionalization of everyone is a bit of sociological romance." Interestingly enough, both of these seemingly antagonistic conclusions are correct. They are both correct because they are basically arguing on different levels. Foote is really discussing individual professionalism and Wilensky is discussing occupational professionalism. Foote (1953: 372) says that "the professionalization of labor in Detroit is . . . what is happening to the laboring men themselves." Thus as *individuals,* laborers are becoming more professional. For example, Foote notes that the laborers are using an increasing amount of general theory. Wilensky, on the other hand, details the barriers to professionalization on the occupational level. Both writers are correct; as individuals some laborers are becoming more professional, but as an occupation laborers face insurmountable barriers to professional status. By differentiating the individual and occupational levels of professionalism we can clarify this controversy and other debates in the literature on professionals.

REFERENCES

BARBER, B. (1967) "Some problems in the sociology of the professions," pp. 15-34 in K. S. Lynn (ed.) The Professions in America. Boston: Beacon Press.

CAPLOW, T. (1964) The Sociology of Work. New York: McGraw-Hill.

COGAN, M. (1955) "The problem of defining a profession." Annals of the American Academy of Political and Social Science 297 (January): 105-111.

FOOTE, N. (1953) "The professionalization of labor in Detroit." Amer. J. of Sociology 58 (January): 371-380.

FREIDSON, E. (1960) "Client control and medical practice." Amer. J. of Sociology 65 (January): 374-382.

GOODE, W. (1961) "The librarian: from occupation to profession?" Library Q. 31 (October): 306-318.

GREENWOOD, E. (1957) "Attributes of a profession." Social Work 2 (July): 44-55.

HALL, R. (1968) "Professionalization and bureaucratization." Amer. Soc. Rev. 33 (February): 92-104.

HAUG, M. and M. SUSSMAN (1968) "Professionalism and the public." Sociological Inquiry 39 (Winter): 57-64.

HUGHES, E. (1967) "Professions," pp. 1-14 in K. S. Lynn (ed.) The Professions in America. Boston: Beacon Press.

——— (1958) Men and Their Work. New York: Free Press.

RITZER, G. and H. TRICE (1969) "An empirical study of Howard Becker's side-bet theory." Social Forces 47 (June): 475-478.

SMIGEL, E. (1954) "Trends in occupational sociology in the United States: a survey of postwar research." Amer. Soc. Rev. 19 (August): 398-404.

——— et al. (1963) "Occupational sociology: a re-examination." Sociology and Social Research 47 (July): 472-477.

STRAUSS, G. (1963) "Professionalism and occupational associations." Industrial Relations 2 (May): 7-31.

WILENSKY, H. (1964) "The professionalization of everyone?" Amer. J. of Sociology 70 (September): 136-158.

Chapter 4

THE GROWING INDUSTRIALIZATION
OF THE PROFESSIONS

GLORIA V. ENGEL and RICHARD H. HALL

Society is increasingly aware of the contributions made by
the professions and has become more dependent upon the services
professionals render than ever before (Lynn, 1963). While there
has been a growth in both number and kinds of professions, the
demand for professional services in our highly industrialized,
urban society has been rising even more rapidly (Hughes, 1963). A
number of social scientists have shown concern over the impact of
societal forces on this vital occupational grouping. In this paper an
attempt will be made to show that professional work patterns are
undergoing a restructuring, a revolution much like that experienced centuries ago with the industrialization of the crafts, and
that this restructuring permits, in some respects, a more faithful
adherence to professionalism and is not as detrimental to
professions as some writers claim.

Traditional definitions of the professions posed by students of
occupations are strikingly similar in content, with differences
based primarily on emphasis, rather than being actual contradictions (a review of this literature can be found in Hall, 1969: ch. 4).
Goode (1960) provides a definition developed from the constella-

Authors' Note: *The authors acknowledge the constructive criticisms and
editorial assistance contributed by Eliot Freidson of New York University.*

tion of characteristics to which the majority of the students of professions adhere. Unmentioned in most definitions, however, is the way professional work has been characteristically organized. Nonetheless, implicit in the discussions is a conception of professional work as typically entrepreneurial and individualistic. The professional is viewed as servicing clients in a one-to-one relationship on the basis of his own individual knowledge and skill, with little or no assistance from members of other occupations or professions.

This conception of professional work is reminiscent of the guild as it existed during the Middle Ages. The craftsman produced a total product, rather than repeating a single, specialized task on an assembly line. The carpenter skillfully performed all processes connected with the creation of his product, meeting his customer's request for a chair, table, sideboard, etc. Much like the traditional model of the physician, dentist, or attorney, the master craftsman did not fashion his product as part of a complex work force providing a composite service, but furnished it to his customer on a one-to-one basis (Pirenne, 1936; Ashley, 1925; Schneider, 1957).

The social organization of both the professions as traditionally conceived and the old crafts results in work situations which are, and were, in the Weberian (1940) sense, irrationally structured. Routinization, standardization, and mechanization were not yet required for delivering services or turning out products. However, both the professions and the crafts built in certain control mechanisms. In addition to constraints imposed by society, membership for craftsmen in their respective guilds was compulsory, and membership in the professional organization, if not compulsory, was nevertheless considered to be highly desirable. Appointed and elected officials in both the guilds and the professional associations were given power to dispense judgments and punish wrongdoers. Guilds, like the professional associations, were multipurpose, regulating not only quality but also the quantity and price of the product for, so they claimed, the public's benefit.

CHANGES ALTERING THE WORK PATTERNS OF THE
GUILD SYSTEM AND THE PROFESSIONS

Several societal changes led to the breakdown of the guild system and opened the way for the reorganization of production. Among these were (1) an increase in knowledge and technology, (2) a greater demand for more and newer products, (3) the economic need to increase output and lower unit cost, and (4) pressures by occupations whose entry into the system was blocked. The model which evolved led to the structuring of work in a more rational fashion, expressed in terms of external control, discipline, and such refinements as a hierarchical division of labor and mechanization.

It should be noted that the consequences of this reordering have not been universally viewed as entirely advantageous. Starting with Marx, many have claimed that bureaucratization has led to worker alienation (for a concise exposition on the basic Marxian position with respect to bureaucracy, see Mouzelis, 1967. Also see Seeman, 1959, discussion of alienation).

As to the professions, greater rationalization of the organization of their activity is giving it much of the character and flavor of the modern industrial work model which is basically organized bureaucratically, as depicted by Weber (Gerth and Mills, 1946). In order to meet contemporary demands, the various professions now require access to complex items of equipment and increased specialization, establishing a need for both a greater division of labor and teams of hierarchically organized work groups functioning within and across professional lines. Professionalism, like craftsmanship, is by necessity becoming bureaucratically organized (for a discussion of professional and bureaucratic work patterns as alternatives and conflicting models, see Stinchcombe, 1959: 168-187, and Vollmer and Mills, 1966: 267-275). Individuals who work in isolation are frequently less able to cope with current client needs.

As occurred with the old guilds, present-day professions have been influenced by a vast knowledge explosion in nearly all areas, advances in technology, and a greater demand for services. New types of professions have appeared, there has been an increase in the absolute number of professionals, and many more are working as employees in formal organizations (Hall, 1969). Moreover, the internal patterns of relationships are undergoing transformation. For example, in the past several years, the trend toward large, bureaucratically organized medical, dental, and legal practices has increased. Although the majority of professional groups are still composed of three to five men, such large-scale units as the Kaiser Permanente medical groups, union-sponsored closed-panel medical and dental clinics, and large law firms as described by Smigel (1964) have found greater acceptance by both professional associations and the public. Similarly, modifications in interactive patterns have been noted among those professions which have traditionally been housed in bureaucracies. The team approach adopted by many teachers and scientists is an example of such alterations.

As the organization of professional work alters, some students of the professions respond negatively (a summary statement of the antibureaucratic view was made by Hickson, 1966: 224-251). Writers such as Mills (1951), Lewis and Maude (1953), Merton (1957), and Whyte (1957) take a dim view of this transition and conclude that the hierarchical relationship and task specialization required within an organization are tending to make the professional indistinguishable from the bureaucrat. They feel that the professional, like the old craftsman, is the only one who is capable of making, in his singular fashion, the decisions required for properly servicing his client. They argue that administrative aspects restrict the professional's freedom and make him dependent upon the organization which, in turn, controls the utilization of his knowledge and skills. His association with the bureaucracy could therefore prevent the professional from fulfilling a fundamental requisite of professional behavior, serving the best interests of his clients.

Empirical evidence supplied by Goldner and Ritti (1967) supports this position. In their study of engineers, they found that the dual promotional ladder which has been adopted by many organizations to provide professional personnel with a means for advancement has not been successful. They attribute failure to the organization's inability to provide the individual with the autonomy he needs to determine the course of his work activities.

Only partially supporting the antibureaucratic position, Kornhauser (1962) tends to view the relationship between the professional and bureaucracy as interdependent, with organizations as well as professionals making accommodations as organizations become increasingly dependent on professionals' services. Hall (1968), after studying both structural and attitudinal data from several types of occupational groupings located in a variety of organizations, finds that there is, generally, an inverse relationship between professionalization and bureaucratization.

Other investigators (Barnard, 1938; Blau, 1955; Goss, 1957; Janowitz, 1960; Dalton, 1961; Perrow, 1967) are among those who stress the informal and adjustive or flexible character of the way bureaucracy actually works (also see Udy, 1962: 299-308, and Perrow, 1965: 910-971). They generally consider it to be a dynamic type of organization which permits more individual freedom than has been acknowledged heretofore and find that professionals are able, in some degree, to alter the structure of the organization as they carry out their work activities. Blau (1955: 2) states that, "In the course of operations new elements arise in the structure that influence subsequent operations."

Several writers (Gouldner, 1954; Litwak, 1961; Etzioni, 1964; Scott, 1966) challenge the uniformity attributed to the concept of bureaucracy. Some suggest that it varies according to the kinds of tasks required and/or the workers who perform them. Bucher and Stelling (1967), studying a private hospital, two state mental hospitals, and a university medical school and hospital, find that the professional does not always step into a preexisting role but builds his own, and that roles are less clearly defined in a "professional" bureaucracy than in other types. Engel (1970), examining the relationship between degree of bureaucracy and degree of professional autonomy, concludes that there is an optimal level of bureaucratic organization with respect to professional autonomy.

THE EVOLVING CHARACTER OF PROFESSIONALISM

While there is some support for both the positive and negative perspectives on the relationships between professions and bureaucracies, if the consequences of the reorganization of professional work patterns are carefully examined, it appears that work in bureaucratic organizations can provide the professional with the opportunity to be more faithful to the ideals of professionalism in several ways.

First, many present-day professionals who are salaried employees in organizations are largely freed from the economic pressures which solo professionals encounter. Within the organization the opportunity for such a nicety as altruism is increased since, relatively free of financial concerns, the professional is better able to participate in a reward system of a different type, one which is based on work achievement as an end in itself, not merely as a means to personal gain (Barber, 1963).

Second, the replacement of individualistic service with a hierarchically organized team approach increases visibility of professional performance and opens the way for greater peer and public evaluation. The old, unwritten tenet of secrecy, or the protection of one's deviant colleagues from lay evaluation, can give way to open assessment. Unlike the solo practitioner, the organizational professional must interact with superiors, peers, and subordinates, all within a more formally structured setting. For example, during client-care conferences the professional must expose himself and his performance.

Although, in many cases, clients may ultimately be treated one-to-one under conditions of privacy in the consulting room, many of the criteria which the current organizational professional uses to make critical decisions are now a matter of wide knowledge. Collaborative treatment of a client requires the use of services and data collected by other professionals and/or paraprofessionals. Therefore, both colleagues and subordinates within an organization are better able to evaluate the work of professionals, and incompetence can more readily be discovered.

It should be noted, however, that since the client interacts not only with the individual professional but with all members of the service team, "the intensity of the link between the [individual] helper and the helped may be attenuated" (Horwitz, 1970: 116). This increased distance between professional and client could lead to a lack of direct responsibility to and for the client. Whether this possible drawback is counterbalanced by the advantages of more open evaluation of professional services achieved through collaborative client care remains to be studied.

Because of these new arrangements, quality control does not depend as heavily on the traditional system of self-government as adhered to in the past by professions and the old craft guilds. This is not meant to imply that a totally open and rational evaluation process is now with us, as it has been shown that in group medical practice the knowledge of one's colleagues' performance, outside of narrow specialty lines, is considerably less than exact (Freidson and Rhea, 1965). Rather, the conditions are such that a more open evaluation system is possible. The manner in which university department faculties evaluate each other suggests that a totally rational system is probably impossible and even undesirable, but that excessive secrecy can be avoided, at least with regard to nontenured personnel. The issue of incompetence and deviance among tenured colleagues has still not been faced in the academic setting and probably will be equally avoided in other professional organizational work settings.

Employment of the team approach is particularly descriptive of the generic professional model, medicine. The privacy of the physician-patient relationship is beginning to diminish. All members of the medical team must interact with, and collect information directly from, the patient. Ultimately, the physician uses these data to determine treatment procedures, but his is no longer an exclusive, private, doctor-patient relationship.

If present trends continue, the physician will have even less direct contact with patients, acting rather as a superconsultant. Assistants or physician surrogates will be trained and licensed to carry out diagnostic and treatment activities which heretofore have been performed solely by physicians and will seek out the physician only when they believe they are in need of consultation for proper patient care. The physician superconsultant role already exists in several fields and involves other professionals as well. Psychologists, social workers, and lay therapists service many patients directly, consulting with the psychiatrist only as circumstances dictate.

In addition to the training of paraprofessionals, some professions are instituting other measures to increase productivity and thereby meet increased client demands. A group discussion technique was recently initiated in an obstetrical practice (Daugherty, 1970). Rather than asking questions and dicusssing their problems on an individual basis, groups of new or expectant mothers interacted with each other and with the physician. Although this group approach to patient care is new in the field of obstetrics, it too has long been an integral part of psychiatric and clinical psychological practice.

In a like manner, the private, individualistic relationship between the priest and his parishioner in the confessional is beginning to undergo alteration. Recently, a papal proposal was submitted to the church bishops which advocates partial adoption of group confession practice. If this practice is initiated, Catholic congregations will seek absolution of their sins through joint prayers of general confession (Los Angeles Times, 1971).

With respect to the legal profession, Johnstone and Hopson (1967: 546) suggest that lawyers modify traditional work patterns by borrowing certain techniques from industry, such as standardizing procedures and permitting less costly personnel (legal assistants?) to handle the routine jobs.

Along with the team approach, the employment of exotic tools and other items of equipment have had an impact upon the professions, on the one hand enhancing the possibility of increased public evaluation and on the other, diminishing the individualistic and personal client-professional relationship. For example, the use of computers has radically changed the ways in which clients' data are obtained, stored, and retrieved. While the professional may continue to integrate and interpret the findings, subordinates also have access to this material and share in the responsibility for serving the client. Modern accounting firms utilize computers to prepare clients' balance sheets, profit and loss statements, tax returns, etc. One member of a team collects pertinent information from the client and feeds it into the computer to be synthesized. Another team member, on the basis of the computer output, produces the finished product.

Clearly, one can imagine as many problems as benefits to flow from such change, but we know little about these in fact. Research is needed to determine the extent to which the diminution of the intensity of the professional-client relationship has resulted in depersonalization and lowered quality of interaction for either the client or the professional and the extent to which the addition of other "persons in contact" would have a reverse impact.

An inherent, structural weakness of traditional professionalism noted by Freidson (1970) is the professional's tendency to develop a type of "tunnel vision" which can prevent his utilization of all appropriate knowledge and skills for problem solving. Group biases can end up in "jurisdictional," rather than "functional," disputes, thereby reducing the quality of the service rendered. However, the previously described knowledge explosion and the more sophisticated and complex problems to which it has given rise have, in many instances, forced the interdisciplinary pooling of knowledge and skills. The lines which, in the past, appeared to separate the various disciplines are beginning to blur. Now there is an increasing interdependence between and within professions, each contributing to the furtherance of the other. In the building industry, architects and engineers are now integrating their disciplines, combining abilities and experience to cover all aspects of master planning, design, and construction.

It should be noted, however, that this forced pooling does not necessarily occur in a rational or congenial way, despite its inevitability as seen from the outside. Further, technical inter- dependence does not automatically result in equality for all participants. The increased dependency on the part of the professional tends to reduce his power and control. While he still can be viewed, in many instances, as the captain of the service team who sets goals and standards in order to accomplish vital aims,: he depends upon the expertise of other professionals and paraprofessionals. If the nerve-damaged patient is to walk again by means of an orthopedic appliance, the talents and contributions of the prosthetic engineer and physiotherapist, as well as those of the physician, are needed.

A major source of the professional's power, exclusive and encompassing knowledge about the subject matter, is threatened by the facts that (1) neither he nor anyone else can have all the knowledge necessary for treatment, and (2) he is in interaction with other professionals who also have important, specialized knowledge. At the same time, of course, factors other than knowledge enter the power situation, and it is most unlikely that any professional group will voluntarily give up some of its power just because to do so would be rational or because it is demanded by other participants. Lawyers oppose accountants' incursions into the tax field, and professors resist students who feel that they have worthwhile contributions to make toward the process of higher education. While the discussion of these internecine warfares are interesting in and of themselves, the illumination of the essence of the conflicts, and perhaps their outcome, depends upon our acknowledging the changes taking place in the work structure of the professions.

The major shifts in the nature of the elements of professionalism discussed in this section are summarized in Table 1. It can be observed that some of the attributes of professions have not been eliminated, as claimed by those who hold an antibureaucratic view, but rather have experienced a change in character which, in some instances, permits a more faithful adherence to the professional ideal.

THE NEW ORGANIZATION OF PROFESSIONAL WORK: ITS COMPATIBILITY WITH BUREAUCRACY

Although Hughes (1958) differentiates between scientists and professionals on the basis of social contacts, with the professional generally interacting with his clients and the scientist interacting with his colleagues, the changes in professional work patterns

TABLE 1
EVOLVING PROFESSIONAL CHARACTERISTICS

Traditional Characteristics[a]	Modified Characteristics
1. Isolated individual provides service	Teams provide service
2. Knowledge from a single discipline typically utilized	Knowledge from diverse fields typically utilized
3. Remuneration predominantly fee-for-service	Remuneration predominantly by salary
4. Altruism: Selfless service limited by entrepreneurialism	Altruism: Increased opportunity for selfless service
5. Restricted colleague evaluation of product	Increased opportunity for colleague evaluation of product
6. Privacy in client-professional relationship	Decreased privacy in client-professional relationship

a. Each of the following authors has associated one or more of these characteristics with the professions: Carr-Saunders and Wilson (1933), Marshall (1939), Cogan (1953), Lewis and Maude (1953), Goode (1957), Hughes (1958), Bucher and Strauss (1961), Becker (in Henry, 1962), Wilensky (1964), and Sherlock and Morris (1967).

which have been discussed reveal that such a distinction is no longer as meaningful as it once was. The industrialization of the professions has resulted in a work pattern which is somewhat more like that of the scientist since, as illustrated, many professionals must engage in search behavior for the appropriate knowledge for a particular issue and are now required to interact with colleagues as well as, or instead of, clients in order to provide service. Additionally, they are forced to make critical decisions based upon data systematically collected by others. Since the personal and individualistic quality of the client-professional relationship is diminishing and the services rendered by the professional are becoming more open to colleague evaluation or more visible to members of other professions in interaction, it therefore appears that both the interactive patterns and the product of personal service workers are becoming more like those of the scientist.

There are those who allege that the current scientific emphasis among professionals, particularly in contemporary medicine, leads to greater impersonality and the dehumanization of the client (Kendall, 1962; Reader, 1963). This accusation is not entirely valid. Babbie (1970) empirically demonstrates that the traditional professional norm of humane patient care is still adhered to by the new scientist-physician, even though he no longer maintains the typical one-to-one relationship with the patient. Hall's (1969) data also show that personal service professionals believe that they are serving the public, and apparently hold strongly to that norm.

It is important to note that the perspective offered here does not make the scientist the new image of the professional. Instead, it is an attempt to describe just how professional work is reorganizing. The issue is that search behavior of the professional is now collaborative rather than individual. Since much professional work now tends to be structured bureaucratically, the bureaucratically organized setting in which many professionals now work may not be as restrictive or conflicting with professional objectives as has been claimed. This is not to suggest the total absence of conflict between the professional and his organization, but rather to indicate that both the organization and the professions are adapting to current societal forces. Kornhauser (1962) has defined the professional-bureaucracy relationship as one of interdependency. It appears that a more appropriate term for describing this relationship, as it is developing, may be "increased compatibility."

Recognition of the existence of a modified professional work model does not mean that closure has been achieved, since continuing broad social changes will inevitably create a situation in which the modified work pattern will itself undergo modification. Nevertheless, it would appear that some earlier writers overemphasized the negative aspects of the industrialization of the professions.

REFERENCES

ASHLEY, W. J. (1925) An Introduction to English Economic History and Theory, Vol. I. New York: Longmans, Green.

BABBIE, E. R. (1970) Science and Morality in Medicine. Berkeley: University of California Press.

BARBER, B. (1963) "Some problems in the sociology of the professions." Daedalus (Fall): 672-673.

BARNARD, C. I, (1938) Functions of the Executive. Cambridge: Harvard University Press.

BECKER, H. (1962) "The nature of the profession," pp. 27-46 in N. B. Henry (ed.) Education for the Professions. Chicago: University of Chicago Press.

BLAU, P. M. (1955) The Dynamics of Bureaucracy. Chicago: University of Chicago Press.

BUCHER, R. and J. STELLING (1969) "Characteristics of professional organizations." J. of Health and Social Behavior 10 (March): 3-15.

――― and A. STRAUSS (1961) "Professions in process." Amer. J. of Sociology 66 (January): 325-334.

CARR-SAUNDERS, A. M. and P. A. WILSON (1933) Professions. London: Oxford University Press.

COGAN, M. L. (1953) "Toward a definition of a profession." Harvard Ed. Rev. 23 (Winter): 33-50.

DALTON, M. (1961) Men Who Manage: Fusions of Feelings and Theory in Administration. New York: John Wiley.

DAUGHERTY, R. (1970) "Techniques in medical practice: a practice profile." Washington, D.C.: United States Department of Health, Education and Welfare.

ENGEL, G. V. (1970) "Professional autonomy and bureaucratic organization." Administrative Sci. Q. 15 (March): 12-21.

ETZIONI, A. (1964) Modern Organizations. Englewood Cliffs: Prentice-Hall.

FREIDSON, E. (1970) Professional Dominance. New York: Atherton Press.

――― and B. RHEA (1965) "Knowledge and judgment in professional evaluation." Administrative Sci. Q. 10 (June): 107-124.

GERTH, H. and C. W. MILLS (1946) From Max Weber: Essays in Sociology. New York: Oxford University Press.

GOODE, W. J. (1960) "Encroachment, charlatanism and the emerging profession: psychology, sociology, and medicine." Amer. Soc. Rev. 25 (December): 902-914.

――― (1957) "Community within a community: the professions." Amer. Soc. Rev. 22 (April): 194-208.

GOSS, M.E.W. (1963) "Patterns of bureaucracy among hospital staff physicians," pp. 170-194 in E. Freidson (ed.) The Hospital in Modern Society. New York: Free Press.

GOLDNER, F. H. and R. R. RITTI (1967) "Professionalization as career mobility." Amer. J. of Sociology 72 (March): 489-502.

GOULDNER, A. (1954) Patterns of Industrial Bureaucracy. New York: Free Press.

HALL, R. (1969) Occupations and the Social Structure. Englewood Cliffs: Prentice-Hall.

――― (1968) "Professionalization and bureaucratization." Amer. Soc. Rev. 33 (February): 92-104.

HICKSON, D. J. (1966) "A convergence in organization theory." Administrative Sci. Q. 11 (September): 224-251.

HORWITZ, J. J. (1970) Team Practice and the Specialist. Springfield, Illinois: C. C Thomas.

HUGHES, E. C. (1963) "Professions." Daedalus (Fall): 655-668.

――― (1958) Men and Their Work. New York: Free Press.

JANOWITZ, M. (1960) The Professional Soldier. New York: Free Press.

JOHNSTONE, Q. and D. HOPSON, Jr. (1967) Lawyers and Their Work: An Analysis of the Legal Profession in the United States and England. Indianapolis: Bobbs-Merrill.

KENDALL, P. (1962) The Relationship Between Medical Educators and Medical Practitioners. Evanston: Association of American Medical Colleges.

KORNHAUSER, (1962) Scientists in Industry: Conflict and Accommodation. Berkeley: University of California Press.

LEWIS R. and A. MAUDE (1953) Professional People in England. Cambridge: Harvard University Press.

LITWAK, E. (1961) "Models of bureaucracy which permit conflict." Amer. J. of Sociology 67 (September): 177-184.

Los Angeles Times (1971) Article. January 9, Part I, p. 3.

LYNN, K. (1963) Introduction to the issue, "The professions." Daedalus (Fall): 649-653.

MARSHALL, T. H. (1939) "The recent history of professionalism in relation to social structure and social policy." Canadian J. of Economics and Pol. Sci. 5 (August): 325-340.

MERTON, R. K. (1957) Social Theory and Social Structure. New York: Free Press.

MILLS, C. W. (1951) White Collar: The American Middle Class. New York: Oxford University Press.

MOUZELIS, N. P. (1967) Organization and Bureaucracy: An Analysis of Modern Theories. Chicago: Aldine.

PERROW, C. (1967) "The impact of technology upon influence and discretion–some problems." Prepared for Organization Theory Conference (April). Cape Cod.

––– (1965) "Hospital technology, structure and goals," pp. 910-971 in J. G. March (ed.) Handbook of Organizations. Chicago: Rand McNally.

PIRENNE, H. (1936) "European Guilds," in Encyclopedia of the Social Sciences, Vol. 7. New York: Macmillan.

READER, G. (1963) "Contributions of sociology to medicine," in H. F. Freeman (ed.) Handbook of Sociology. Englewood Cliffs: Prentice-Hall.

SCHNEIDER, E. V. (1957) Industrial Sociology. New York: McGraw-Hill.

SCOTT, R. W. (1965) "Reactions to supervision in a heteronomous professional organization." Administrative Sci. Q. 10 (June): 63-81.

SEEMAN, M. (1959) "On the meaning of alienation." Amer. Soc. Rev. 24 (December): 783-791.

SHERLOCK, B. J. and R. T. MORRIS (1967) "The evolution of the professional: a paradigm." Soc. Inquiry 37 (Winter): 27-46.

SMIGEL, E. O. (1964) The Wall Street Lawyer: Professional Organizational Man? New York: Free Press.

STINCHCOMBE, A. L. (1959) "Bureaucratic and craft administration of production." Administrative Sci. Q. 4 (September): 168-187.

UDY, S. H. (1962) "Administration, rationality, social setting and organizational development." Amer. J. of Sociology 68 (November): 299-308.

VOLLMER, H. M. and D. L. MILLS (1966) Professionalization. Englewood Cliffs: Prentice-Hall.

WEBER, M. (1947) Theory of Social and Economic Organization. A. M. Henderson and T. Parsons (trans.), T. Parsons (ed.) New York: Free Press.

WHYTE, W. H., Jr. (1957) The Organization Man. Garden City: Doubleday.

WILENSKY, H. (1964) "The professionalization of everyone?" Amer. J. of Sociology 70 (September): 137-150.

Chapter 5

PROFESSIONALIZATION
AND UNIONISM
A Jurisdictional Dispute?

MARIE R. HAUG and MARVIN B. SUSSMAN

Unionization and professionalization are two processes by which
members of an occupation seek to achieve collective upward
mobility. Such combined efforts at job advancement are the
analogue, on a group scale, of individual striving for a better
job—one with higher pay, pleasanter working conditions, more
freedom from supervision, and higher community status. Where
individual upward mobility is blocked or hindered, occupational
incumbents often turn to collective efforts with the same
generalized goals of increased earnings, autonomy, and prestige. In
short, individuals unlikely to get better work tend to join with
others similarly situated to make their work better.

The particular upward mobility route chosen historically has
varied with the nature of the tasks, along the manual/nonmanual
dimension. Blue-collar workers have formed unions, while white-

Authors' Note: *This article is adapted from a paper presented at the
American Sociological Association, Washington, D.C., September, 1970. It
was written in connection with a larger study on the Career Contingencies of
the Rehabilitation Counselor, supported in part by the Rehabilitation
Services Administration, Project RD-1726-P-69-C4, and Case Western Reserve
University.*

collar workers have been more apt to strive for professionalization, particularly if they were in a social service field. Teachers, social workers, counselors, nurses, and librarians were interested in professionalization, while plumbers, mechanics, assemblers, and welders unionized. Even though collective upward mobility strivings of the blue-collar worker along strictly occupational lines was more characteristic of an earlier era of craft unionism when combinations were formed on the basis of a particular type of work, the occupational mobility model still holds in the more recent case of industrial unionism. When various occupations join in one organization on an industry rather than on a craft basis, incumbents combine at two levels, within occupations and across occupations, in order to put together a more powerful instrument in securing the same occupational mobility goals.

MODELS, ROLES, AND DEFINITIONS

Conceptualizing unionism and professionalization as alternative forms of collective upward mobility does not mean that there are no differences between the two processes. Indeed, differences can be distinguished in goal priorities and explicit definitions, in strategies of achieving these goals, and in relationships to the public.

Workers who choose the union road undertake to gain their ends through a publicized power struggle with specific work systems. Using the mechanisms of collective bargaining, within-organization pressures, public attitude change through public relations and the press, and occasional strikes, employees in bureaucracies extract higher wages, more comfortable job conditions, and a delimited corporate span of authority over their work lives. An expected side benefit of these improvements is higher status in the eyes of the immediate community as a result of the more affluent workers' new patterns of consumption and expanded leisure, although higher prestige in terms of the public at large may not be forthcoming. Similarly, although management's authority to hire, fire, discipline, and upgrade may be stringently circumscribed by a successful union, the power to define actual work performance is a jealously held bureaucratic prerogative, rarely if ever fully relinquished in industry.

Relationships to the public also have a problematic character. Unions have been charged with ignoring the public interest in their concern with the interests of their members, and, certainly, where public services are involved, the withdrawal of labor inconveniences the users of these services. However, the more modern unions have learned to appeal to the public and to use them as allies against obstinate employers. Today's unionized worker makes a case for the consumer of services and his so-called disregard for the public is more the complaint of the establishment than of the rank and file.

Persons in occupations striving to professionalize are also in a power struggle, but on a societal level. They have, at least in the past, attempted to persuade the public at large,[1] rather than a particular bureaucratic hierarchy, that they are due various emoluments. Because of their mysterious specialized knowledge, communal power over members, shared role definitions, and their dedication to service, professionals lay claim first and foremost to autonomy and independence on the job, with attendant control over the client, and expect as inevitable secondary benefits both large financial rewards and exalted prestige. Organization takes the form of a professional association rather than a union. Instead of engaging in a power contest between haves and have-nots, the association undertakes to protect and expand the profession's knowledge base, enforce standards of learning, entry, and performance, and engage in similar activities designed to enhance the position of the practitioners while simultaneously purporting to protect the welfare of the public in the person of the client. Indeed, professional claims concerning the primacy of the public good over the practitioner's own private benefit might be viewed as a critical difference between the professionalizing and unionizing modes of mobility, were it not for considerable evidence that the claims are watered with rhetoric.

Professionalization may imply a concern for service to individuals, but it is built around a neutralist ideology that has potentially elitist consequences. The tendency is to move away from extensive involvement with the client and into a "community of one's peers" from which client concerns are barred. It is a curious anomaly that the unionized service worker may actually be more involved and identified with his client's concerns than is the professional, even though there is an element of self-interest, in that he also seeks client support for his goals, and thus anticipates a payoff from a reciprocal relationship of collective power.

The model of professionalization and unionization as alternate roads to collective mobility has not included the issue of conflict between these two modes of occupational behavior, yet this may be the most problematic issue in terms of the contemporary scene. More and more professions are being pursued in bureaucratic settings. Even for the physician and the lawyer, the last of the "free professionals," practice is increasingly a group enterprise, boxed in with various organizational constraints. Private practice as a style of professional work is rapidly disappearing, while many new and emergent professions have never practiced in anything except a bureaucratic setting. Under these circumstances, it is a particular bureaucratic structure, not some vague public or segment of a public, which must be dealt with, and from which money, autonomy, and other perquisites must be extracted.

The role of the professional association and of the union overlap in this context of bureaucratic controls, and the tension between the two forms of collective action then becomes similar to a jurisdictional dispute. It could be argued that, while the general aims are the same, the differences in goal weights as between money and autonomy, the variations in value systems with respect to the public, and the disparity between the pressure tactics used are too wide for there to be any real contest. The fact is that professionals like engineers, teachers, nurses, social workers, and others who work in organizations, are turning to unionism, with or without the consent of their appropriate professional association and with apparent disregard for differences in goal emphasis or values, even adopting classic union tactics, such as strikes, slowdowns, sick calls, and picketing.

These organizational and attitudinal tensions are explored in a sample of rehabilitation counselors, an occupational group where the leaders are seeking to professionalize, but whose work locus is almost exclusively in large state and federal bureaucracies, where union organization daily grows more common. Specifically, this paper examines the relationship between willingness to join a union as the outcome variable, and professional association commitment, perceived level of professionalization of the occupation, status, and autonomy as job attributes, and various demographic variables such as age, income, and position in the work bureaucracy.

RESEARCH ON REHABILITATION COUNSELORS

Rehabilitation counselors have been selected as a strategic research population because their "occupation-in-transition" situation is expected to maximize tensions between the professionalizing and unionizing modes of action and thus permit a sharper analytic focus. Since their practice is carried on in government settings, these counselors are exposed to union-organizing efforts. The American Federation of State, County and Municipal Employees, for example, has brought many similarly situated state employees into the organized labor field. Government unionization is a very rapidly developing phenomenon.[2] At the same time, counselors are subject to the pressures of two professional organizations—one related to the guidance and one to the rehabilitation field—both vying to advance the professional level of the occupation by sponsoring training programs, educational workships, ethical codes, research, in-group commitment, and the like.

Furthermore, rehabilitation counseling is strategic to the researcher because this occupational category is similar to the many new professions emerging from the expansion of human service systems. It represents, perhaps, a labor trend of the future, since its birth and growth have been entirely under the wing of the government bureaucracy, a history which may well be repeated as new divisions of labor are created to deal with proliferating social needs. Employees who enter such an expanding occupation, undergirded by governmental dollars, may do so with the expectation that chances for quick personal advancement are good, as appears to have been the case among rehabilitation-counseling recruits. If professionalizers and unionizers are both to claim "jurisdiction" over this type of upwardly striving employee, the attitudes, behaviors, intentions, and ultimate allegiances of rehabilitation counselors may well be typical of future processes of collective upward mobility.

Data were collected from two groups of rehabilitation counselors: the entire cohort of students scheduled to graduate from an M.A.-level training program in the field in 1965, and a subset of those with M.A. degrees taken from a larger national sample randomly selected from practitioners already employed in the field in 1965.[3] As part of a longitudinal study design, these groups were surveyed by mailed questionnaires in late 1968. The ex-student response rate was 90%, providing 292 cases, and the practitioner response rate was 95% for an n of 333.

RESULTS OF THE SAMPLING

The findings indicate that the two sample groups are very similar in attitudes toward unionism, despite the fact that they are in different stages of their careers. In response to the question "Would you favor a union for rehabilitation counselor?" about 21% of the student cohort and nearly 17% of the national sample of practitioners agreed, about a fifth from each category replied "maybe," and 59 to 63% opposed a union. Since the differences between the groups are minimal and can be attributed to sampling error, the students and practitioners are combined for most of the analysis which follows.

Like career stage, location in the occupational hierarchy, age, and current earnings are also unrelated to views on unionism. While those in local front-line offices of the federal Rehabilitation Services Administration are somewhat more likely to favor a union than those in the state or regional offices, the differences are within chance expectations. Similarly, those under forty are only slightly more likely to be union-oriented than their older colleagues. Further, the mean salaries of those who favor unionization differ little from those of the opponents', with variations attributable to sampling error.

With respect to professionalism attitudes and activities, however, a relationship to views on unionism does exist. One measurement of the professional level of the occupation is the nature of its roles and role relations, as viewed by the incumbents. Five levels of agree-disagree responses on seventeen role elements were scored and combined in an Index of Professionalized Counselor Roles. It is apparent that there is an inverse relationship between favoring unionism and the professional role image of rehabilitation counseling (Table 1). Among those who score high on the Index, only 11% favor a union for their occupation, while more than 25% of the low scorers support unionization. The relation, as evaluated by X^2, is linear and beyond chance expectations.[4] It is apparent that a belief in the professionalism of one's work is not, in this group, conducive to an interest in unionism. The disparity suggests conflict between unionization and professionalization as alternative collective upward mobility models.

The point is underscored in an analysis of the respondents' professional activities as related to their union views. Since membership in a professional association may be almost a mechanical accompaniment to employment, particularly in certain public agencies,[5] this variable alone is inadequate as an indicator of attachment to the association. Thus, an index was devised combining membership, attendance at meetings, and journal readership as a measure of individual commitment to professional association activities. This Index of Individual Commitment also has an inverse relationship with attitudes toward unionism (Table 1). A third of those with low commitment favor union organization, as against less than 15% of those with high commitment. The differences and the linear structure are statistically significant. The divergence between union and professional association attachment is clearly evident. Indeed, among those who oppose a union for rehabilitation counselors, the explanation given by nearly 65% is that it would be unprofessional.

Yet some of the same motivational factors seem to underlie both union support and beliefs concerning appropriate profes-

TABLE 1
ATTITUDES TOWARD UNIONISM BY TWO MEASURES
OF PROFESSIONALISM

Professional Level of Counselor Roles—Index Score	Attitudes Toward Unionism				
	Oppose %	Ambivalent %	Favor %	Total n	%
Lowest	45.1	29.4	25.5	51	100.0
Low middle	57.2	21.6	21.1	194	99.9
High middle	65.1	17.4	17.4	281	99.9
Highest	67.6	21.6	10.8	74	100.0
Total	61.2	20.3	18.5	600	100.0

$$X^2 = 11.9253, \text{df } 6, p < .10$$
$$X^2 \text{ for linearity} = 3.9887, \text{df } 1, p < .05^a$$

Individual Commitment to Professional Activities[b] Index Score

	Oppose %	Ambivalent %	Favor %	Total n	%
Lowest	37.8	28.9	33.3	45	100.0
Low middle	61.0	18.4	20.6	136	100.0
High middle	63.5	19.2	17.3	266	100.0
Highest	64.5	21.0	14.5	152	100.0
Total	61.3	20.2	18.5	599	100.0

$$X^2 = 13.8314, \text{df } 6, p < .05$$
$$X^2 \text{ for linearity} = 8.3741, \text{df } 1, p < .01^a$$

a. The X^2 test for linearity of ordinal data is given in A. E. Maxwell, Analysing Qualitative Data, John Wiley: New York, 1961, pp. 63-72.
b. Measured by Index of Individual Level of Professionalism.

sional activities. One of the main reasons given for favoring a union, mentioned by 81% of those with at least quasi-favorable views, was the need for securing higher pay. Respondents were also asked to indicate whether professional associations should enforce standards concerning salaries, working conditions, and fringe benefits—the issues more frequently believed union concerns—as well as educational requirements, agency accreditation, best practices, and ethics. Those who were favorable to union organization were overrepresented among the group who believed that professional associations should address monetary issues and working conditions (Table 2), and the differences were beyond chance. The implication is that the financial pressures in this emerging profession are so severe as to move certain incumbents to favor *any* organized effort—whether union or professional association—to improve their incomes. However, the set of respondents already highly involved in professional association activities tended to be *under*represented in the group favoring economic concerns for professional movements. Apparently some of those who have already made the professional association choice have not done so because of any expection of direct financial reward.

One possible explanation is that the individual who perceives himself as a professional, having taken on the imagery of the role, uses a rhetoric which is basically different from the pro-union occupational holder. Both want the best wages and working conditions for themselves and their colleagues. The latter employs an open dialogue of rights, demands, grievances, needs, and privileges, while the former cloaks his hidden agenda of higher pay and ideal work environment behind the words of service, reward, skill, mystery, and privilege.

A more detailed examination of the factors related to union support is possible for the student cohort, since data were collected on relevant work attitudes and experiences not studied among practitioners. The students were asked to rank desirable elements of any job by order of importance. There is considerable variation in the percentages favoring unionism according to items ranked first and second (Table 3). Union supporters are overrepresented among those rating independence on the job, responsibility for leadership, or high pay among the two most desirable work characteristics. The salience of earnings is an already noted concomitant of union interest, but the concern for independence and leadership are more expected as indicators of professionalism than of union organization. In fact, those highly involved in professional association activities are overrepresented among students favoring independence on the job.

Although these variations fall short of statistical significance, and thus may be attributable to random error, they do support the notion that autonomy needs are felt by persons open to the idea

TABLE 2
ROLES ATTRIBUTED TO PROFESSIONAL ASSOCIATIONS,
ATTITUDES TOWARD UNIONISM AND PERSONAL PROFESSIONAL
ACTIVITIES INDEX

Role Attribution	Attitudes Toward Unionism		Personal Professional Activities Index	
Professional Associations Should Enforce Standards With Respect To:	Ratio of % Favorable per Category to Total % Favorable (18.5%) (base n in parenthesis)		Ratio of % High per Category to Total % High (25.2%) (base n in parenthesis)	
Salaries				
Yes	1.36	(202)[a]	.84	(212)[a]
No	.79	(389)	1.09	(402)
Working conditions				
Yes	1.48	(164)[a]	.94	(173)
No	.80	(427)	1.02	(441)
Fringe benefits				
Yes	1.65	(85)[a]	.89	(85)
No	.88	(506)	1.02	(529)
Educational requirements				
Yes	.98	(504)	1.10	(523)
No	.99	(87)	.44	(91)
Agency accreditation				
Yes	1.00	(290)	.98	(302)
No	.97	(301)	1.02	(312)
Best practice				
Yes	.84	(302)	1.09	(310)
No	1.14	(289)	.91	(304)
Ethics				
Yes	.92	(487)	1.08	(506)[a]
No	1.30	(104)	.62	(108)

a. Difference beyond chance expectations at .05 level or better, as evaluated by χ^2

of union organization, as well as by those oriented toward the professional association. Since the issue of autonomy is sharpest at the point where practice and supervisory roles intersect, the relationship between evaluation of supervision and unionism was examined, and data revealed that rehabilitation counselors who consider those above them in the hierarchy to be poor supervisors are likely to favor unionism. More than half are ambivalent toward

TABLE 3
RELATIVE RATING OF DESIRABLE JOB ELEMENTS, ATTITUDES
TOWARD UNIONISM, AND PERSONAL PROFESSIONAL
ACTIVITIES INDEX, AMONG STUDENT COHORT

Element Given Rank of 1 or 2 in Job Importance	Attitudes Toward Unionism		Personal Professional Activities Index	
	Ratio of % Favorable per Category to Total % Favorable (20.5%) (base n in parenthesis)		Ratio of % High per Category to Total % High (25.3%) (base n in parenthesis)	
Challenging work	.88	(205)	1.04	(209)
Independence on the job	1.13	(134)	1.14	(138)
Service to humanity	.91	(96)	.86	(96)
High pay	1.14	(60)	.99	(60)
Responsibility for leadership	1.14	(47)	.76	(47)
Job security	.73	(20)	.99	(20)

or support union organization, as against a third of those who find their supervisors adequate or better, a difference which is beyond chance expectations.

In addition to financial and autonomy concerns, the need for status has also been viewed as a spur to organization. An index combining three indicators of the respondents' views on the status position of rehabilitation counseling revealed that those who believed the occupation has not achieved sufficient status are more likely to favor unionization than those who consider its status already high. Nearly 50% of those who rated rehabilitation counseling as low status either favored, or were at least ambivalent to, unionism, as compared to less than 25% of those rating it high, a statistically significant difference. Moreover, status views also relate to professional association activity. The former students who denigrated the prestige of their work were more likely to be moderately or very active than those who saw its status as already high.

Here are some apparent anomalies: Among rehabilitation counselors, career stage, age, present earnings, even occupational position, have no meaningful relationship to union support, but the image of the professionalism of their occupation and of their own professional association activity level is related to unionism views. Those who consider rehabilitation counseling a profession and are involved in their associations' activities and those who feel that they can make it careerwise through this groove tend to reject unionism, suggesting tension between these modes of upward mobility. On the other hand, those who think the professional association should be involved in economic issues also favor unionism, chiefly for economic reasons. Further, autonomy needs and the belief that the occupation has not achieved sufficient status are indicators both of union support and professional association activism. In terms of satisfying demands for money, independence, and prestige, professionalism and unionism thus appear to offer equally attractive strategies.

INTERPRETATIONS

Interpretations of these exploratory findings are necessarily tentative and little more than suggestive of further lines of inquiry. One possible conclusion is that the type of mobility mechanism, union versus professional association, is perceived by many emerging professionals in a bureaucracy to have no inherent qualities which would selectively affect autonomous behavior or public prestige. It may be that unions and professional associations have sufficiently changed their images and practices in recent years so that they are viewed as more similar than dissimilar in goals, structure, and functions, despite being social systems vying with one another for followers. Professionalization and unionization can thus be seen as contending processes in the struggle of an occupational group to achieve work autonomy on the job and parallel recognition of status among the public at large, along with the narrower focus on wage and security issues, in which neither process carries any particular moral or political advantage. Explanation for a choice of one method over another by job incumbents or occupational groups must be sought elsewhere.

One explanation is that two competing systems of authority and control over the work place and its product provide one additional option for individual practitioners for upward mobility.

Those who cannot "make it" via normative establishment routes (professional association) can vie for power and status by way of a second path, with appropriate rhetoric on the moral superiority of the union's ideology.

Another possible explanation for a particular selection, it might be argued, is differential concern for the client. Those whose major work interests are humanitarian and client-centered would supposedly be more apt to choose the professionalizing route. This factor, however, does not distinguish between individuals who opt for one path or the other (see Table 3), and thus might not distinguish between occupational groups. Further, it is a dubious rationale in comtemporary context as well. There is widespread suspicion among clients concerning professional good will and expertise.[6] At the same time, bureaucratic constraints on particularized attention to individual clients make it difficult for persons in government service to claim better care for clients if staff are professionalized than if they are not. Everyone, after all, is supposed to get a fair shake.

Indeed, it could be argued that financial reward is in any event the major motivator in upward mobility efforts, with the concern for the client secondary, if in the picture at all. In this view, the emphasis on service is chiefly rhetoric, and thus available both to professionalizers and unionizers. The professional claims that his greater knowledge and autonomy will provide more benefits to the client and meets the charge of elitism and client-practitioner distance by shunting the blame onto the functionaries of bureaucratic work settings. The union supporter also claims that his goal is to provide better service to the client, and explains any short-run inconveniences suffered by the client as the product of bureaucratic intransigence in the power struggle. In the long run, it is held, the satisfied practitioner, whether a professional or a union member, can afford to be more concerned about the client: such involvement provides the rationale for high economic rewards. Only when it comes to timetables does the unionist have a slight edge; he can maintain that his route to monetary payoffs is the faster, since professionalization is a painfully slow process.

Although the occupational or individual attitude toward the client may not, especially in bureaucratic settings, explain the outcome of the professionalizer-unionizer contest, the implication *for* the client of the direction taken may be identifiable. The linkage is in the varying impact of collective mobility styles on individual mobility patterns. Occupational groups seeking collective advancement through professionalizing provide a built-in mechanism for *individual* mobility within the collective process. Persons may gain credentials through formal schooling, specialized training, or advanced degrees, and move up the occupational ladder, because the professionalizing ethos allows and even encourages such efforts. No comparable procedures obtain in the unionizing mode. Indeed, the slogan of "all for one and one for all" suggests disapproval of individual climbers. The repercussion for the client of personalized mobility-striving among professionals may thus be further social distance between client and practitioner, or even complete loss of contact as the newly polished graduate moves up into an administration position. No similar consequences follow from unionizing norms. This is not to say that union members do not try to better themselves on an individual basis, but rather that such activity is not part of the organizational value system.

Another possible explanation for the outcome of the professionalism-unionism jurisdictional dispute is the stage in the division of labor at which the issue is joined, and the nature of the bureaucratic system in which the contest occurs. Rapidly expanding service occupations, which are in flux and not clearly defined, are particularly open to the persuasive professionalizer, because he offers a process for outlining the dimensions of the occupation, marking out the boundaries of its knowledge base, and locating it vis-à-vis other occupations and professions. Under these circumstances, new recruits to the burgeoning field enter a professionalizing system and will tend to be socialized in this direction in the course of being acculturated to the job and the organization. In more established lines of work, where incumbents are more certain of interoccupational relations in the work hierarchy, and where bureaucratic limitations on tangible benefits have been found relatively impermeable to professionalism appeals, the tendency toward unionism could be more pronounced. This may explain why school teachers have organized more frequently than rehabilitation counselors. Similarly, in more solidly entrenched and stratified service bureaucracies, old-line professionals might be happy to let aspirers be bought off with more money, as long as they, "the true pros," are permitted to keep their power and authority. If they had to make a choice, would physicians be happier to have hospital nurses unionize for more tangible gains, or professionalize and demand autonomy in their piece of the patient-care turf?

Complicating the problem of choice between the professional and union routes is the supply and demand for occupational holders and the promises made to incumbents, the latter's expectations of success, and the subsequent experience in the field. Union growth is, in general, related to conditions of the labor market. Specifically, in professional fields, a high rate of unemployment may well lead to accelerated unionization, since individual upward movement is limited in periods of labor oversupply. A labor shortage, on the other hand, favors the option of professionalization, with its greater opportunities for personal advancement. Under these circumstances, however, novices are often promised too much during their period of training, and may experience "reality shock" with the field after entry; in turn, this disenchantment may lead them away from professionalizing, despite their prior socialization in this direction. Under different market conditions, therefore, there may be shifting inequalities in the salience of the two mobility options.

CONCLUSION

For occupational sociologists, all these questions and speculations must presently remain problematic. The conditions under which work independence and wage gains are more likely to be pursued by the power battles implied by unionism, or the appeals for submission to esoteric knowledge implied by professionalism, are essentially undetermined. In light of the spread of unionization to professional fields and rising client rejection of professional rights to unique expertise, the estimate may well be that professionalization is no longer the preferred route to job autonomy, high income, and social status for occupations with knowledge claims. The concomitants, as well as the effects, of such trends on the whole occupational system cannot be lightly dismissed. It has often been hypothesized that ours is a professionalizing society. This paper suggests that the hypothesis is not necessarily supported by the course of history.

NOTES

1. Specialized publics which utilize the services of the "professional" are most important in winning professional acceptance (Haug and Sussman, 1969a).

2. A discussion of the implications of this development may be found in Kassalow (1969).

3. In selecting this subset, those employed by the Veterans Administration were omitted, since such personnel are almost exclusively counseling psychologists with Ph.D. degrees or equivalent and thus not comparable to the student cohort.

4. The X^2 test for linearity, as described in Maxwell (1961: 63-72), is suitable for ordinal data and is based on the formula $\dfrac{b_{yx}^2}{V_{byx}}$.

5. In some regions, the top administrators become involved in campaigns and vie with other regions in trying to attain 100% professional association membership.

6. See for example, Haug and Sussman (1969b).

REFERENCES

HAUG, M. R. and M. B. SUSSMAN (1969a) "Professionalism and the public." Soc. Inquiry 39 (Winter): 57-64.

——— (1969b) "Professional autonomy and the revolt of the client." Social Problems 17 (Fall): 153-161.

KASSALOW, E. M. (1969) "Trade unionism goes public." Public Interest 4 (Winter): 118-130.

MAXWELL, A. E. (1961) Analysing Qualitative Data. New York: John Wiley.

Chapter 6

PROFESSIONAL INNOVATION
IN POST-INDUSTRIAL SOCIETY

ALBERT L. MOK

A number of sociologists have predicted the coming of a new type of society in which knowledge plays an unprecedented role. Lane (1966), for example, describes what he calls the "knowledgeable society" as one where there is much knowledge and where many people are employed in the business of research and scholarship. Citing Machlup (1962), he points to increases in personnel and expenditures on knowledge, and concludes that knowledge occupations—producers as well as distributors of knowledge—have grown more rapidly than others. The knowledgeable society encourages and rewards men of knowledge more than it does men of affairs (Lane, 1966: 652).

Whether any particular society has become fully "knowledgeable" in character is a question Lane does not answer, but one gets the impression that in his view the United States is not far from it:

The prodigious and increasing resources poured into research, the large and increasing numbers of trained people working on various natural and social "problems," and the expanding productivity resulting from

Author's Note: *Revised version of a paper read at the Seventh World Congress of Sociology, Varna, Bulgaria, September 14-19, 1970. I wish to thank Eliot Freidson and Jerry Rosenblum for their criticism of an earlier draft of this paper.*

this work, is, at least in size, a new factor in social and . . . . in political life. This "second scientific revolution," as it is sometimes called, reflects both a new appreciation of the role of scientific knowledge, and a new merger of western organizational and scientific skills [Lane, 1966: 653].

Etzioni (1967, 1968) visualizes a similar development. He characterizes the post-modern society as an active society which is master of itself and which realizes to the full the goals it has set for itself. Control of knowledge is an essential element in this mastery, but there is not such a clear division between the producers of knowledge and the decision-making elites as is sometimes supposed. He claims (1967: 176) that the producers of knowledge play an active role in forming the judgments of decision makers, and thus in fact guide societal action. He distinguishes between "stable" and "transforming" knowledge, the former elaborating and respecifying what is known, taking the basic framework of knowledge itself for granted, and the latter concerned with exploring potential challenges to the basic assumptions of a system. Decision-making elites, claims Etzioni, tend to prefer "stable" over "transforming" knowledge and seek closure on basic knowledge assumptions.

Finally, we may note Bell's characterization of yet another, though similar, model—that of the post-industrial society. Such a society is based on a service economy, and is composed of predominantly white-collar workers, with the professional class most prominent. The most striking dimension of that emerging new society is to be found in the preeminence of theoretical knowledge, characterized by a "new fusion between science and innovation" (Bell, 1968: 182). "It is the altered awareness of the nature of innovation that makes theoretical knowledge so central" (Bell, 1968: 155). Indeed, the chief resource of the post-industrial society is its scientific personnel. Bell predicted that by 1975 15% of the labor force in the United States will be engaged in professional and technical work. This figure may rise to 25% in the year 2000, when 75% of all 18- to 25-year-olds will have attended college. And according to Bell (1968: 153), the United States is the first nation to have reached the post-industrial state, though a limited number of other nations—Japan, Canada and Sweden, suggests Servan-Schreiber (1969: 57)—are likely to join this exclusive club in the forseeable future.

All three of these characterizations of the emerging society of the future emphasize both the important role of specialized knowledge in its governance, and thus the role of the professions, and the importance of innovation in the development of new forms of knowledge. But the existence of specialized knowledge in itself does not mean that innovation follows, nor does it follow inevitably from the existence of a professional class. If scientists and professionals are to be the mainstay of this new, emerging society, what will guarantee that they will be innovative rather than conservative in their work? How will their work be organized, what will be the source of their standards of performance, and what will be the consequences for the kind of knowledge they use and produce? In this paper I wish to distinguish two kinds of professional roles and indicate their implication for the kinds of knowledge they will involve, evaluate the way current trends encourage the adoption of one or the other role, and finally, assess the likelihood that the new society discussed by such writers as Lane, Etzioni and Bell will possess the innovative characteristics they suggest.

TWO PROFESSIONAL ROLES

The literature on professions is enormous. In his recent book, Moore (1970: 245-301) lists over 850 references to the literature, and there are many more in existence if we were to add European sources. As large as the literature is, however, there seems to be general consensus that two basic role models are to be found in the professions. Both have been suggested in one way or another by a number of prominent scholars.

Hughes (1958: 139-144) has distinguished among three occupational models—science, profession and business—of which only two are relevant for our purposes. He sees science as the discovery and systematization of knowledge, which derives its value from convincing communication to colleagues. In contrast, profession is the giving of esoteric services to clients who, as laymen, cannot handle their problem themselves, and who are said not to be able to evaluate the work of the professional.

This distinction is extended further by Geiger (1949: 12-19) and, following him, Ben-David (1964: 249), in discussing the differences between the creators and the reproducers of knowledge. The creative intellectuals, the artists and the scientists are the producers of knowledge, while the practicing professions are the reproducers, appliers and users. Freidson (1970: 74) made a similar distinction between the scholarly and learned professions which create and elaborate the formal knowledge of a civilization, and the practicing or consulting professions which have the task of applying that knowledge to everyday life. Elsewhere (Mok, 1969a) I made yet another but analogous distinction between a "modern" and a "traditional" model of professional work.

In considering this distinction, however, it must be noted that no actual profession is likely to be composed entirely of people whose work is represented by only one of those professional roles. Present-day professions contain elements of both models. There is no professionalization process which leads to but one type of role, measurable with some sort of scale of professionalization (Wilensky, 1964; Moore, 1970). Kairat (1969) has pointed out that in a highly developed society with a complex knowledge system, professionalization will almost always lead to the partition of individual professions into two subsystems, one of which deals with the development of knowledge and theory, and one with the application of knowledge, or praxis. In accordance with Geiger's terminology, I would call the professionals engaged in the former kind of activities the producers of knowledge, and those engaged in the latter type users of knowledge.

As Kairat sees it, the two subsystems of a profession have a constant mutual exchange relationship even though they each have different goals. The goal of the producers of knowledge is innovation; the goal of the users of knowledge is the solving of the problems put to them mostly by a lay clientele. Thus, in any particular profession, essentially two professional role-models can be found from which the individual worker, or cohorts of workers, must choose. Which role-model is chosen makes the difference between emphasis on innovation or on mere application of available knowledge. The pressure which can be brought to bear on this choice appears to be a central structural element in assessing the creation of new knowledge as opposed to those for the application of old, for an "active society" or a static one.

THE CHOICE OF ROLE-MODELS

Every profession's members are confronted with the necessity of choosing a role-model. Every discipline has its producers and its users, its innovators and appliers. One cannot say that a certain profession as a whole—like physics—fits the producer model, and another—like medicine or architecture—the user model. What one can say is that every profession has these two segments in which professional norms are institutionalized and prescribed to the incumbents of the positions in that segment. The relative power of one of these segments to give dominant role prescriptions to the profession as a whole is an important question for research. What structural conditions exist that make professionals adhere to certain institutionalized norms? What role models do librarians (Goode, 1966), nurses (Katz, 1969), pharmacists (Denzin and Mettlin, 1968; McCormack, 1956), and others choose, and from where do they derive their professional identity? Does the librarian become an information specialist or does he concentrate on service to the client, accepting the limitations which the client imposes on him? Does the nurse take part in the power structure of the hospital by controlling knowledge via the structuring of relationships, or is she merely a mediator between physician and patient? And in pharmacy, does one choose to be a research pharmacist or a shopkeeper? A number of factors lead me to believe that in the emerging society, the tendency will be to choose the model of the user of knowledge rather than that of the producer or innovator.

Pressure toward choice to be a user of knowledge exists within the professions themselves. For one thing, the user or applied segments tend to dominate professions. Even the scientification (Mok, 1969b) of established professions like medicine, law and architecture has not led to serious challenge to the power of the user segment. The clearest example of this is the profession of medicine, of which Freidson (1970: 163) has said that it is characteristically oriented to applying science rather than to creating or contributing to it, and applying it to the concrete problems of individual clients. There are producers of knowledge within the profession of medicine, but they compose a small and relatively powerless segment (Rayack, 1967). Science and technology constitute the seeds of conflict in medicine, medical practice has changed considerably, specialization has grown tremendously, but still there is strong resistance to change in institutionalized medicine. When new medical specialties come into being as a result of the scientification of medicine, the incumbents of such new specialties as pathology, (Bucher, 1962) radiology and anesthesiology (Lortie, 1958), far from taking the role of the scientists of medicine, adopt the traditional clinician's role for the sake of establishing professional credibility and identity with the public, and for the sake of the financial rewards (Katz, 1968: 95).

Some of these pressures stem from choice of clientele. Fisher (1969: 433) has observed that the decision about which client group to serve is the most important one an occupation or worker can make. The client, of course, need not be an individual person, but can be any person or social subsystem that has an asymetrical relationship with the professional. This may be the government, a business firm, or whatever. Indeed, Van Doorn (1965) has designated the state as the client of the military. Understanding, then, that client means more than a person or class of persons, it can be noted that the choice need not be to serve a client at all, but only one's colleagues. The producer of knowledge is concerned with pursuing knowledge for its own sake, by criteria established by his peers, rather than, like the user of knowledge, seeking solution to problems brought to him or suffered by a clientele. But there seems to be an ever-increasing tendency for even the elite scientists working in universities to become more and more dependent upon the state for the support of their work. Such a tendency encourages the producers of knowledge to forsake their role-model by formulating their proposals for research support in terms of the problems with which the state as client is concerned, and in terms of finding practical solutions which rest on "stable" rather than "transforming" knowledge.

Indeed, Rex (1970) has argued that the institutionalization of science may be detrimental to innovation and scientific discovery, for it tends to encourage what Merton (1957) has called the ritualist and to discourage the innovator. Rex calls this the pathology of the professionalization of science, which leads to the domestication of the scientist by sponsors, consumers and the government. As Etzioni (1967: 176) has said, innovations form potential challenges to the basic assumptions of a system. Domestication prevents the scientist from reaching conclusions which may be disruptive to the existing system. If domestication is successful, there will be strong pressure on the scientist to merely apply existing knowledge and to adopt the user of knowledge model.

Rex (1970: 158) gives a striking illustration of how sponsorship may lead the scientist to bow to the wishes of the "client" by limiting his research questions.

> If a sociologist in Britain or the United States seeks to analyse racial conflict in terms of a model which begins by seeking to make an objective estimate of the likely behaviour and motivation of all the participants in the situation including not merely that of the white racist extremists and various negro groups, but also of those in governmental positions and those holding so-called "liberal" views, he is bound to impinge on what is an ideological field. If, however, he accepts that what he can do qua sociologist and scientist is to analyze small-scale correlations and causal sequences, then he is likely to find himself engaged on a project estimating, say, the effect on public attitudes on fair practices procedures. A sociologist, salaried in a university or a research institute, is far more likely to be supported in the latter type of work than he is in the former.

Finally, I may point out the implications of Etzioni's analysis (1968: 213), which suggests that the emerging society will be more concerned with the uses of knowledge than with its production. If such were the case, it would mean that the producers of science will have more difficulty in establishing their credibility and their worthiness for support than the users of science. This is strengthened by another factor. Etzioni (1968: 136) mentions two functions of knowledge: informational and normative. The information function provides factual statements about reality, the normative function gives an evaluative interpretation of that reality. Etzioni suggests that the knowledge used (and thus, I would add, expected of their guides, interpreters and mediators in the field of knowledge) by societal actors commonly mixes information with evaluative interpretation. Thus the public puts pressure to bear on the scientists not to stay aloof, which means that in an "active society" scientists do not enhance their identity by insisting on objectivity. To establish their credibility scientists have to convince their most sceptical observers—the public they serve—of the vital function of their work (Haug and Sussman, 1969). This is yet another pressure toward adoption of the user of science model.

THE FATE OF KNOWLEDGE IN THE NEW SOCIETY

If knowledge growth is as rapid and exponential (Price, 1963: 5) as can be expected from the descriptions of the post-industrial society, the relationships between the two subsystems of knowledge in the knowledge professions is bound to be rather one-sided. The user of knowledge, confronted with ever more complex problems, and the increasing demands of clients who have high expectations of expert service, is likely to become more and more dependent on the producers of knowledge to keep him qualified for his practice. Or, as Kairat (1969: 82) puts it, the more innovation in a profession is institutionalized independently, the more the practitioner becomes dependent on the creative institutions for the production of new knowledge.

But at the same time another process weakens the producers of knowledge. As knowledge becomes more complex and the development of it therefore becomes ever more costly, the producers of knowledge will become more dependent on external institutions for material support. This dependence is likely to lead the innovating scientists to deny the charge that they develop knowledge merely for its own sake and to emphasize instead their contribution to the immediate solution of practical societal problems. Thus, they identify themselves with the practitioners, or the users of knowledge, not with the task of basic creative innovation. In this way the relationship between the subsystems is reversed, or at least the differences vitiated, with the producers seeking legitimation by pointing to the utility of their knowledge to the institutions which support them. This constitutes a denial of the special content of the innovating scientist's role, a shift in role-model emphasis, for it seeks legitimation from a clientele rather than from a collegium of peers.

Turning to the client for legitimation may occur in any profession, even if it is "natural" only to the user-of-knowledge segment. The client, whether an individual person, a bureaucratic organization like a business firm or a government agency, or the public at large, lends creditability to the activities of the professional man and helps him establish his claim of value. By definition, the professional-client relationship is asymmetrical (Katz, 1968: 28), the client lacking the knowledge he seeks from the professional. But this asymmetry is only one of skill or knowledge which does not, in itself, create a situation favorable to the profession. If the professional becomes highly dependent on client groups or policy makers for his rewards, financial or otherwise, his autonomy is bound to be limited severely. Indeed, it is in fact my argument that, in the emerging society of the future, the professional who has in the past produced highly creative innovations in knowledge, when confronted with the need to make a clear choice of role-models, will tend to choose that of the user rather than the producer of knowledge, for it is the former which will gain him the support he seeks. He will not do this because he is so inclined, but because he will have to yield to the external pressure which grants legitimation on the basis of utility.

If this is true, it seems that the prospects for the innovating capacity of the post-industrial society are gloomy indeed, for who will produce the new knowledge and innovation necessary for the survival of that new society if scientists turn away from the creative role? The applied role, the user of knowledge model, though not antithetical to innovation, is less suited for structural and cultural change than the producer model, for the diffusion of innovations takes longer in the user model than in the producer model (Rogers, 1962; Coleman et al., 1966), and the amount of cognitive reorganization required to integrate new information with previous knowledge is greater in the user than in the producer model (Crane, 1969). And if this too is true, it means that the emerging society, highly dependent for its existence on innovation, will nonetheless create the conditions which discourage the very pursuit of knowledge for its own sake which is most likely to be innovative.

REFERENCES

ARAN, L., and J. BEN-DAVID (1968) "Socialization and career patterns as determinants of productivity of medical researchers." J. of Health and Social Behavior 9 (March): 3-15.

BELL, D. (1968) "The measurement of knowledge and technology" pp. 145-246 in E. B. Sheldon and W. E. Moore (eds.) Indicators of Social Change. New York: Russell Sage.

BEN-DAVID, J. (1964) "Professions in the class system of present-day societies." Current Sociology 12: 247-330.

BUCHER, R. (1962) "Pathology: a study of social movements within a profession." Social Problems 10 (Summer): 40-51.

COLEMAN, J. S., E. KATZ, and H. MENZEL (1966) Medical Innovation. A Diffusion Study. Indianapolis: Bobbs-Merrill.

CRANE, D. (1969) "Fashion in science: does it exist?" Social Problems 16 (Spring): 433-441.

DENZIN, N. K. and C. J. METTLIN (1968) "Incomplete professionalization: the case of pharmacy." Social Forces 46 (March): 375-381.

DOORN, J. VAN (1965) "The officer corps: a fusion of profession and organization." European J. of Sociology 6: 262-282.

ETZIONI, A. (1968) The Active Society. A Theory of Societal and Political Processes. New York: Free Press.

——— (1967) "Toward a theory of societal guidance." Amer. J. of Sociology 73 (September): 173-187.

FISHER, B. M. (1969) "Claims and credibility: a discussion of occupational identity and the agent-client relationship." Social Problem 16 (Spring): 423-433.

FREIDSON, E. (1970) Profession of Medicine. A Study of the Sociology of Applied Knowledge. New York: Dodd, Mead.

——— (1968) "The impurity of professional authority," ch. 3 in H. S. Becker et al. (eds.) Institutions and the Person. Essays presented to Everett C. Hughes. Chicago: Aldine.

GEIGER, T. (1949) Aufgaben und Stellung der Intelligenz in der Gesellschaft. Stuttgart: Ferdinand Enke Verlag.

GOODE, W. (1966) "The librarian: from occupation to profession?" pp. 34-43 in H. M. Vollmer and D. L. Mills (eds.) Professionalization. Englewood Cliffs, N.J.: Prentice-Hall.

HAUG, M. R. and M. B. SUSSMAN (1969) "Professionalism and the public." Soc. Inquiry 39 (Winter): 56-64.

HUGHES, E. C. (1958) Men and Their Work. New York: Free Press.

KAIRAT, H. (1969) "Professions" oder "Freie Berufe?" Professionales Handeln im sozialen Kontext. Berlin: Duncker & Humblot.

KATZ, F. E. (1969) "Nurses," pp. 54-81 in A. Etzioni (ed.) The Semi-Professions and Their Organization. Teachers, Nurses, Social Workers. New York: Free Press.

——— (1968) Autonomy and Organization. The Limits of Social Control. New York: Random House.

LANE, R. E. (1966) "The decline of politics and ideology in a knowledgable society." Amer. Soc. Rev. 31 (October): 649-662.

LORTIE, D. C. (1958) "Anesthesia: from nurse's work to medical specialty," pp. 405-412 in E. G. Jaco (ed.) Patients, Physicians and Illness. New York: Free Press.

MACHLUP, F. (1962) The Production and Distribution of Knowledge in the United States. Princeton N.J.: Princeton University Press.

McCORMACK, T. H. (1956) "The druggists' dilemma: problems of a marginal occupation." Amer. J. of Sociology 61 (January): 308-315.

MERTON, R. K. (1957) Social Theory and Social Structure. New York: Free Press.

MOK, A. L. (1969a) "Alte und neue Professionen." Kölner Zeitschrift für Soziologie und Sozialpsychologie 21: 770-781.

——— (1969b) "Continuities and discontinuities in the nursing profession." International Nursing Rev. 16: 296-309.

MOORE, W. E. (1970) The Professions. Rules and Roles. New York: Russell Sage.

National Academy of Sciences (1969) The Invisible University. Post-doctoral Education in the United States. Report of a Study conducted under the auspices of the National Research Council, Washington D.C.

PRICE, D. J. DA SOLLA (1963) Little Science, Big Science. New York and London: Columbia University Press.

RAYACK, E. (1967) Professional Power and American Medicine. The Economics of the American Medical Association. Cleveland: World.

REX, J. A. (1970) "The spread of the pathology of natural science to the social sciences," in P. Halmos (ed.) The Sociology of Sociology. Sociological Review Mongraph No. 16, 1970: 143-161.

ROGERS, E. M. (1962) Diffusion of Innovations. New York: Free Press.

SERVAN-SCHREIBER, J. J. (1969) The American Challenge. New York: Avon.

STORER, N. W. (1966) The Social System of Science. New York: Holt, Rinehart & Winston.

WILENSKY, H. L. (1964) "The professionalization of everyone?" Amer. J. of Sociology 70 (September): 137-158.

PART II

PROFESSIONS
TODAY AND TOMORROW

Chapter 7

ENGINEERING
Professional Servant of Power

ROBERT PERRUCCI

The extent to which the United States has become a technological society is reflected in the periodic predictions concerning the possibility of a technocratic elite taking control of the country. The increasing complexity of production systems, managerial decision-making, and military preparedness has made the technical expert, with his esoteric knowledge, a key figure in our society. Even the realm of political decisions has become so overwhelmed with information, study groups, and research reports that legislation and political decisions have come under the influence of the expert.

Sometimes the prospect of a technocratic elite controlling the nation has been seen in very positive terms. Over fifty years ago, Thorstein Veblen eagerly predicted the emergence of a "Soviet of Technicians" as a revolutionary class dedicated to recapturing American industry from financial and business interests. The engineer, with his "instinct for workmanship," with his faith in the scientific method, and with his commitment to rationality and efficiency, would sweep away the business interests that were controlling American industry and were seen as responsible for the waste, inefficiency, and chaos that plagued industry.

A modern version of Veblen's vision can be found among engineers who see technological solutions to many of the social problems of advanced societies. Ramo (1969), for example, enthusiastically recommends the application of systems analysis to problems of air and water pollution, city riots, poverty, race problems, crime, medical care, mass transportation, urban decay, and education. Ramo carries forward an optimism based upon engineering's technological achievements in space and weapons systems and assumes that technology is the main hope for solution of the problems of what he terms "civil systems." This eagerness to seek technological solutions to social problems is also reflected in the changing content of papers in engineering journals and those presented at professional meetings. "Engineering and the Urban Crisis" was the theme of the 1968 meetings of the Indiana Society of Professional Engineers; a casual perusal of engineering and systems-oriented journals will reveal an abundance of such titles as "The Need for a Systems Analysis in Welfare," "Automation and Fingerprint Retrieval," and "Systems Analysis: A Rational Approach to School Management."

A less sanguine view of technology and its potential for solving social ills is found in the recent writings of Boguslaw (1965) and McDermott (1969). Rejecting a benign definition of technology as nothing more than organized knowledge for practical purposes, McDermott perfers to look at technology as an institutional system with an ideology, elites, and supportive links with other social institutions. Similarly, Boguslaw raises questions about the growing power of system specialists as decision-making organizations created by system designers take over the responsibilities formerly reserved for informed publics and elected representatives.

An assumption which runs through these predictions of an emerging technocratic elite is that such elites as engineers constitute a homogenous collection of professionals dedicated to the same values, motivated by the same noble goals, and constrained by all powerful professional associations. A second assumption is that such elites have access to the sources of power in society which would make it possible to apply their knowledge in a manner which reinforces their control over important economic and political decisions.

The problem with such assumptions, whether they are made by those who applaud or those who express caution concerning technology, is that they fail to distinguish between the nature of technology itself and the technological elites alleged to control technology. For example, when modern technology, in the form of systems analysis or any other technique, is prescribed as a solution to crime, poverty, or urban decay there is a failure to see that (1) the solutions to many social problems are political rather than technological; and (2) the decisions of whether or not any social problem will be put on the national agenda for solution are made by corporate and political elites, and not by technological elites.

In this essay, I will suggest that one of the major problems facing American society is that its technological elite—i.e., its engineers—*do not* constitute an independent power base which shares in decisions governing the uses to which engineering talents are put. The growing size and increasing centrality of engineering in industry, defense, and governmental activities is but a glimpse of the future programs in system design that engineers will design and operate in the areas of health systems, urban development, crime and delinquency, welfare, and education. Yet, as the importance of engineers has increased to the point where major segments of the society are dependent upon their expertise, we have also observed a corresponding decline in the possibilities for the development of engineering as a genuine profession committed to the service of man in the provision of useful and necessary products. These contradictory trends may also reveal something about the role of power in the development of a profession.

The factors operating against the development of engineering as an independent and autonomous profession are the background and motivational characteristics of persons attracted to the occupation, and the segmentation and diversity of the professional community itself. More specifically, I will suggest (1) that the social origins and consequent mobility experiences of persons entering engineering lead to the reinforcement of business rather than professional values, thereby inhibiting the emergence of a service ethic which focuses upon human welfare; and (2) the increasing specialization and fragmentation of the profession, in terms of educational experiences, professional associations, and organizational careers serve to limit the chances for the emergence of a professional organization with sufficient power to shape its own activities.

POWER AND THE PROFESSIONS

The theory of the professions, as treated in much of the sociological literature, has developed along two distinct lines. The first and more established view, often referred to as the functional theory of professions, gives central attention to the unifying impact of a professional education in which both selection and socialization serve to reduce variability among practitioners. Professionals are thus seen as distinctive from other occupational groups in their specialized knowledge, service ethic, and communal values, emphasizing the importance of colleague contact and control over their activities.

The second view of professions is reflected in the so-called "process" model in which occupational groups are found to follow an orderly sequence of stages and events leading to professional status. Wilensky (1964) has looked at this sequence in terms of such things as the development of university-based training schools, professional associations, license laws, and the like, and suggested that the hypothesized sequence is often not present in "occupations aspiring to professional status . . . where the organization push often comes before a solid technical and institutional base is formed; the professional association, for instance, typically precedes university-based training schools, and the whole effort seems more an opportunistic struggle for the rewards of monopoly than a 'natural history of professionalism.' "

Regardless of the particular model used to understand the professions, a basic *resource* that is necessary for any occupational group seeking to transform itself into a profession is *power*. Professions must have the power to influence legislation regarding licensing and protective laws; they must have the power to have university-based curricula established in universities operated by public monies; they must have the power to establish the collegial body as the sole judge of the performance of any practitioner. The basic source of the power commanded by professions is found in the knowledge they have and the utility of that knowledge as it is applied to specific problems. Yet, while expert knowledge may be a factor in initiating the power of an occupational group, that same power is also used to maintain exclusive control over the knowledge of the profession and the legal right to use that knowledge in practice. Thus, while the knowledge base of an occupational group may be critical for creating a profession with the power to control its activities, the knowledge base is not a sufficient explanation for the continuation of this power. To understand the continuation of power, we must look elsewhere; namely to the nature of the target group or users of the profession and to the context in which the professional's activities are carried out.

The established professions of medicine, law, and the clergy best exemplify occupational groups with sufficient power to shape their own affairs with a minimum of interference from other segments of society. Aside from the importance of its knowledge base for this power, of which we have already spoken, we might also take note of the fact that these established professions have traditionally been concerned with the problems of individuals, and have been concerned with society only in the aggregate sense. The power of the professional in dealing with his individual client is not very problematic from the point of view of *misuse* of power, or the use of power to intrude upon the prerogatives of other groups or organizations. This may be most clearly seen in an examination of the critical issues set loose by those doctors, lawyers, and clergymen who have taken to applying their knowledge to the problems of society, and, in so doing, have challenged the power claims of other groups in society. Doctors in the area of public health, or those dealing with the reorganization of medical care systems; lawyers setting up storefront law firms to challenge established judicial practices; clergymen who have taken to the streets to deal with the temporal needs of their congregations—each has raised questions about the misuse of the power granted them by society. If such professionals were today seeking to establish their power to deal with the problems of society as they have defined them, it is highly unlikely the legislatures, trustees, and political leaders would support their requests for protective legislation, licensing, educational programs, and autonomy in the conduct of their affairs. In fact, the doctors, lawyers, and clergymen who have chosen to define society, rather than individuals, as their clients face the possibility of having their professional status withdrawn by their professional associations.

An examination of some of the main features of the engineering profession gives an indication of its potential for developing a power base from which it can acquire control over its activities. With approximately one million practitioners, the engineering profession carries out its activities primarily in private industry. About 85% of all engineering graduates are in industry, with some 13% in government (Perrucci et al., 1966a). Of those in private industry, over one-third are directly employed on government projects. Working in these organizational settings on group projects and government contracts limits the engineer's ability to determine what he works on and how he works on it.

In contrast to medicine, law, or the clergy, engineers do not as a profession maintain exclusive jurisdiction over their practice. Graduates from a number of physical science fields are employed as engineers, a condition which reflects the similarity of their educational preparation and one reason for engineers' limited identification with their profession (National Opinion Research Center, 1965: 72-75). When asked questions about some specific aspects of their work, engineers tend to feel that their talents are not always being properly used and that what they do work on is not really a contribution to society. Two-thirds of a national sample of engineers indicated that the work they are doing could be done by someone with less technical training. And in response to a question of how important it was to them to make significant contributions to society, only one-quarter said it was "very important," and only twelve percent said their present work allowed them to make such contributions (Perrucci et al., 1966a).

Given such limited autonomy over their work, control over who may and may not practice engineering, and doubts about how their talents are being used, engineers find themselves with a body of specialized knowledge that is for sale to any client who seeks to hire them. It would also probably be more correct to speak of the buyers of engineering talent as employers rather than as clients, for the latter term usually implies that the professional exercises some measure of control over the services he performs for clients.

However, just as the established professions are embarking upon new enterprises that will bring them into greater conflict with society, so is engineering moving in directions that will challenge its existence as a profession that serves society. In addition to growing numbers, recent engineering graduates have been occupying positions of greater responsibility and importance than did their colleagues of an earlier vintage. It also seems probable that the decades ahead will find engineers having an even greater impact upon American society as they continue to apply scientific knowledge to a wide variety of societal problems. The key issue, however, is whether engineers will develop a service ethic of such strength as to require them to serve the human welfare of the American people, or whether they will continue to serve *employers*, who will determine the uses to which they put their talents.

MOBILITY, BUSINESS VALUES, AND HUMAN WELFARE

A notable characteristic of occupational groups classified as professions is that the prestige and power of the profession closely corresponds to the proportion of the practitioners that are recruited from high socioeconomic origins. Engineering recruits more of its students from lower social origins than do medicine, law, clergy, dentistry, or teaching (More, 1960; Adams, 1953; Charters, 1963; Perrucci et al., 1966a). Moreover, there has been a steady increase in the proportion of engineers coming from lower socioeconomic origins. Engineering graduates prior to 1940 were recruited in large part from sons of proprietors and managers (30%), while in the post-1950 period the proportion dropped to

24%. For the same period, engineering graduates from blue-collar origins increased from 30 to 40%.

Looking at geographical origins, over two-thirds of the engineers were born in the Midwest and East, which is higher than the proportion of the eligible population in these areas at any time in this century. Overselection of engineers also seems to come from small-town America. Recruitment from rural areas (under 5,000 population) is in proportion to the population in these areas, but a higher proportion of engineers come from communities of 5,000 to 50,000 population than would be expected from the general population distribution. This small-town recruitment pattern is further reinforced by examination of temporal trends which indicate that engineering recruitment has not followed the population movement to the large metropolitan areas (Perrucci and Gerstl, 1969).

These data on the social origins of engineers indicate that a sizable proportion of the persons who become engineers experience a significant degree of social mobility. They have an occupation that allows them to enjoy considerably more prestige than their fathers, and they make considerably more money. The mobility experience of these engineers is probably more conducive to maintaining or enhancing their personal gains than it is to the development of altruistic impulses and the promotion of human welfare.

An examination of some historical data supports the general hypothesis that professionals who experience social mobility will not be especially concerned with using their professions to serve society as much as to serve themselves. In the established professions and in engineering at the turn of the century, most persons were drawn from high social origins and therefore already had the security of established status (Calvert, 1967). The big push for creating and building a professional society that would enhance the prestige and income of engineers came from those practitioners for whom becoming an engineer meant upward social mobility. Those with the security of established status will in contrast not seek to secure their newly acquired status through the activities of professionalization of their occupation. A further hypothesis would be that the humanitarianism and service ethic of the established profession can be partly traced to the noblesse oblige of elitist groups in response to the needs of the less fortunate.

It is suggested, therefore, that the desire to contribute to human welfare—to develop a service ethic—preceded the desire to establish the security, autonomy, power, or prestige of an occupational group. The reason for this is that the early practitioners in each profession were persons of established status (e.g., sons of professionals) and hence had little reason to seek to protect or enhance the rewards of their recently acquired positions.

A second consequence of this mobility experience is found in the particular loyalities of engineers to their employers and to organizational careers, rather than to their colleagues. When a national sample of engineers was asked whose judgment should count most in evaluating their professional performance, some 54% said it should be their immediate superiors in their companies, as compared to 26% who named their fellow engineers (Perrucci et al., 1966a). Further, one-third of the graduates indicated that they would take a business or management educational program as an addition to their engineering degree, and another 40% indicated a strong preference for a management career. This loyalty to employers, management careers, and organizations is reflected in the settings in which engineers work. Some 35% of engineers work in organizations with 10,000 or more employees; another 38% are in organizations with between 1,000 and 10,000 employees.

An additional indication of how the mobile orientations and aspirations of engineers lead them to identify with organizational careers rather than with colleagues is revealed in their actual current and anticipated salaries. Salary data from 1966 shows that 40% of engineers earn less than $10,000; 41% earn between $11,000 and $15,000; 15% earn between $16,000 and $20,000; and the remaining 4% earn over $21,000. Expectations on anticipated peak career salaries are: 16% between $51,000 and $90,000; 18% between $26,000 and $50,000; 37% between

$21,000 and $25,000; 20% between $16,000 and $20,000; and the remaining 8% expect to earn less than $15,000 as a peak career salary (Perrucci et al., 1966a).

Aside from the fact that such expectations are very unrealistic (median salary for engineers with twenty years' experience is about $15,000), it would suggest a career orientation that is less concerned with service and human welfare than it is with personal status and income. Moreover, the emphasis on career and income combined with little interest in colleagues is probably not conducive to the development of a strong service ethic to go along with the increased involvement in dealing with social rather than with technical problems.

Finally, a barrier to the development of an engineering profession committed to service is found in the view that the concept of professionalism, with all its noble meanings, is not the creature of engineers, but of management. Goldner and Ritti (1967) have suggested that professionalism is encouraged by management as a device for further cementing the engineer's commitment to his employing organization:

Management thus attempts to impose professionalism as a definition of success within the organization in order to maintain commitment on the part of those specialists who would ordinarily be considered failures, for not having moved into management. Identification as a professional has become a way to redefine failure as success [Goldner and Ritti, 1967: 490].

An investigation of what professionalism means to engineers indicates that there may be some support for Goldner and Ritti's findings but perhaps not for the reasons they give. Professionalism is encouraged by management for some of its engineering employees, as evidenced by the number of organizations that encourage (and sometimes reward) attendance at professional meetings, publication of papers in professional engineering journals, and membership in professional societies (Perrucci et al., 1966a). However, involvement in professional activities and support of the values of professionalism are not, as Goldner and Ritti suggest, exhibited by those engineers with unsuccessful, dead-end careers. On the contrary, there is a moderate and positive association between professionalism and several measures of career success (Perrucci and Perrucci, 1970). Available evidence also clearly indicates that engineers with doctoral degrees give much greater support to professional values reflecting the importance of colleague contact, belonging to a professional community, and contributing to scientific knowledge and less support to the importance of pecuniary rewards and career advancement than do engineers without doctoral degrees (Perrucci and Gerstl, 1969: ch. 4). However, since engineers with doctoral degrees constitute only about two or three percent of all practicing engineers, it is clear that the profession does not have a strong foundation in the values of professionalism from which a strong service ethic could emerge.

SEGMENTATION, DIVERSITY, AND PROFESSIONAL COMMUNITY

In an examination of the role of division of labor in industry and the way it results in extensive specialization and role fragmentation, Gouldner (1961) put forth the interesting hypothesis that management's interest in specialization has less to do with efficiency than it does with control. Workers whose jobs have been reduced to a few basic movements or operations find themselves without valuable skills, but reduced to joining an army of workers who are interchangeable and easily replaceable. Without needed skills, workers have little control over their work and must fall back upon the power of the labor organizations that represent them. Yet, even when labor is strong and jobs are secure, specialization proceeds, and worker control and discretion are lost.

Specialization of engineering activities can also function to reduce the importance of any particular engineer in any particular organization. It can also serve to create differences and divisions among engineers that work against the development of a unified, strong profession. The roots of specialization are found in industry; yet these roots are nourished and strengthened by the wide variety of educational programs at engineering schools, and the great diversity of professional associations representing engineers.

The engineering profession is probably more diverse in formal education, work activities, and collegial associations than are other professions. There are approximately 250 institutions of higher learning that award a baccalaureate degree in engineering. Approximately 170 of these programs are formally accredited by the Engineers Council for Professional Development. There are four-year baccalaureate degree programs, five-year programs, evening school, and work study programs. Curricula at these schools also differ in the emphasis they give to mathematics, basic science, humanities, engineering science, and technology. All this diversity results in approximately 35,000 baccalaureate degrees, 10,000 master's degrees, and 2,000 doctoral degrees annually, scattered across some 24 engineering specializations.

The existence and continuation of this diversity in the engineering profession stems from two sources: (1) The dramatic changes in the content of engineering education that were put into effect in the mid-1950s and created distinct educational generations separated by technical knowledge and conceptions of engineering. The traditional conception of the "nuts and bolts" engineer whose education prepares him for immediate productivity in industry has long dominated engineering education. Engineers were men who worked with "things"; the type of person "who can roll up his sleeves and get down on the floor and make something work." The last decade has seen this traditional conception of the engineer come in conflict with a curriculum which stresses mathematics, computer science, physical sciences, and engineering sciences. Such engineers often know more about general scientific theories and technical principles than they do about concrete principles of design and technical processes. (2) The varied needs of organizations that employ engineers are expressed through the American Society for Engineering Education. Industry is represented in the ASEE through the formal arrangement of the Industrial Members of ASEE. Each member organization provides a representative for the specific purpose of working with educators whose job it is to shape engineering education. Some industries seek engineering graduates who can immediately fit in with the production needs of the organization without costly, time-consuming, on-the-job training. Such industries support the maintenance of engineering specializations that are closely tied to the needs of industry. Those who tend to support continued specialization also tend to deemphasize the importance of advanced degrees for engineers.

Support *for* the continuation of all engineering specializations and *against* the proposal to make a graduate degree the first professional degree is substantial in both industry and the professional associations. The views of top management from a national sample of organizations employing engineers indicate that approximately one-half of them wish to maintain programs of specialization in the traditional areas of engineering rather than move to a common program with little specialization. In addition, almost one-half of the organizations indicate that a bachelor's degree is all that is needed for engineers to work in their firms (Perrucci et al., 1966b).

These facts are further reinforced by the strong opposition from industry and professional societies to the proposal by the American Society for Engineering Education that the master's degree should be the first professional degree, and it should not be distinguished with adjectives representing the various specializations. The recommendation offered by ASEE in its preliminary report of a national study of engineering education is as follows:

> The *first professional degree* in engineering should be the master's degree, awarded upon completion of an integrated program of at least five years' duration. This degree should be uniformly identified as the Master of Engineering degree, without qualifying adjectives or phrases. It is expected that implementation of this recommendation can be accomplished within a period of five to seven years [Engineering Education Committee, 1965].

Resistance to this recommendation among educators and industry resulted in its revision in the final report (Engineering Education Committee, 1968).

Differences in background and activities of engineers, as well as the manifold allegiances across many professional societies, serve to undercut the chances for the emergence of a unified profession that could also develop its own standards of service. Perhaps the only thing more destructive to a potentially unified profession than the fragmentation of professional associations is the number of engineers without any professional identity reflected in a collegial body. Almost one-third of a national sample of engineers do not report membership in any professional or scientific society (Perrucci et al., 1966a). This is probably due in part to the extreme fragmentation in engineering which inhibits the sense of professional community and colleagueship and encourages the dependence upon, and authority of, employing organizations.

CONCLUDING NOTE

The growing centrality of engineering activities in American society calls for a profession that not only has the technical skills to deal with societal problems, but also has both a strong commitment to serve human welfare and the independent power to determine the way in which its talents are used. Our examination of the present structure of engineering, in terms of the persons recruited to the occupation and its internal diversity, suggests that such a profession does not now exist. Engineers now serve dominant industrial and governmental interests, and they do not attempt to determine whether or not their work contributes to pollution, to international tension, to urban decay, or to the creation of a totalitarian social system.

The existence of an engineering profession with a strong sense of social responsibility and with a commitment to human welfare will not guarantee that our technological society will be directed toward more humane objectives. It might, however, cast the engineering profession in the much-needed role of advocate for the needs and rights of man in a technological age.

REFERENCES

ADAMS, S. (1957) "Origins of American occupational elites." Amer. J. of Sociology 62 (January): 360-368.

——— (1953) "Trends in occupational origins of physicians." Amer. Soc. Rev. 18 (January): 404-409.

BOGUSLAW, R. (1965) The New Utopians. Englewood Cliffs, N.J.: Prentice-Hall.

CALVERT, M. J. (1967) The Mechanical Engineer in America: 1830-1910. Baltimore: Johns Hopkins Univ. Press.

CHARTERS, W. W., Jr. (1963) "The social background of teaching," ch. 14 in N. L. Gage (ed.) Handbook of Research on Teaching. Chicago: Rand McNally.

Engineering Education Committee (1968) Goals of Engineering Education Committee, Final Report. Washington, D.C.: American Society for Engineering Education.

——— (1965) Goals of Engineering Education Committee, Preliminary Report. Lafayette, Ind.: Purdue University.

GOLDNER, F. H. and R. R. RITTI (1967) "Professionalization as career immobility." Amer. J. of Sociology 72 (March): 489-502.

GOULDNER, A. (1961) "Metaphysical pathos and the theory of bureaucracy," pp. 71-82 in A. Etzioni (ed.) Complex Organizations. New York: Holt, Rinehart & Winston.

McDERMOTT, J. (1969) "Technology: the opiate of the intellectuals." New York Rev. of Books 13 (July 31): 25-35.

MORE, D. M. (1960) "A note on occupational origins of health service professions." Amer. Soc. Rev. 25 (June): 403-404.

National Opinion Research Center (1965) The United States College Educated Population: 1960. Chicago, Ill.: Report 102.

PERRUCCI, C. C. and R. PERRUCCI (1970) "Social origins, educational contexts and career mobility." Amer. Soc. Rev. 35 (June): 451-463.

PERRUCCI, R. and J. GERSTL (1969) Profession Without Community: Engineers in American Society. New York: Random House.

PERRUCCI, R., W. K. LEBOLD, and W. E. HOWLAND (1966a) "The engineer in industry and government." J. of Engineering Education 56 (March): 237-273.

——— (1966b) "Organizational views on recruitment, employment, and education of engineers in industry and government." J. of Engineering Education 56 (June): 389-407.

RAMO, S. (1969) Cure for Chaos. New York: David McKay.

WILENSKY, H. (1964) "The professionalization of everyone?" Amer. J. of Sociology 70 (September): 137-158.

Chapter 8

THE PUBLIC ACCOUNTING
PROFESSION
Organization, Ideology, and Social Power

PAUL D. MONTAGNA

Although it is among the oldest and largest of the major professions in the United States, accounting is the least known. The nature of the accountant's work does not bear directly on those human relationships with high visibility or those that take place on a face-to-face level with large segments of the population. The balancing of books, the confirmation of receivables, or the observation of inventories does not produce the Patrick Henrys or the Nathan Hales, the Perry Masons or the Ben Caseys. The image of the accountant as someone perched on a high stool with green eyeshade, poring over long columns of figures, is still held by some. He is the conscience of the businessman, the policeman of industry—hardly a dramatic role. As Elbert Hubbard describes him, he is unimpassioned, conservative, and with eyes like a codfish—minus passion, bowels, and a sense of humor.

Even some financially sophisticated people are unaware of the major division of labor in accounting—that between accountant and certified public accountant. Whereas the noncertified accountant generally is an employee of an organization engaged mostly in detailed measuring and recording of that organization's finances for its own information, only the certified public accountant is licensed by the state to express an overall independent opinion of those recorded measurements to interested parties (stockholders, the public, the government, the company itself, or any combination of these). In addition, he can and does engage himself as an expert in: tax services; the design and installation of accounting systems; production control; mergers, consolidations, reorganizations, and acquisitions; and advice in systems and procedures related to finance and accounting. He offers these services to public and private corporations, partnerships, federal, state, and local governmental units, voluntary organizations, nonprofit organizations, banks, railroads, utilities, and individuals.

Public accounting has existed as an officially recognized profession in this country since the 1890s, when certification of accountants first began. With the advent of the "revolutions" of the twentieth century—mass production, communications, automation, and now, information—their numbers increased rapidly from 5,000 in 1920 to 20,000 in 1940, 70,000 in 1960, 87,000 in 1965, and 107,000 in 1970. The estimated number of practicing noncertified accountants and people in accounting-related positions in the United States today is about 400,000 (American Institute of Certified Public Accountants, 1970b).

Techniques of accounting have changed along with the changes in the types and amounts of information they measure. As the information becomes more complex and numerous, so also do the methods and concepts for measurement of this information. A distinct body of accounting knowledge developed and expanded, and when the corporate form of ownership became dominant, the role of the accountant as a policeman for interested third parties took on increased importance. He was the outsider, able to obtain a fresh view of the organization and able to utilize his accumulated experience of accounting and auditing gained from other similar clients. With the increase in public ownership of corporate stocks, pressure developed for an independent examination of the "state of health" of the business enterprise. The most important event hastening this type of investigation was the economic depression of the 1930s, which instigated a series of federal acts greatly increasing the significance of the accountant's reporting. It became law that all corporations registered with stock exchanges be audited by an independent CPA. Presently, this means that CPAs are required for the auditing of the approximately 2,500 publicly traded corporations (Bevis, 1965: 2) with stock at market value of more than $500 billion.

In short, the public accountant has extended his work into nearly every type of organized economic entity. Most of this has been accomplished during the past fifty years and mainly through two types of organization: professional association and firm partnership. The firm partnership is the most common unit of practice, more than 50% of all CPA units being partnerships (Carey, 1965: 422-425). The largest firms dominate the profession in terms of size, number and size of clients, and influence on the business community. The eight largest firms, known in business circles as the Big Eight, employ approximately 10% of the 110,000 CPAs in the United States, an even greater number of accountants aspiring for the certificate, and several thousand non-CPA technical specialists.[1] In contrast, the remaining twenty-five to thirty firms employing more than fifty CPAs each, are much smaller, altogether comprising only around 2% (3,000) of all CPAs. Together, the Eight perform about 90% of the auditing and its related services to big business in this country.[2] They also perform services for many smaller organizations, as well as for those not required by law to be audited. For example, one Big Eight firm—Peat, Marwick, Mitchell & Co.— audits more than 1,000 banks, 700 savings and loan associations, 700 insurance companies, and 1,200 nonprofit institutions, including universities, hospitals, and local, state, and federal governmental bodies (Wise, 1966b: 91). The average number of clients for a Big Eight firm is 10,000. Its average annual earnings are somewhere around $100 million.

To carry out such a large task, the average firm is comprised of 6,000 persons, which includes a clerical staff of about 900. Because of the size and geographical diversity of its clients, and because the auditor must physically audit and go to the records, each firm has an average of 65 offices, located in the major cities in the United States, and maintains an average of 100 offices, affiliates, or correspondents in 40 foreign countries. The internal division of labor is similar to that in the large law firms (Smigel, 1964), starting with partner at the highest level, followed by manager, senior, and junior. Administrative authority is highly centralized in a national and an international executive office located, with only two exceptions, in New York City (Montagna, 1968: 139). Because these firms are so large in size and in influence on the profession, they are the focus for this paper. They represent what is changing and what is new in public accounting.

THE IMPLICATIONS OF ORGANIZATION

During the past decade, the public accounting profession has been faced with a rapidly increasing rationalization of its body of knowledge. Its auditing procedures have been codified, and attempts are being made to standardize the "generally accepted accounting principles." Procedures for the annual audit have become so routine that it is constantly referred to as the "annual nuisance." Already in some areas the basic audit steps can be completely automated (Dill and Adams, 1964). Accounting educators and practitioners have continually emphasized the need for new areas of challenge to recruit and keep the creative young. The answer to this call has been provided in what the profession calls "management advisory services" (MAS), a broad designation covering such activities as: general management, accounting costs and budgeting, operations research, industrial engineering, organization and personnel, data processing, and marketing. Each of these areas includes several subspecialties.

It is the size and scope of operations of the Big Eight which have allowed the rapid development and specialization in MAS. The average size of a MAS department in one of these firms is five hundred, nearly half of whom are located in the New York City office. They are in all but a few cases nonaccounting specialists, about 50% holding advanced degrees (several at the doctorate level) in economics, law, mathematics, psychology, engineering, political science, and so on. With the advent of electronic data processing and real-time systems, there has been more emphasis on giving the client an "operational audit," (i.e., to integrate the information from the traditional audit with MAS information into a computerized "total information service") or at least to interpret client data in terms of systems analysis. Each of the firms conducts yearly formal training programs in MAS, tailored to its clients and to each major career level in the firm.

With their sights on diversification, these giant firms have also expanded into actuarial work, considered to be an extension of MAS. Of the fifteen largest actuarial firms, two are contained within Big Eight firms: Peat, Marwick, Mitchell & Co., and Lybrand, Ross Bros. & Montgomery. Their work is primarily to advise corporations on the financing of their pension plans, increasingly important because of the amount of annual profits retained there (Wise, 1966a). Most recently, the profession— especially the Big Eight—has experienced a resurgence in auditing with the development of independent examinations in federal government agencies and in banking. Twenty-six government agencies now use independent auditors, including the Departments of Defense; Housing and Urban Development; Health, Education and Welfare; and Transportation. In 1965, these agencies used outside accountants in more than 40,000 cases—double the number of 1959 (see *The Journal of Accountancy* for April of 1966).

These firms, then, offer a wide variety of specialists, organized as temporary work teams around a problem to be solved or a client to be audited. As old problems are solved or discarded, old groups are disbanded and new ones formed around new problems. This is much like Bennis' (1966) description of the adaptive, creative, nonbureaucratic work organization of the future. It is because these firms are so large and organized so well administratively that they are able to capitalize on the new needs of their clients by offering such a wide variety of important services. With such a background in auditing, taxes, and management services, the CPA is depended upon for much key financial information.

Why has the profession developed along these lines, and what are some of the social consequences of such a development in our society? The answer to these questions will provide a view of the nature of a profession which, in turn, will serve as a guide to examine recent developments in accounting and the business professions.

IDEOLOGY AND AUTONOMY

As with most other professions, in public accounting we are dealing with a "knowledge-oriented" work community, one in which "knowledge itself becomes the focus, rather than the mere tool of work" (Holzner, 1968: 126). The historical development of the body of knowledge does not, however, tell us why this work community has maintained its high position in the society. The fact that the amount of auditing expanded following the passage of the Securities Acts of 1933-1934 is not adequate proof of the increasing popularity of the profession. Nor is the increase in MAS sufficient to infuse new ideas at work. What is necessary is an examination of the professional ideology. Included in such an ideology are those beliefs and values which serve to legitimate a group's claims for power and prestige and which serve as a guide to influence its behavior and the behavior of others defined as within its sphere (Holzner, 1968: 144; Krause, 1968: 132). No body of knowledge is completely understood; there are no areas where some uncertainty does not remain. Where there is a question as to the control of that knowledge and its uncertainties, an ideology is formed. "Ideology expresses that point in social knowledge at which interests connect up to a picture of reality" (Horowitz, 1961: 79).

As an auditor, the CPA still makes many important decisions which require considerable judgment. For example, an executive partner of one Big Eight firm stated in an interview with the writer: "On a ten million dollar inventory, if six CPAs were to each judge it separately [as to its worth], there would be a range of judgment of plus or minus 10% of that inventory." Whatever is within the limits of this judgment area of two million dollars is the area of nonmateriality. Whether an item were "material" or not would depend on whether the accounting method of treating it would influence significantly, that is, "make a difference in," the judgment or conduct of a reasonable person (Dohr, 1950; Reininga, 1968).

The area of nonmateriality in all decisions involved in the audit process is the basis for the public accountant's autonomy. The conventions governing this materiality have developed gradually over the years, are spelled out loosely in "generally accepted accounting principles," and are somewhat more structured in "generally accepted auditing standards." The method for transmitting the results of the audit to all interested parties is the CPA opinion, which can take four basic forms: a fully satisfactory "unqualified" opinion of the financial statements of the client; a "qualified" opinion, in which certain selected factors on the financial statement are taken exception to by the CPA; an "adverse" opinion—the financial statements are stated as not in conformity with accounting principles, thus are not presented fairly; a "disclaimer" of opinion—there is not "sufficient competent evidential matter" to give an opinion. Because of the rather wide range given nonmateriality, the latter two types of opinion are exceptions which rarely occur, and the qualified opinion occurs only with moderate frequency.

There are societal beliefs, enacted into the National Securities Acts, which say that only the properly trained *independent* CPA has the right to render these opinions. This limitation is a form of social control of knowledge. Because of its mandate to perform these services, no other group can "set itself out" to compete in this area. Perhaps some corporations would prefer to hire someone other than a CPA firm—say, a management consulting firm—to audit their finances. But the law prevents them from doing so. This affects other types of organization as well. Banks, universities, voluntary organizations, and the like, though not required by law to be audited, are going to the CPA firms to take advantage of their accumulated experience. What has been created and controlled in the audit field by this occupation, then, is largely determined by its ideology, as supported by the public—i.e., that only the independent public accountant can properly deal with problems of materiality and remain both competent and objective while doing so.

However, the beginnings of a "client revolt" (Haug and Sussman, 1969a) against this control may be forming. The independent CPA has assumed a special responsibility to "third parties"—that part of the public interested in his opinion of the client's financial statements. In effect, these third parties are part of the clientele of the profession. A clash between the two occurred when, in 1970, the federal courts denied an appeal in a criminal case (*U.S.* v. *Simon,* F.2d, CCH Fed. Sec. L Rep., 92, 511 [2nd Cir. 1969], known as the Continental Vending Case) involving two partners and an associate from one of the Big Eight firms, who were convicted on three counts of mail fraud and conspiracy for assorted deficiencies. The national association of CPAs, the American Institute of Certified Public Accountants, bitterly fought the case, objecting to the trial by jury by repeatedly stating the need for expert analysis in the complex issues involved, and noted in a brief, submitted *amicus curiae* to the U.S. Supreme Court (subsequently rejected):

> So far as diligent research discloses, this is the first case, criminal or civil, to hold that conduct governed by professional standards may be measured otherwise than by those standards [American Institute of Certified Public Accountants, 1970a: 71].

In this case, the public as client was represented on two levels: as a "consumer of financial information" (Olson, 1970), and as active participants as jurists in determining the rights and responsibilities of "the only true profession in the field of finance and management" (Carey, 1969). The major issue in the case involved the method of presenting an affiliate's collateral on the corporation's balance sheet. As the court noted (Court of Appeals, S.D.N.Y. 397 U.S. 1006 [1970]), mere indication in a footnote to the financial statement regarding the irregular source of collateral for this corporation's securities would be an absolutely necessary minimal warning that would have to be given to any reasonable person. But the deviation was not considered material by members of the profession. Eight CPAs, described by the court as "an impressive array of leaders of the profession," testified that the method of presentation was in no way inconsistent with the profession's accounting principles or auditing standards.[3]

Seen in this light, the public accountant is viewed as leaning on his corporate client (the man who pays him); he becomes "implicated with the established structure because he uses it to his own ends" (Haug and Sussman, 1969a: 155). The public no longer believes independence is being adequately maintained, regardless of whether it is or not. As some in the profession have recently commented, it is a question of *perceived* independence (Carmichael and Swieringa, 1968). Taking this landmark case as a precedent, the public accountant will no longer have the choice as to how the collateral covering securities will be reported. His judgment potential is being reduced in this area, and, more important, it may serve as a guide to reductions in other areas as well.

MANAGEMENT ADVISORY SERVICES: THE CONFLICT OVER NEW KNOWLEDGE

Management consulting is an old profession in the United States, but it remains an ideologically undeveloped one. Management consulting firms compete on the open market with engineering firms, architectural firms, private and public foundations, and especially with the Big Eight public accounting firms, for the services of big business and big government. In 1965, the Big Eight devoted 20% of its total professional man-hours to management advisory services (the profession's name for management consulting). Less time (18%) was given to one of its more traditional functions, tax services. Auditing commanded the largest part—52%, administration, 8%, and "other," 2%. All indications are that MAS has increased significantly in proportion to other activities and will continue to do so. This in no small way is due to the efforts of the AICPA and a number of leading practitioners and theorists to professionalize this area. The AICPA has created a committee on management advisory services, with full powers to legislate on matters pertaining to its areas of concern. The committee has already issued the rudiments of a code of ethics and is recommending that MAS specialists who are not CPAs be admitted to full membership in the AICPA. This service orientation is emphasized as well. The director of MAS for Lybrand, Ross Bros. & Montgomery feels that the public accountant should practice forensic accounting where reasonable because, if not, he *prevents* independence. He would purposely narrow his vision so much as to fault the client in needed "perception, discrimination, or moral judgment" (Kaufman, 1967: 719). Also being discussed is the possibility of some form of training program and testing procedure. These are among the commonly cited attributes of a profession, which are the tools for obtaining control of an area of knowledge through the public's acceptance (Freidson, 1970: 77-82). The latter's role is crucial (Haug and Sussman, 1969b), for the AICPA's conferring a status on the MAS specialist means little or nothing to those not connected with the profession. The public's acceptance, formal (through licensing via the state) or informal (through acquiescence), will alone permit the control of expertise in this area.[4]

Public accountants are in a unique position to obtain this mandate, if it is forthcoming. For they are the only persons who yearly audit the internal control systems of American business. And in the smaller companies, where sophisticated techniques of internal control in most cases do not exist, the auditor fills the role that is normally assigned to the comptroller in a larger organization. MAS is a natural extension of the audit role; it is the logical combination of electronic data processing and systems analysis. When combined and synthesized with audit, management, and employee information, a total administrative service can be offered.

The profession receives help from another source—those of its members who have defected to the client. CPAs have become top executives in many of the largest businesses.[5] Each of the Big Eight maintains a placement bureau for those who leave the firm every year, and clients usually receive first choice of applicants.

One writer (Wise, 1966b) reports that Peat, Marwick holds within it the world's largest executive placement agency and may well be the largest management consulting operation in existence.

For the Big Eight, generally, MAS is expanding at 15% annually, whereas for the 45 "elite" management consulting firms (defined by membership in the Association of Consulting Management Engineers) expansion is approximately 10%, and for the consulting business in general, it is 4% (Forbes, 1966). Every Big Eight MAS department is included among the twenty largest management consulting groups in the country (Kaufman, 1967). Some of Peat, Marwick's MAS activities in a single year include (Wise, 1966b): arranging mergers and acquisitions for approximately 250 clients; placement of 250 executives in corporations; placement of 300 men from its own firm with client firms; advising foreign governments on such things as new industrial projects (India) and computation of price and cost values in industry nationalization (England); preparation of programs on construction and maintenance costs and management methods to highway departments of ten states, with fees ranging from $75,000 to $250,000.

It is thus that some in the profession have begun to consider their role to be that of an "entrepreneurial counselor," as a generalist to advise and assist management in recording, classifying, and interpreting information, and, in some cases, to suggest organizational goals and assist in their implementation. It is generally assumed that there is room for only one profession of this kind, destined to emerge in the near future.

FUNCTIONALISM IN PUBLIC ACCOUNTING

In the 1960s, most of the social science professions experienced a resurgence in theories which emphasized conflict, strain, and power as central factors in ongoing social systems. These theories are generally in opposition to the functionalist view of society, the latter being essentially conservative in character, concerned with preserving the status quo. There are beliefs underlying these theoretical perspectives that operate as ideologies. One observer (Gouldner, 1970: 47) calls them "domain assumptions . . . beliefs about what it is possible to *do* . . . what courses of action are desirable and thus shape conduct." The domain assumptions (or ideology) of functionalism predominate in the public accounting profession. As the title of an information pamphlet (American Institute of Certified Public Accountants, 1970b) states, CPAs are the "Designers of Order." It points out that "proper discharge of the [audit] function obviously requires . . . complete objectivity." This implies value freedom, a "methodological dualism" (Gouldner, 1970: 495-498), which is the assumption that the researcher can separate his biases and commitments from what he is studying.

These domain assumptions are built into the methodology of the discipline itself. In the case of methodological dualism, knowledge is viewed as information and nothing more. For example, information in accounting is described as "data evaluated for a specific use . . . .An accounting estimate is improved by reducing the uncertainty under which it is made" (Bedford and Onsi, 1966: 15). The emphasis is on the reduction of ignorance rather than on the creation of knowledge. This fits very well for computerized accounting and auditing—the highly rationalized areas that can easily be quantified. This economic approach to information is now being applied to a form of macro-accounting known as social accounting, basically a system of accounting for changes in any social system. The result is an equilibrium theory for social action in which individuals are utility maximizers and will expend that effort necessary to maintain the system as it is.

One of the most ambitious projects in social accounting has been a systems analysis approach to Detroit's war on poverty, in which a team from Touche, Ross, Bailey & Smart worked with the Mayor's Committee for Human Resource Development. The supervisor of this team (Ruff, 1966) stated that "the War on Poverty does not have a profit motive in the business sense; but in all other respects the similarity is striking." A poverty "market" is defined, "market information" is collected, "performances" of poverty areas are measured through the success of Community Action Programs (Bruns and Snyder, 1969), and on this basis the team "reviews the allocation of resources procedure" and provides "internal management": information, as well as "data which will satisfy public demand" (Ruff, 1966). Poverty area "perform-ances" are determined by measuring police department offense complaints and arrests, city welfare relief rolls and stamp operations, clinic venereal disease and tuberculosis cases, health department birth, deaths, and stillbirths, unemployment and old-age statistics, truancy and dropouts, and the like. A major purpose of the program is to "anticipate trouble before it erupts and to make changes and adjustments as required" (Beyer, 1969: 40). There is no consideration of the more subjective elements affecting the program, those judgments that are normatively and politically motivated at the highest levels (Etzioni, 1968: 266; Etzioni and Lehman, 1969).

Many accountants are aware of these problems of measurement; nevertheless they feel that they can be overcome in time. They ask that the profession become more involved in the "developing social systems," as well as in the developed ones, and to seize this opportunity by going beyond business parameters to develop techniques for measuring basic social and economic causes rather than just symptoms (Linowes, 1970: 64-65). The overlap with other social sciences is considerable. A *Journal of Accountancy* editorial in July of 1970 notes that, as MAS experts, CPAs can be of "substantial help" in suggesting ways to "unclog institutional channels" of the maze of social institutions now interposed between man and his environment—namely, to give expert advice on problems of bureaucracy and large-scale organization. A sociologist (Campbell, 1970: 36) asks for essentially the same development by members of his discipline, adding that, if we do not respond, other professions will fill the slots.

THE 1970s: THE DECADE OF THE CPA?

It has been suggested (Marx, 1969: 84) that there is a second generation of ideologies developing in the West following the exhaustion of the first generation of political ideologies. These new ideologies are spawned in "multiprofessional areas" of the applied social sciences and policy sciences—e.g., medicine, law, education, business—and deal with the important social problems and their political and ethical implications. As the field of administration becomes more fully developed, it is likely that many such arenas will contend for the power inhering in its strategic role of adviser to the nonresident directors of social and economic institutions. In fact, some (Gouldner, 1970: 444; Friedrichs, 1970: 296; Wheeler, 1970: 3) suspect that administration, in terms of systems theory, will become a dominant arena in itself. In the process, it may engulf one or more of those professions now engaged in developing this discipline.

What is most disturbing about the development of this field is not its growth—much of its technique is necessary with the increasing rapidity of social change—but its domain assumptions. Public accounting, a serious contender for this position, is highly instrumental in its orientation, with emphasis on systems analysis. Although few in accounting believe that everything in a social system can be objectively and quantitatively measured, recorded, and thereby predicted, the idea persists that close approximations to this ideal can and should be achieved, and that the better we are at this, the more "efficient" our democracy becomes. Behind this objectivity, there is a measure of alienation (as Gouldner, 1970: 440, emphasizes), that society, as an independent force, shapes man rather than man shaping society, that the socializing process of the system is so efficient as to eliminate the potential for conflict. Through the ideology of consensus, one travels, in Saint-Simon's words, "from the governance of men to the administration of things." The professional autonomy of adaptive, fluid systems of diverse experts may limit bureaucracy or make it less rigid in some instances (Bucher and Stelling, 1969; Engel, 1970), but at what price? The power over systems of control in terms of what they are, how and why they interrelate, and how and why they should be interrelated, mediated by an extreme functionalism of systems analysis, by its nature serves as an apology for the established elite. There is technically one best way, and the planners become part of the elite—*la trahison des clercs.* In this sense, power is knowledge, for knowledge which gives the power to bring about a desired future state of affairs is derived by the methods prescribed (Rytina and Loomis, 1970).

Though the public accounting profession is highly instrumental in its approach to socioeconomic events and activities, it is not to say it will remain this way. An increasing number of accounting researchers and educators are aware of the problems attached to this position and have begun to ask serious questions about it (for example, see Willingham and Carmichael, 1969). Also, it would be rash to suggest that the profession will be the only one of significance in administration if systems analysis should continue to gain in popularity. However, because of their unique position as auditors and advisers in financial and related areas to major American and world institutions, they are destined to play an increasingly important role in social policy and planning. As a knowledge-oriented work community, and thereby a power-oriented work community, public accounting promises to become a major force in the social construction and elaboration of reality. There may be another and larger client revolt in reaction to the public accountant's often stated desire to become a generalist,[6] but it could be too little, too late, if the elements of knowledge control are known and used against those who wish to change the ordered and orderly society.

NOTES

1. Alphabetically, the eight firms are: Arthur Andersen & Co.; Ernst & Ernst; Haskins & Sells; Lybrand, Ross Bros. & Montgomery; Peat, Marwick, Mitchell & Co.; Price Waterhouse & Co.; Touche, Ross, Bailey & Smart; Arthur Young & Co. Unless otherwise cited, all references to these firms are based on the writer's study of them (Montagna, 1966). Statistics on size have been updated.

2. This amounts to $300 billion+ in total sales and net revenues, and $400 billion+ in total assets, based on the lists of the 500 largest industrial corporations, the fifty largest merchandising firms, the fifty largest transportation companies, and the fifty largest utility companies, as listed in *The Fortune Directory* (1965), when compared to the listing of auditors in the 1965 series of Moody's industrial, public utility, and transportation manuals, *Poor's Register of Corporations, Directors and Executives* (1965), and personal telephone calls. This percentage is relatively stable over the span of a few years. A check on 1968 industrial corporations revealed no change from 1964.

3. For publicized cases involving similar issues, see Whalen (1965); Fortune (1958).

4. This would explain the more pessimistic view of accounting historians (for example, see Carey, 1965: 378) that the profession is not yet an established or "higher" profession, as compared to the more optimistic results of a quantitative analysis of public accounting, limited to measures of attributes of the profession (Wilensky, 1964).

5. There are no data for CPAs, but accountants are generally found in more top management positions than are any other profession. Results are from a questionnaire mailed to the 500 largest companies in the United States (includes industrial, merchandising, and transportation firms listed in *The Fortune Directory*, with a return of 57.4%). The results (Bradish, 1970) in percentages were: accounting, 23.3%; engineering, 16.5%; law, 12.7%; liberal arts and social science, 10.8%; industrial management, 10.1%; economics, 6.8%; science, 4.7%; marketing, 3.2%; miscellaneous, 11.9%.

6. The attempt to become a generalist is considered an important factor aiding the development of client revolt (Haug and Sussman, 1969b: 159-160).

REFERENCES

American Institute of Certified Public Accountants (1970a) "AICPA brief in Continental Vending." J. of Accountancy 129 (May): 69-73.

––– (1970b) Designers of Order: The Story of Accountancy Briefly Told. New York.

BEDFORD, N. M. and M. ONSI (1966) "Measuring the value of information: an information theory approach." Management Services 3 (January-February): 3-18.

BENNIS, W. G. (1966) Changing Organizations. New York: McGraw-Hill.

BEVIS, H. W. (1965) Corporate Financial Reporting in a Competitive Economy. New York: Macmillan.

BEYER, R. (1969) "The modern management approach to a program of social improvement." J. of Accountancy 127 (March): 37-46.

BRADISH, R. D. (1970) "Accountants in top management." J. of Accountancy 129 (June): 49-53.

BRUNS, W. J., Jr. and R. J. SNYDER (1969) "Management information for community action programs." Management Services 6 (July-August): 15-22.

BUCHER, R. and J. STELLING (1969) "Characteristics of professional organizations." J. of Health and Social Behavior 10 (March): 3-15.

CAMPBELL, E. Q. (1970) "Recruiting tomorrow's sociologists." Amer. Sociologist 5 (February): 36-37.

CAREY, J. L. (1969) The Rise of the Accounting Profession. Volume I. New York: American Institute of Certified Public Accountants.

––– (1965) The CPA Plans for the Future. New York: American Institute of Certified Public Accountants.

CARMICHAEL, D. R. and R. J. SWIERINGA (1968) "The compatibility of auditing independence and management services—an identification of the issues." Accounting Rev. 43 (October): 697-705.

DILL, S. L. and D. L. ADAMS (1964) "Automated auditing." J. of Accountancy 117 (May): 54-59.

DOHR, J. L. (1950) "Materiality—what does it mean in accounting?" J. of Accountancy 90 (July): 54-56.

ENGEL, G. V. (1970) "Professional autonomy and bureaucratic organization." Administrative Sci. Q. 15 (March): 12-21.

ETZIONI, A. (1968) The Active Society. New York: Free Press.

——— and E. W. LEHMAN (1969) "Some dangers in 'valid' social measurement," pp. 45-62 in B. M. Gross (ed.) Social Intelligence for America's Future. Boston: Allyn & Bacon.

Forbes (1966) "Are CPA firms taking over management consulting?" 98 (October 1): 57-61.

Fortune (1958) "The mess at Atlas Plywood." Volume 57 (January): 118-119, 234-236.

FREIDSON, E. (1970) Profession of Medicine. New York: Dodd, Mead.

FRIEDRICHS, R. W. (1970) A Sociology of Sociology. New York: Free Press.

GOULDNER, A. W. (1970) The Coming Crisis of Western Sociology. New York: Basic Books.

HAUG, M. R. and M. B. SUSSMAN (1969a) "Professional autonomy and the revolt of the client." Social Problems 17 (Fall): 153-160.

——— (1969b) "Professionalism and the public." Soc. Inquiry 39 (Winter): 57-64.

HOLZNER, B. (1968) Reality Construction in Society. Cambridge, Mass.: Schenkman.

HOROWITZ, I. L. (1961) Philosophy, Science and the Sociology of Knowledge. Springfield, Ill.: Charles C Thomas.

KAUFMAN, F. (1967) "Professional consulting by CPAs." Accounting Rev. 42 (October): 713-720.

KRAUSE, E. A. (1968) "Functions of a bureaucratic ideology: 'citizen participation.' " Social Problems 16 (Fall): 129-142.

LINOWES, D. F. (1970) "The need for accounting in developing social systems." J. of Accountancy 129 (March): 62-65.

MARX, J. H. (1969) "A multidimensional conception of ideologies in professional arenas: the case of the mental health field." Pacific Soc. Rev. 12 (Fall): 75-86.

MONTAGNA, P. D. (1968) "Professionalization and bureaucratization in large professional organizations." Amer. J. of Sociology 74 (September): 138-145.

——— (1966) "Bureaucracy and change in large professional organizations." Ph. D. dissertation. New York University.

OLSON, N. O. (1970) "The auditor in legal difficulty." J. of Accountancy 129 (April): 39-44.

REININGA, W. (1968) "The unknown materiality concept." J. of Accountancy 125 (February): 30-35.

RUFF, J. A. (1966) "Poverty programs—a business management approach." The Quarterly / Touche, Ross, Bailey & Smart 12 (June): 24-25.

RYTINA, J. H. and C. P. LOOMIS (1970) "Marxist dialectic and pragmatism: power as knowledge." Amer. Soc. Rev. 35 (April): 308-318.

SMIGEL, E. O. (1964) The Wall Street Lawyer. New York: Free Press.

WHALEN, R. J. (1965) "The big skid at Yale express." Fortune 72 (November): 146-149, 226-236.

WHEELER, J. T. (1970) "Accounting theory and research in perspective." Accounting Rev. 45 (January): 1-10.

WILENSKY, H. (1964) "The professionalization of everyone?" Amer. J. of Sociology 70 (September): 137-158.

WILLINGHAM, J. J. and D. R. CARMICHAEL (1969) "Innovation and change in accounting: testing a behavioral hypothesis." Working Paper 69-70. Austin: University of Texas Graduate School of Business.

WISE, T. A. (1966a) "Those uncertain actuaries." Fortune 73 (January): 164-166, 184-186.

——— (1966b) "The very private world of Peat, Marwick, Mitchell." Fortune 74 (July 1): 88-91, 128-130.

Chapter 9

THE EROSION OF MEDICINE
FROM WITHIN

IRVING KENNETH ZOLA and STEPHEN J. MILLER

> *A history of medicine is a history of human society and culture, of its metaphysics as well as its physics, of its basic philosophy of nature, of its ideas of health and disease, of the processes of therapy, and its notions about the proper economy and distribution of goods and services, including healing services and facilities.*
>
> *—Everett Cherrington Hughes*

INTRODUCTION

The character of any profession can be explicated only by reference to the conditions that limited or facilitated its development in our society. Medicine is prototypal and provides many examples of the social conditions and contemporaneous change which have influenced the character of modern professions. This paper is thus devoted to tracing some of the wherefores and implications of four basic challenges to medicine:

(1) on license and mandate

(2) on independent practice

(3) on the doctor-patient relationship

(4) on social responsibility

THE CHALLENGE TO LICENSE AND MANDATE—THE MANY VOICES OF MEDICINE

As Everett Hughes (1958) has long since delineated, the key to understanding the essence of a profession is to realize what sets it apart from other occupations. Simply put, this separation is based on its claim that it knows more about some matters than do other people, that it is able to do something so much better than anyone else that its members should be given a monopoly over doing it, and that they are so devoted to giving good service that the taker must trust them and leave to them not only the exclusive right to deem who is qualified to give such services, but also the sole right to discipline any of their number who have failed to warrant such trust. The nature and "justice" of medicine's claim to such license has been critically analyzed in Freidson (1970). While his book may do much to undercut the base of medicine's license and mandate, it also seems apparent that the uniform edifice of this license and mandate is also being eroded from within—by long-term developments within the medical profession itself.

A necessary condition for the successful claim of a mandate by a profession is group self-consciousness and the resulting solidarity (for development of this notion see Rose, 1965). On medicine's part, much of this solidarity might well have been defensive and yet there is some justice to the claim that until virtually the late nineteenth century, there was a sufficiently limited corpus of knowledge, modes and locations of practice to ensure a certain agreement on the nature and function of medicine in society. With, however, both a growing body of knowledge and practitioners, it was not long before many different types of careers opened for the medical practitioner and with this came differences in the appropriate mission or primary aim of medicine. Thus today some physicians believe the purpose of medicine to be scientific investigation which would provide information to control or eradicate acute, episodic disease. These are the physicians who most often choose careers of teaching at medical schools or research positions at laboratories, institutes, and hospitals. Other physicians think teaching or research to be less important than applying available knowledge directly to the problems of distressed patients. Similarly, while the often idealized general practitioner may symbolize medicine for the public, the medical profession actually consists of many kinds of physicians who differentially define medicine and its purpose in society. Thus, the highly esteemed general practitioner, the ideal model of a physician, is less valued among physicians and enjoys less prestige than medical educators, scientists and specialists.

Further, it became increasingly difficult for anyone to master all the accumulated knowledge or the increasingly complex technology. Thus, the formation of subgroups within medicine which were organized around special knowledge and particular skills (Galdston, 1958, 1959). Today, though physicians have an exclusive license for the practice of medicine, no one physician can claim to know it all. The members of a specialty do, however, possess the knowledge relevant to the particular work their specialty claims as its own and, in matters pertaining to those special interests, can claim intellectual superiority.

When a subgroup of physicians can claim intellectual superiority they are recognized as a specialty within the medical profession. The subgroups (segments) of the medical profession are not all of the same kind. Some are established and their claims to intellectual or technical superiority have been recognized. Internists and surgeons are examples of recognized specialties or established subgroups within medicine. Other subgroups of physicians are not as well established—for example, psychiatry and physical medicine. Some segments are only emerging, like community medicine; they try to gain recognition for the work the members do and claim superiority over other members of the profession. At any particular period in the history of a profession these different kinds of subgroups are engaged in activities and tactics that will establish or entrench them further in medicine. The groups that are most successful in doing so may be expected to be the subgroups of medicine whose work is of most public concern because the practices of their members are most influential for many aspects of life and for the definition of health that will obtain in society.

The members of a specialty are a constituency within medicine whose common interests and purpose lead them to wield power to guide the policies and practices of medicine, supposedly for the good of all but particularly to advance their special interests and facilitate the purpose of their group. When referring to the organization of the medical profession, we have in mind the interrelationships of these subgroups and assume the actual organization of medicine to be, at any time, determined by the activities and tactics of those subgroups.

In light of the conditions which presently obtain in society, some sociologists (Bucher and Strauss, 1961) have suggested a focus on conflict of interest which accompanies diversity of activity, rather than a focus on homogeneity of the professions. The study of conflict should not be limited to its consideration within professions, but also between professions. The implication of license as originally conceptualized was that it was granted to only one work group who, during the course of making use of their license, further had a moral and intellectual mandate to define the terms of how they would implement the license granted by the public (Hughes, 1958). A division of labor was, therefore, effected by granting exclusive licenses to varied work groups. Today, however, licenses are somewhat less exclusive. Although much of the practice of medicine is still the sole province of the physician, there is a challenge to this inclusivity on two levels: first a competition wherein other occupations are today claiming to deliver similar services and second, where more and more responsibility is being delegated (if not taken over) by ancillary health workers, the so-called paramedicals. As to the first challenge, this is perhaps seen most clearly in the mental health field where psychiatrists, clinical psychologists, psychiatric social workers, members of the clergy, and now an amalgam of family therapists and group workers are all engaged in some form of counseling or therapy (Gurin et al., 1960: Kadushin, 1969). As a result, no one of these groups is recognized as having the sole mandate to determine what is good and right counseling or what is good mental health (Szasz, 1961). That psychiatry has an especially weak link to medicine or that mental illness is not really "illness" is an argument which attributes a specificity and a narrowness to the notion of physical illness or health which is simply not true. For whether we take the World Health Organization (hardly a psychiatrically oriented group) definition postulated in 1948 that "health is a state of complete physical, mental and social well-being and not merely the absence of disease or infirmity" or look carefully at the history of medicine, we see that the very categories and measurement of physical health and illness are in constant flux (Dubos 1959, 1965). Certainly in the 1970s it begins to look as if physical culturalists, yoga enthusiasts and many of the ecology-oriented (e.g., food sellers to food growers) may give orthodox preventive medicine and public health a run for their money in establishing the prerequisites and requirements of a healthy life and environment.

The second challenge is really a division of labor phenomenon and embodies a certain irony. For at one time the bonesetter, the apothecary, the nurse, the barber-surgeon were autonomous. Medicine by its claim to greater knowledge and through the judicious aid of the state brought virtually all auxillaries under their hegemony. Now, however, partly because of the increased technical division of labor and because of the increased separation of the physician away from direct patient care, there is an increasing delegation of responsibility (for certain dilemmas see Levy, 1966). Moreover, some of this delegation is not merely to technical efficiency but to an albeit grudging recognition that not only can these paramedicals do the job better than existing professionals, but that they are in a better position than the orthodox medical profession to determine the health wants, health needs of the patient and, in some cases, even successfully challenging the priorities of the medicine in this regard.

This is not to say that the medical profession does not hold exclusive license for many kinds of activities. Rather, it is to say that as other occupations successfully lay claim to a license, for example, legal permission to carry on counseling, to give injections, to perhaps even prescribe or alter certain medical regimes, the medical profession has to share the mandate for defining health in society. No longer are physicians permitted the presumption of a broad mandate defining all matters of health, the relationship of other health practitioners to the physician and each other, or to determine the conditions of work of all other health workers.

In sum, the relative simplicity of the work claimed by the profession in the past made it possible for its members to achieve solidarity which, in turn, facilitated a collective claim by the medical profession to license and mandate. The knowledge which medicine accumulated and its increasingly complex technology required first specialization and then division of labor introducing diversity and subverting the collective claim to a mandate. Advances toward professional status made by other occupations, though not negating license, are forcing reconsideration of the exclusive mandate previously granted to medicine. Partly by virtue of their being there first and taking full possession, medicine remains firmly in control. For in virtually all the above examples, medicine colors the basic definition of the problem and treatment, medical men provide the basic teaching to these occupations and hold important positions even in their very licensing boards.

THE CHALLENGE TO INDEPENDENT PRACTICE–ON THE POSSIBILITIES OF BEING AN ISLAND

The medical profession is usually thought to be a group of practitioners who are alike and more or less agree on what it is they should do for the public. But unanimity is no more characteristic of physicians than of any group of professionals. The medical profession is a heterogeneous group of workers and distinctions must be made between kinds of physicians and the kinds of work that they do on behalf of the public.

When we refer to the independent practice of medicine we refer to the kind of work that is more consultation than scientific or scholarly. Specialists whose medical careers are directed toward specific scientific ends achieve status by establishing their intellectual superiority over other segments of their profession. Physicians who are engaged in the delivery of service, on the other hand, direct their efforts less toward scientific endeavors and more toward solving the problems of health posed by laymen. The usual medical career is one of consultation to the layman and practicing physicians must, for that reason, make what they do and the manner in which it is done attractive to the public. "The contingency of the lay public," concludes Freidson (1970: 188), "is thus critical to the development of medicine as a [practicing] profession . . . and to the professional performance of physicians."

What is ironic is that the impact of contemporary public opinion has been greatest on the scientific segments of the medical profession. Clinical investigators have been increasingly concerned that new government funding policies are reducing the amount of money available for the support of basic medical research (Medical World News, 1966). The governmental policies are based on the public's increased demand for direct service rather than the more nebulous benefits of research.

Medicine, in the past, was most often practiced by the entrepreneur in privacy—in the office. More and more of medical practice, however, is taking place within the health institutions of society. Members of the medical profession always had to obtain hospital privileges to have a successful practice. Today, more than ever before, they must arrange affiliations with the hospitals and clinics which house the increasingly complex technology of health care. The medical center provides the practicing physicians not only the technical support he requires, but also the access to other specialists he needs to supplement his own knowledge and skill.

The rise of modern medicine has made it difficult, if not impossible, to practice alone and, for that reason, the practice of medicine is less often private. Practicing physicians are involved in circles of colleagues who control the appointments to hospitals in their community, without which most physicians could not practice. Hospitals were not always so completely monopolized by circles of colleagues. But, today, physicians occupy varied positions in health institutions and control access to the hospital and determine patient referrals between themselves and their colleagues. The modern practitioner is dependent upon other physicians for career assistance and they are a source of patients, without whom he has no practice. Simply, dependence on colleagues in one way or another is the rule (Coleman et al., 1966), for special advice, hospital facilities and patient referrals are essential to the contemporary medical practice (Freidson, 1963).

With the rise of specialization patients required the assistance of more than one physician. The solo practitioner had of necessity to arrange for other physicians to assist him in the provision of medical care. What evolved was a system of reciprocal arrangements between general practitioners and specialists, who together constituted a colleague circle. The general practitioner was the patient's port of entry to a loose federation of physicians who together could provide the needed care. A practitioner could, when it was required, refer a patient to his colleagues who were specialists and be assured that his practice would not be subverted. He could, in other words, depend upon his colleagues to provide a patient with the expert care which was required and then return that patient to him for general care.

The general practitioner faced with an increasingly complex technology and accumulated knowledge could not claim to know it all. He turned to other physicians for assistance, and what emerged was an informal collaboration between two or more general practitioners and a cohort of selected specialists. The general practitioners had reciprocal arrangements for "covering" each other during illness, days off, and vacations. The specialists provided expertise which supplemented the general practitioner's limited knowledge and skill. Specialists, in their turn, depended upon the general practitioners for referrals. The general practitioner was assured that specialists would not subvert their practices because to do so would be to deny themselves a continuing source of clients. The reciprocity implicit in these arrangements assured both general practitioners and specialists stable practices and was the basis of cooperative medical practice.

The solo practice exists almost exclusively in geographic areas which have a scarcity of physicians. The exigency of contemporary practice requires cooperation if not actual collaboration among a variety of physicians. Further, the general practitioner has become less important to the circles of physicians who constitute a cooperative practice.

> The time has passed in the United States when the general practitioner was in a strong enough position to be the key "feeder" to a network of specialists. As the patient has developed more sophistication and the number of accessible specialists has increased, the patient circumvents the general practitioner and seeks out his own specialists. Indeed, the general practitioner's place is being taken by the internist and the pediatrician, and nonprofessional referrals are the major source of patients in urban settings for the average opthamologist, otorhino-laryngologist and orthopedist, if not the obstetrician-gynecologist, allergist, and dermatologist [Freidson, 1963: 304].

The early form of cooperative practice has been replaced by a variety of more sophisticated arrangements. The informality of implicit reciprocity has given way to more formal arrangements between physicians, physicians and consumer groups. The most elementary contractual arrangement is the hiring of physicians by the established practitioner—so to speak, the proprietary practice. The established physician with a large practice simply hires the assistance he needs and, in that way, facilitates the maintenance of his practice by contracting for routine care and the covering of his practice. The partnership is a more common form of cooperative practice, where two or more physicians share the labor and expense of maintaining a practice for proportionate shares of the profits of that practice. Another common cooperative arrangement is the group practice. The group practice permits physicians to have their own patients and collect their own fees while sharing the expenses of maintaining equipment and offices. A further advantage of the group practice is that a variety of specialists can participate and make the group a somewhat self-sufficient colleague system. Physicians within a group serve as referring agents for each other, providing each with a source of clients without subverting the practice.

The group practice is more bureaucratic than the partnership, though it is often difficult to distinguish between extended partnerships and limited group practices. What is most significant is that such practice arrangements are becoming more common and that the introduction of bureaucracy has many implications for the delivery of medical care. The most obvious implication is that the bureaucratic practice can be of significant size to contract with a third party to provide medical care to a selected population of patients. When this is done, the third party obtains a modicum of control—that is, for economic reasons, it can negotiate the conditions of medical care. Hospitals themselves are more and more encouraging physicians to establish groups which they would back with supportive services and facilities to meet the expressed needs of the public.

Many developments outside the medical profession itself are influencing its practice. The Office of Economic Opportunity, which was established to conduct the War on Poverty, has financed community health centers, a departure from the traditional delivery of medical care. Made aware of the problems of the poor and the rising cost of health services, Congress had made money available for innovative systems of getting medical care to the people who need it. Medical care in the future will not be the exclusive responsibility of hospitals. There are now and will be more facilities that provide regular care to ambulatory patients and, when necessary, special care. Many new service organizations are emerging as the hospitals did in an earlier period.

The hallmark of the full-fledged physician is the right he is granted to work independently, without supervision and subject to little if any control. Autonomy of this sort is based on the assumption of an unusual degree of technical knowledge, skill, and experience with the management of disease. But it is very difficult to establish a specialty practice without referrals, and next to impossible to practice all but the most basic medicine without hospital affiliations. Also, the amount that there is to know fosters specialization which, in turn, makes physicians depend more on each other. It is paradoxical that the very circumstances which make it possible to claim autonomy also more or less preclude not only solo and general but any autonomous practice.

If a physician attempts to go it alone, he has greatly increased the control his patients have over his work. He is totally dependent upon the opinion of the public, and must perform in accord with the expectations of his patients. On the other hand, if he engages in cooperative practice, he increases his dependence upon his colleagues and accordingly increases their control of his work. When faced with this dilemma, physicians chose practice arrangements which protected them from the public but which all but precluded the independent practice of medicine.

The needs of the public and the influence of third parties further redice the physician's ability to set the conditions of his practice. The third party can stipulate not only the kind of payment, as health insurance does, but the method of payment. Many reject the traditional notion of fee-for-service and insist on salaries or stipulate a per capita sum for continuing and comprehensive medical care. Other third parties will stipulate the kind of medical care. All of these developments serve to more or less control the mechanics of providing medical care and serve to reduce the physicians' control not of what care he will provide but of the way in which he will provide medical care.

THE CHALLENGE TO THE DOCTOR-PATIENT RELATIONSHIP—FROM A ONE-WAY TO A TWO-WAY STREET

The medical profession is also undergoing change in its basic therapeutic relationship with its clientele. Broadly speaking, the shift involves the dilution of the exclusiveness and directionality of this relationship. To borrow a term from the diplomatic realm, there is a shift in the balance of power. As many observers (Bloom, 1963; Entralgo, 1969; Szasz and Hollender, 1956) have noted, there was a time in the not-too-distant past, when the doctor did come close to a perceived image of omniscience and omnipotence in his relationships with his patients. At a time when the major illnesses that afflicted, debilitated and killed men were mostly the acute infectious variety, the very situation supported both an enormous differential in power as well as social distance. In terms of the medical armaentarium available, what was mostly necessary was for the doctor to do, to dose, to purge, to cut and the patient to cooperate and for the most part suffer in silence. While there were always an abundance of marginal practitioners and "curers" outside the pale of medicine, within it, the team was pretty much doctors and nurses with both their tasks fairly well circumscribed and the latter clearly subservient and dependent on the former. As for the patient, outside of refusing to cooperate, or seeking aid outside the pale, there was little he could do. Finally, the possibility of questioning or challenging the doctor was difficult not only because of the greater difference in social status, but also in direct knowledge. For much of its history, medicine and its allied professions has literally fostered a knowledge and communications gap, hiding its methods and its recipes in both a highly technical and foreign (i.e., Latin) oral and written language. Thus, in a real sense, the patient did not know either the why's or what's of his treatment.

But the times are changing. More people than ever before are over 65, and they, because of health plans, are able to demand continuing and comprehensive care. Other people consider health care a right and are demanding and, also because of insurance and a variety of prepayment plans, are able to meet the cost of regular, preventive, comprehensive care. And while no single force alone has altered this relationship one of the most pervasive factors has been a change in the very nature of the problems which the physician treats. For whether we look at general mortality statistics or the morbidity figures of the National Center for Health Statistics or large-scale epidemiological studies, it is evident that the major disorders of today can be broadly classified as chronic diseases. While there are from time to time epidemics of flu and other contagious diseases and while upper respiratory infections still seem the bane of everyday existence, today's health problems are primarily arthritis, diabetes, cancer, heart disease, mental illness. Several of these will never lead directly to death, and those that do usually do so over a considerable period of time.

The implications of this shift to chronicity for the relationship of the physician to his clientele are manifold. In these diseases, there are few opportunities for a "magic bullet"–the dramatic intervention which cures the patient. Cure as the measure of success fades slowly into the background, instead the figures speak of "improvement" or "in remission"—an acknowledgment that at best the problem is still there though temporarily held at bay. (The frustrating nature of this for physicians and their consequent dislike of working with such disorders and patients is widely documented.) In any case the treatment of such disorders involves not only a longer period of time (in many cases for "life") but also a fundamental change in the role of the patient. For not only must he be *continually* motivated to cooperate, but he must *actively* participate in his own treatment. Thus he must not only in some sense treat himself (give himself injections, take pills, watch his diet) but where there is anything "psychosocial" in either his treatment or his disorder, he finds that he must even supply the basic data and tools. We are not claiming that this shift has either been easily acknowledged or accepted by patients and doctors (Speigel, 1959), but rather that a new course and direction has been set.

The chronicity of illness has diluted the exclusive control of the physician in still another way. For while the very complexity of today's medicine has expanded the team that deals with the patient and his illness, the nature of chronic disease by spreading out the course of treatment has set the stage for the involvement of a series of other independent (and non-M.D.) practitioners. The case so ably delineated by Fred Davis (1963) in his study of polio patients is being essentially repeated in any disorder requiring both long convalescence, rehabilitation and even lifetime care. In the course of such long-term disorders, the doctor recedes further and further into the background, eventually assuming the role of occasional medical consultant. With this, the physiotherapist, visiting nurse, dietician, prosthetist becomes essentially "the doctor" not only in terms of primary day-to-day management, but in terms of the transference relationship as well.

Finally, the social distance gap itself is closing in certain ways. For while the doctor is still hardly a man of the people, the ethnic and social class representation is widening, particularly with the current self-conscious efforts of medical schools to recruit more students from the "disadvantaged classes." Moreover, while admittedly limited, there is a movement among those new recruits to the ranks of community medicine (1) to live and become part of the lower class area where he practices, (2) to play down the insignia and perquisites of his office, and (3) to level his income either to that of his immediate community or abolish different rates among "the medical team." But perhaps the greatest general foreshortening is in the knowledge-communications gap. By this we do not mean that the lay public is in any position to be its own doctor, but nevertheless that the functional ignorance and awe of medical knowledge and techniques has certainly decreased. With greater literacy, the American public has become such avid readers, that in the publishing industry the books about sex, dogs, and doctors are sure sellers (no interconnection implied). But this is not the only exposure, for where the public does not buy books they can learn about the latest medical advance in the mass periodicals and daily newspapers. And finally for those whom even these writings might miss, there is television. Anyone who tries to understand the public perception and "knowledge" of medicine without examining the decade-long exposure of the Doctors Casey and Kildare, the Medical Centers and the Bold Ones is certainly ignoring one of the great levelers and disseminators in modern society. The result of this continual input, while largely undocumented, has reached the level of medical backroom anecdote where doctors repeatedly tell of patients asking for, suggesting, and occasionally demanding certain drugs and services—a relatively infrequent event prior to World War II. Perhaps not unrelated to this accumulation of knowledge is a newfound confidence in what the patient can directly contribute to his improvement and care. For another post-World War II development is the profusion of patient mutual aid groups—groups which have not only "organized" to lobby for better medical services but which have shown that they have an expertise in the day-to-day management of chronic disease often unknown if not inaccessible to the medical practitioner (Zola, 1971). In short, as far as power is concerned, the age of the patient has arrived not with a whimper but with a bang.

THE CHALLENGE TO ITS SOCIAL
RESPONSIBILITY—THE DILEMMAS OF EXPERTISE

Finally we turn to perhaps the most far-reaching of all changes effecting the license, mandate, and function of medicine—namely, its involvement in "the social." As Sigerist (1943) has aptly claimed, medicine at base was always not only a social science but an occupation whose very practice was inextricably interwoven into society. Yet even as he noted, this "social relationship" was primarily evidenced through the ramification that the practice of medicine has had on everything from the demographic structure of society, to the outcomes of wars, to developments in art and literature. What we are contending, however, goes further, for medicine is grudgingly being pulled into greater and greater explicit involvement in the society of which it is a part. This involvement can perhaps best be seen in the undermining of one of professional medicine's basic tenets—its functional specificity (Parsons, 1951; but see Freidson, 1970). For by the latter was meant the unspoken rule which limited the attentions and activities of the physician to a rigidly circumscribed sphere— toward those things "strictly medical" and away from religious, political, social, economic, and psychological or personal circumstances of the patient and his illness. While specialization perhaps carries this mandate to its logical extreme, the increasing emphasis on "treating the whole patient" has forced the physician to consider an ever widening range of nonmedical factors. Thus Robert Wilson (1963: 285) concludes that "the line separating the medical sphere from the non-medical is a shifting one; especially in psychotherapy the practitioner may at times be drawn into a set of global concerns more nearly comparable to those of the priest-healer than those of the hospital technician."

What was once claimed for psychotherapy has become increasingly true for all medical therapies. Thus, one of the greatest pushes for social involvement has come just from where Wilson said it would, in the awareness of what it takes to practice good medicine in today's society. Whether it be those whose research links "the stress of life" to a whole series of disorders (Langner and Michael, 1963; Levine and Scotch, 1970) or those whose community orientation imposes a social reality, there is a similar cry for more social intervention. Those involved in "ghetto medicine" echo this most clearly (Norman, 1968).

Thus regardless of any political ideology that such physicians may represent, they are saying that medicine must get involved in changing society, for without it any good that its methods might produce will soon be undone. Some physicians have obviously gone further and see the explicit relevance of their expertise to issues not so directly related to their ability to practice but rather their own and their patients' ability to survive. Such sentiments have been directly manifested in the formation of such organizations as the Medical Committee for Human Rights, the Physicians for Social Responsibility and such newsletters as the Health PAC Bulletin.

Two branches of medicine have had a built-in social emphasis from the very start—psychiatry (Szasz, 1961; Foucault, 1965) and public health—preventive medicine (Rosen, 1958). Today's social involvement seems with hindsight almost a logical outcome. Public health was always committed to changing social aspects of life from sanitary to housing and working conditions and used legal (and thus nonmedical) methods to gain its ends (e.g., quarantines, vaccinations, required reporting of certain communicable diseases). In recent years, the social involvement has become more open for where legal recourse was impossible, social law helped psychiatry regarding his job: commitment proceedings; and psychiatry aided the law regarding his: insanity as a defense. Perhaps it is from the latter experience that springs psychiatry's current expansion into the realm of social problems. Thus we are now witnessing a shift of enormous import wherein a number of acts hitherto defined as crimes are being claimed in reality to be symptoms of a disease if not a disease in itself—alcoholism, drug addiction, homosexuality, prostitution, gambling, and murder. The magnitude of this shift can be seen in the mere fact that such a shift (i.e., legally regarding this problem as a disease rather than a crime) in regard to alcoholism alone could result in a reduction of nearly 40% in national arrest figures.

The ultimate in social involvement is in the changing definition of health. For it looks as if the World Health Organization's 1948 credo on health is beginning to be accepted. Thus it is not merely that health has social, psychological, vocational aspects but that good health involves the greatest possible achievement and satisfaction in all these spheres. Still another way of stating this "sanctifying" of health is in the claim that health is no longer considered a means to an end, but an end in itself. Today, health becomes the benchmark by which we continually evaluate the work we do, the way we travel, the food we eat, the plants we save, and the games we play.

On the whole the trend described in the previous pages is a mixed blessing: for it reflects the same dilemma heard about the relationship of the university to the outside world—isolated citadel of learning vs. involved agitator for social justice. It is difficult to predict the direction of either the university or of medicine. What is perhaps most clear is that both institutions will never be able to retreat again behind some narrow definition of their social responsibility. Where medicine is concerned, it seems almost on an inexorable path towards becoming a major institution of social control. In the short run, as many inhumane practices cease because of the added perspective and medicine, the trend is beneficial. On the other hand to the degree that medicine becomes involved in social issues because of its supposed "objectivity" (as previously religion and the law were to some extent perceived) then it is a dangerous course. For as many are beginning to argue there is little objective or even value-neutral about the terms and practices of modern medicine. To regard it as such can only lead to the obfuscation of underlying social and moral issues.

CONCLUSION

What has been delineated in these pages is a series of challenges to several traditional aspects of medicine. In some ways our claims may seem contradictory. For on the one hand we see an erosion of medicine's license and mandate while on the other hand we see medicine spreading its influence even farther in terms of its becoming a major institution of social control. Our point is that medicine is being challenged on many fronts and that as a result it is changing, not that it is crumbling. For whether we look at the new arrangements of service or relationships with patients, at greater reliance on external institutions or on paramedicals, medicine remains on top, in control, at very least the first among equals.

Yet we are concerned with some of the directions in which medicine may go, particularly if it is one either chartered by a select few or the result of an insidious almost unconscious drift. To this end, what at very least seems necessary in medicine as well as all professions is the institutionalization of the gadfly, a periodic Flexner Report. For it is well to bear in mind two cautionary statements. The first is Dubos' (1959):

> Organized species such as ants have established a satisfactory equilibrium with their environment and suffer no great waves of disease or changes in their social structure. But man is essentially dynamic, his way of life constantly in flux from century to century. He experiments with synthetic products and changes his diet; he builds cities that breed rats and infection; he builds automobiles and factories which pollute the air; and he constructs radioactive bombs. As life becomes more comfortable and technology more complicated, new factors introduce new dangers; the ingredients for utopia are the agents of new disease.

Thus the battle against disease and suffering will ever continue. But the weapons as well as the problems will change, for as Eisley (1965) has noted:

> The long, slow turn of world-time as the geologist has known it, or the invisibly moving hour hand of evolution perceived only yesterday by the biologist, has given way in the human realm to a fantastically speeded up social evolution induced by industrial technology. So fast does this change progress that a growing child strives to master the sociological moves of a culture which might compared with the pace of past historys, compress centuries of change into his lifetime. I myself like many among you, was born in an age which has already perished. At my death I will look my last upon a society which, save for some linguistic continuity, will seem increasingly alien and remote. It will be

as though I peered upon my youth through misty centuries. . . . I will not be merely old: I will be a genuine fossil embedded in onrushing man made time before my actual death.

Our main weapon against stagnation then is awareness. To be forewarned is, hopefully, to be forearmed.

REFERENCES

BLOOM, S. (1963) The Doctor and His Patient. New York: Russell Sage Foundation.

BUCHER, R. and A. STRAUSS (1961) "Professions in process." Amer. J. of Sociology 66: 325-334.

COLEMAN, J. S., E. KATZ and H. MENFEL (1966) Medical Innovation: A Diffusion Study. Indianapolis: Bobbs-Merrill.

Commission on Chronic Illness (1957) Chronic Illness in A Large City. Cambridge: Harvard University Press.

DAVIS, F. (1963) Passage Through Crisis. New York: Bobbs-Merrill.

DUBOS, R. (1965) Man Adapting. New Haven: Yale University Press.

––– (1959) The Mirage of Health. Garden City, New York: Doubleday.

EISLEY, L. C. (1965) "The Freedom of the Juggernaut." Mayo Clinic Proceedings 40: 7-21.

ENTRALGO, L. (1969) Doctor and Patient. New York: World University Library.

FOUCAULT, M. (1965) Madness and Civilization. New York: Pantheon.

FREIDSON, E. (1963) "The organization of medical practice" pp. 299-319 in H. Freeman, S. Levine, L. Reeder (eds.) Handbook of Medical Sociology. Englewood Cliffs, N.J.: Prentice-Hall.

FREIDSON, E. (1970) Profession of Medicine. New York: Dodd, Mead.

GALDSTON, I. (1959) "The natural history of specialism in medicine," J. of the American Medical Association 170 (May 16): 294-298.

––– (1958) "The birth and death of specialties," J. of the American Medical Association 167 (August 23): 2056-2061.

GROB, G. (1966) The State and the Mentally Ill. Chapel Hill: University of North Carolina Press.

GURIN, G., J. VEROFF and S. FELD (1960) Americans View Their Mental Health. New York: Basic Books.

HUGHES, E. C. (1958) Men and Their Work. New York: Free Press.

KADUSHIN, C. (1969) Why People Go To Psychiatrists. New York: Atherton.

LANGNER, T. and S. T. MICHAEL (1963) Life Stress and Mental Health. New York: Free Press.

LEIFER, R. (1969) In The Name of Mental Health: Social Functions of Psychiatry. New York: Science House.

LEVINE, S. and N. SCOTCH [eds.] (1970) Social Stress. Chicago: Aldine.

LEVY, L. (1966) "Factors which facilitate or impede transfer of medical functions from physicians to paramedical personnel." J. of Health and Social Behavior 7: 50-54.

Medical World News (1966) "Is basic research threatened" 7 (December 2): 108-119.

NORMAN, J. C. [ed.] (1969) Medicine in the Ghetto. New York: Appleton-Century-Crofts.

PARSONS, T. (1951) The Social System. New York: Free Press.

ROSE, A. M. (1965) "Group consciousness among the aging," pp. 19-36 in A. M. Rose and W. A. Peterson (eds.) Older People and Their Social World. Philadelphia: F. A. Davis.

ROSEN, G. (1958) A History of Public Health. New York: MD Publications.

SIGERIST, H. (1943) Civilization and Disease. New York: Cornell University Press.

SPEIGEL, J. (1959) "Some cultural aspects of transference and countertransference," pp. 160-182 in J. H. Masserman (ed.) Individual and Familial Dynamics. New York: Grune & Stratton.

SZASZ, T. (1961) The Myth of Mental Illness. New York: Hoeber-Harper.

––– and M. H. HOLLENDER (1956) "A contribution of the philosophy of medicine: the basic models of the doctor-patient." AMA Archives of Internal Medicine 97 (May): 585-592.

WILSON, R. N. (1963) "Patient-practitioner relationships," pp. 273-295 in H. Freeman, S. Levine, L. Reeder (eds.) Handbook of Medical Sociology. Englewood Cliffs, N.J.: Prentice-Hall.

ZOLA, I. K. (1971) "Helping–does it matter? The problems prospects of mutual aid groups." Cleveland Ostomy News.

Chapter 10

PRIESTS AND CHURCH

The Professionalization of an Organization

THOMAS P. FERENCE, FRED H. GOLDNER,
and R. RICHARD RITTI

> *The problems of vocations are the most serious in the Church today.*
> *Without priests and nuns, how could the Church carry out its mission?*
> *What would become of the preaching of the gospel? What would*
> *become of the salvation of the world?*
>
> *—Pope Paul VI, Summer, 1970*

The drop-off in recruits and the increase of withdrawals among the
diocesan priesthood present the Roman Catholic Church with a
crisis. But the reduction in numbers of its cadre is only the most
publicized part of the crisis. There are a number of changes in
both the Church as organization and the priesthood as profession
to threaten the belief structure of its members, the structure of
the organization, and the services members provide.

The Roman Catholic diocesan priest is a professional engaged in
the provision of a spiritual service to his clients. That is, by virtue
of extended training, esoteric knowledge, dedication, and acceptance of a particular code of ethics and practices, he is acknowledged to be a legitimate practitioner in the profession of religion.[1]

The priest engages in the performance of his professional
functions as a member of a professional organization: his services
are provided under the auspices of an aggregate of individuals

Authors' Note: *We thank Arlene Kaplan Daniels for her comments.*

joined into an organization whose product is the professional service. Although the priest is generally recognized as a professional—and one of the oldest ones at that—the conceptual literature about professionals in organizations is of limited aid in understanding behavior and change in organizations which encompass professionals.[2] By focusing on the crisis in the Church we hope to shed more light on organizations composed of such high-talent manpower and on the processes of internal organizational change.

THE PROFESSION AS ORGANIZATION

The distinctive nature of the Catholic Church among Christians is its universality and its claim to being the linear descendent of the church founded by Christ. It appears to its members as the embodiment both of Christ and of the People of God. All of these have depended on the Church's unity and, hence, its organization. The organization and high degree of centralization provide this unity which both legitimates the Church in the eyes of its followers and is a key part of the service it provides.

We have been discussing priests as if they were individual professionals. They are not. For example, we have identified the unity of the Church as a service that is provided to its lay members—its clients. That contradicts the model of the independent professional. We suggest that the professional-client relationship is, in this case, more accurately depicted as a relation between client and "profession as organization." One of the major services the Church provides is that it is an organization and not just an independent professional or an association of them. It is an organization in the strict sense that its existence and ability to provide services do not depend on the identity of particular members. In fact, the quality of the spiritual service provided the client is independent of the particular professional providing it.

We use the strained nomenclature of "profession as organization" to distinguish this organization from those called professional organizations (Etzioni, 1964: 81-87) because the latter, although composed of and dominated by professionals, still relate to clients as individual professionals. We use the term to indicate professional occupations without an institutional structure that transcends the containing organization. It applies when the organization becomes more important than either the individual practitioner or any association of participants.

The Church provides the service, not the individual priest. This is certainly true of sacramental duties, although not quite as true of pastoral ones. If we look at those services provided by this profession, we find most of them coming from the organization: administering the sacraments, maintaining the religious order, maintaining a place of worship and opportunity for community, and helping the poor.

Unlike other professions, and even unlike other clergy, the priests are not involved in a professional-client relationship between individuals. Rather, the Church is the profession vis-à-vis the laity. It is a corporate and organic body with the priest only a representative within and of it. For example, the sacraments can only be administered by someone ordained in the Church. And the Church has the right to withdraw this permission from a priest.

The internal legal structure of the Church, canon law, specifies the behavior of the priest as well as his relations to the members of the larger Catholic community. There are a number of proscriptions which make it clear that the priest is not to be perceived as an individual practitioner—even by himself. Recent events have highlighted this issue. Some priests have continued to administer the sacraments even after leaving the active ministry. A few evidently are able to do so by securing their own clientele. The refusal of the organization to permit such independent practice creates an interesting struggle not seen in other professions.

Competition to serve this clientele is not among individual professionals but among organizations—or at least among religious organizations. The client does not follow an individual (except at the birth of religions). Thus, when parishioners develop too great an attachment to one clergyman, there is a perceived danger to the institution. Preference for one cleric over another, however, is not a great threat unless laymen follow a priest from parish to parish or even out of the Church.

The individual priest is supposed to immerse himself in the

organization on the basis of sacrifice and complete devotion to the clientele. Anything that appears self-serving is denounced. There is even a strain of anti-intellectualism among some diocesan priests based on the notion that it encourages "individualism" and leads a priest to more narrowly define what he should be doing instead of being a "soldier of the Church"—willing to go anywhere. Others have noted similar bases for anti-intellectualism, but they usually refer to groups with extreme disparity in education (Schurmann, 1968: 52, 565). In this case, it occurs in a group where all members have at least a college degree.

This is not the only profession where the client comes to the organization first and only then is "assigned" to an individual professional. It occurs in medical clinics, public health facilities, social welfare agencies, and especially in schools. But clients may be referred to a specialist in those organizations. And, unlike most of these examples, there is no such thing as an independent practitioner in the Church. More importantly, the priest does not move from one organization to another. In all the other examples, the individual professional may move to another agency, another hospital, or another school. Further, in Catholicism it is possible to be a member of the Church and receive its services without any personal interaction with the priest beyond that of receiving Communion and occasional confessions behind a barrier.

Whatever the distinctions between priests and other professions, it remains that many others have attributes of a "profession as organization."[3] However, the implications of such an arrangement have been little enough explored in any of these areas. In fact, we would maintain that it is an increasing phenomenon and that many so-called professional organizations are being transformed in this direction. We now look at some of the implications of this by examining organizational changes in the internal structure of this profession.

ORGANIZATIONAL CHANGE: INTERNAL PRESSURES AND MECHANISMS

We have emphasized that the main characteristic of the Catholic Church and a major reason for its strength is its unity—without which it loses its claim to legitimacy as inheritor or direct descendent of the Church of Peter. As with almost any organization, such unity is only obtained with a hierarchical form and a centralized authority structure. The hierarchical system, developed through interaction with the exigencies of various historical periods, came to be thought of as having sprung full-blown from the mind of Christ. The result was an increasingly self-contained Church, with preservation and justification of traditions and hierarchical structure attaining the status of autonomous goals.

As the Church as institution continued to grow, the priesthood as organization, originally created to provide consistent and responsible service to the spiritual needs of believers, was led to develop administrative procedures for coordinating the organization itself. The priesthood, as an organization, contains mechanisms for recruiting, training, placement, promotion, and control of organizational members, as well as mechanisms for the production, packaging, and distribution of the organizational product which is, in this case, the spiritual services demanded by members of the Church as institution.

The current and popular image of the Church's centralized authority following from this is of the Pope as an absolute ruler located in Rome along with his Curia (administrative staff). At the diocesan level, the bishop, subject to the Pope, "rules" over the priests. All of these leaders, however, are still priests and professionals, though they are concerned with administrative duties and organizational necessities rather than with individual professional or religious duties.

The conflict between serving the people and serving the organizational needs of an institutional church has been an endemic problem in the Church for some time. There are now, additionally, powerful forces of decentralization and counterforces, in turn, which together threaten the unity of the Church. The forces of decentralization come both from needs of the people and as a reaction to the organizational excesses of the institution. The question of birth control is an example of an issue where the organization's official reaction did not meet the needs of parishioners (New York Times, 1968). And the response was seen as excessive in the management of those priests who voiced the disagreement felt by many more (Morris, 1968).

CHANGE: ENABLING MECHANISMS

The long-term secularization trends in industrial society have exerted continual external pressure for changes in the Catholic Church. Internal pressures have also been present for over a century (O'Dea, 1968). But it was not until Vatican Council II (1962-1965) that any of these changes were realized (Rynne, 1968). But since then there have been a number of changes brought on by the continual interplay between ideas and institutional arrangements which originated with Vatican II.

Change in the Church, as elsewhere, frequently comes about through "enabling mechanisms" which either permit pressures to surface or which create new situations and definitions. Vatican II was both the origin and the best example of a number of such mechanisms in the Church. It was the first time that most of the attending bishops were together as a body for legislative purposes. During their stay, they were removed from their administrative duties and the responsibilities of "handling" those below them. As O'Dea (1968: 123) has put it, they were there to "discuss."

Issues that had not been previously discussed in public were raised, as were those for which bishops, in their administrative role, had had neither the occasion nor time to consider. Unconfined by day-to-day administrative chores, they were able to call upon the ideal values that appealed to the core of their religion but that so often were submerged by what appeared to be organizational necessities. As one attending bishop reported (in a private conversation with one of the authors) about the final documents: "If the council documents were given to the 2,000 bishops at the beginning you couldn't have gotten 100 signatures—including mine."

The Council increased the bishops' awareness of their common interests and illustrated their ability to promulgate change even over the opposition of the Curia. Accordingly, they attempted to

institute a similar arrangement by providing for regularly scheduled synods composed of representative bishops from each country.
However, the Curia preceded them by urging irregular synods to
be called only by the Pope and with his agenda. Previous to a
recent synod, one of the bishops recounted (in a private
conversation) how it had come to be created and how they now
hoped to change it:

> Debate in the Council was leading inexorably to a synod but not this
> kind [rather]—a synod of bishops in collegiality. Before it happened,
> the Pope announced the setting of a synod he could call. Everyone
> applauded, but we were had. They [the Curia] walked all over us. Now
> we have to fight it to change it to a statutory meeting. This is where we
> were headed. You have to give them credit. We were innocents abroad.
> They were the experts in infighting.

No longer did the bishops confront the administrative center of
the Church only as individuals. In concert, they realized their
common interests and, during that subsequent synod, they
arranged to meet regularly and to originate agenda items. Even
back in their administrative posts, they were now willing to
decentralize the Church still further—at least to their level in the
organization.[4]

But whether they had intended decentralization to proceed
below them or not, they had now legitimated such pressures in the
eyes of the priesthood. It became increasingly difficult to claim
that decentralization should not apply to the bishop-priest
relationship now that it was in effect at the bishop-Pope and
bishop-Curia levels.

The crisis of the Church is most salient at the level of the priest
and with the governance of this level. But the priests have become
less reverent toward those above them. It has become clearer that
bishops are only "other" priests; they have been divested of any
sense of greater divine nature. Priests are apparently less willing to
recognize that the consecration of bishops confers a higher status
within the spiritual profession. Wide and intense publicity given to
the internal workings of, and political maneuvering among bishops
at Vatican II played a large role in this.[5] It is unusual for an

organization, other than an explicitly political one, to have the deliberations of its leaders openly available to all members. If, as Thompson (1961: 70-71) has maintained, status rank is a function of ignorance, then such publicity will reduce the chances that members of the hierarchy will be held in awe by subordinates.

NEW ORGANIZATIONAL FORMS

The major organizational change at the diocesan level was the creation of priest senates or associations. Following Vatican Council II, Pope Paul VI issued a *Motu Proprio:* "Ecclesiae Sanctae," Article 15 of which provided for the creation in each diocese of a senate of priests which would be representative of that body of priests. In many dioceses the senators were elected by the priests, while in others they were appointed by the bishop. In still others, they were either not created or the bishops refused to recognize them.

Until now, the relations between the priests of a diocese and their bishop or his staff at the chancery were on an individual basis. Occasionally, when there was more than one priest in a parish, they might act jointly, but priests from different parishes seldom acted together. Common problems, such as relations with the laity (their clients) or with their bishops, were discussed informally, if at all, when priests were together socially. No mechanisms existed for joint action, and the formation of one was not perceived as a legitimate endeavor. Besides, there already was a mechanism to take care of any diocesanwide problem—the administrative staff of the bishop. Nothing in their history or value system made any attempt to organize priests an easy one.

Nor, despite their successes, has it been. As long as the priest performed the tasks required by his organizational role within this professional organization, he had quite a bit of time and personal autonomy. This was especially true before the advent of parish councils (described below). A logical form of counterbalancing the organization's power was in an individual direction, rather than joined with other priests. The interpersonal and interprofessional relations required by the former were far less cumbersome than those by the latter.

The creation of senates now legitimated concerted action on the part of priests. For example, associations (as opposed to officially recognized senates) were created in a number of instances when a bishop balked at starting or recognizing a senate. These senates and associations then went one step further when many of them combined to form the National Federation of Priest Councils (N.F.P.C.). This was an even more daring move, for nothing in the formal structure of the Church provided for any nationwide unit. The bishop of each diocese dealt directly with Rome. The dioceses were completely autonomous from each other. Diocesan priests do not transfer from one diocese to another. While there was some form of cooperation among bishops at the national level, it was with regard to the place of the Church in the political structure of America. Although it preceded the N.F.P.C., the nationwide unit of bishops (the National Conference of Catholic Bishops) has only become a more viable unit since Vatican II and with the advent of the synods.

By its very nature, the N.F.P.C. is parallel to, dependent on, and is in some form of opposition to the bishop's national organization; it can now deal with issues that transcend more than one diocese. However, as yet there have not been many such issues. It provides a body to represent priests as a class with bishops as a class, rather than as a body representing the priests of a diocese to their immediate superior.

Some standard of comparison or of potential is important for any new organization, without its own history. The combination of senates or associations into the N.F.P.C. provided a yardstick by which each of them was able to judge itself. What one senate did became at least a potential for any other that knew about it. The N.F.P.C. provided the means for the exchanging of information and experience.

The provision of a comparative framework goes to the heart of the issue of legitimation. It helped each area examine its own basis of legitimation on an issue that was not uniformly accepted by the American bishops. As we have said, there are still dioceses without senates or others where senates are controlled by the bishop. It was not just that one diocese had something another did not, but that activities forbidden in one part of the Church might be conceived and recognized as legitimate in another. Those who had not seen the relative structure of the Church or had only thought about it abstractly were forced to confront it. It taught that what was still considered illegitimate in one area was legitimate elsewhere. Having a senate present and unquestioned in one area made it more difficult to question elsewhere. A precedent had been established.

The creation of these organizations of priests reversed the usual order in the process of professionalization. Occupational groups usually form a professional association as one of the early steps in the attempt at professional recognition and in the attempt to gain exclusivity from official state sources (Wilensky, 1964). The association of priests, as priests, followed long after the existence and recognition of their profession. Instead of being formed to gain professional status, their association was formed as an organizational tool to deal with bishops. As part of the longest-lived profession, they did not have to compete with a welter of established ones in order to gain professional status. The national association was formed to reduce the power of specific others rather than to gain general power. At the least, it was to question the power of the bishops, if not overtly to reduce it.

BUREAUCRATIZATION AND PROFESSIONALIZATION – SIMULTANEOUS PRESSURES

The first order of business for most senates and the N.F.P.C. was with the position of priests as "personnel" in their dioceses. Their first concern was over the assignment and promotion of priests. Heretofore, the frequent transfer of priests had been made by the bishop or, more likely for the younger ones, by a chancery official. In any case, the moves were made largely on the basis of personal knowledge and feelings about individual priests or despite the lack of any knowledge about younger ones. Recourse was provided only by the pleadings of the involved individual.

At first glance, the demands of this group of professionals to produce standardized personnel procedures with uniformly applied criteria appeared to be an attempt to bureaucratize their relationship—a strange request from professionals. A closer look reveals a more complicated picture. If most of the transfers in the past were made on a personal basis—unpredictable and unstandardized—promotions from curate to pastor were almost always predictable because they were largely based on seniority. The exceptions were made for those who stood out at either extreme of the bishop's favor. In neither case were distinctions of merit involved. While seniority met the conditions of being rational, impersonal, and standardized, it was not directed toward improving the organization or the profession.

The issue of differential merit has been a difficult one for most professions. Professionals are usually reluctant to admit to laymen that some members of the profession are without merit.[6] Within the profession, however, they are constantly evaluating others through invidious comparisons. Similarly, priests have readily made distinctions among themselves between those who were good or bad leaders and administrators, but they have been loath to evaluate a man as a good or bad priest. Up to now, however, seniority procedures assumed an identity between spiritual professionalism and leadership or administrative skills. Some priests have now questioned this identity. They have urged the use of merit distinctions among priests as a criterion for promotions to pastor while leaving unchallenged the notion that a man remains a priest for life. At the same time, another group has been urging the elimination of the pastor-curate distinction. Although these simultaneous pressures may be conceptually confusing, they should make it clear that organizations can contain many different and even opposing pressures at the same time. And in this case, the pressures for greater bureaucratization were from the desire for individual autonomy and to further the goals of the profession.

An even more significant and far-reaching attempt at greater professionalization was made by priests in their effort to gain greater control over the assignment of personnel. As we have seen, priests are more a part of an organization than are other professionals. None of them operates as an independent practitioner. The attempt at greater personnel control was much more typical of those in professional organizations than of those professionals who were part of larger, nonprofessional organizations.[7] But some senates went further than almost any professional organizations. They moved toward a system whereby elected representatives from their ranks were responsible for the task of drawing up the criteria for promotion and transfer, utilizing them, and making the moves (although the bishop still held final appointive power). This went beyond most professional organizations where, although it is a fellow professional that makes the decision, he does so by right of his hierarchical position and not on the basis of representative legitimation.

For the first time, the diocesan priests have become an association of professionals, although not an association of independent professionals. More importantly for comparison to other professional organizations, they are an association of professionals within the confines of a containing organization, albeit a professional one. They meet as colleagues, as equals, to help run their organization. This, despite the fact that many of them are the subordinates of others. The pastors and curates have equal voices binding on both. And, in a few places, as mentioned above, priests have even begun to talk of doing away with the distinction between pastor and curate. They are professionals in an organization increasingly run by the professionals in combination rather than by a vertical hierarchy. They wanted, then, both greater bureaucratization by altering the mechanisms for personnel decisions and greater professionalization by changing *who* was to be involved in the decision.

ORGANIZATIONAL CHANGE: SHIFTING BOUNDARIES

Vatican II created changes in the Church's relations to the laity that have further complicated organizational relations within the Church. These changes will, in fact, redefine what is internal and what is external.[8] The boundary has already started to shift with the creation of parish councils. Each parish is to have a group of laity who, together with the pastor and curates, will serve as a kind of executive committee to run the parish. While the activities of these councils, where they do exist, range from passivity to complete control over the finances of the parish, there is no doubt that they will encourage greater lay involvement in the Church. In fact, the laymen have created their own national organization to promote lay influence in the Church.[9] Although they may not be influential in any local diocese, the National Association of Laymen has been able to exert pressure through the national press. For example, its report attacking Church financial records was featured on page one of the *New York Times* (New York Times, 1970).

There is ambivalence among priests over the inclusion of the laity, with the younger ones generally favoring it. This ambivalence highlights the tenuous nature of the processes now at work in the Church. For example, the lay members of some parish councils are picked by the pastor, while in others they may be elected. The discussion of these alternative methods came up at a regional meeting of priest associations more generally devoted to greater freedom from bishops, including the notion that bishops should be elected. However, they could not agree that lay council members should be elected by other laity. Instead, their compromise resolution stated they should be democratically "selected."

There is ambivalence even among the proponents. The priests still see themselves as embodying a set of values in human relations not always embraced by their congregation. The spirit in which they wish to include the laity as colleagues among the People of God, they also expect to see embodied in the laity's actions toward the less fortunate and the "minority" groups. They fear that a sharing of power to do good will result in a parochial view.

An argument is thus raised that more power to parishioners—more decentralization—will hurt the chances of the diocesan-level church to carry on good works. Whenever the issue was brought up at the meetings of one senate,[10] the senators were reminded of one of the parishes that insisted on spending a million dollars to build a new building at a time when the Church did not want to expend capital because of the shortage of funds for "good works." They recited the opposition of this parish toward giving their monies to any other groups—especially if the blacks would get part of it. The actual story was not that clear-cut, but it was used a number of times before anyone questioned it. The problem of more power to the people when those people turn out not to think like those who urged it for them has always been with us.

Increased lay participation may appear to be similar to Protestantism on the parish level, but it is highly unlikely the two religious organizations could end up structurally similar. Most religions other than Catholicism are organizationally important at the local level. Few of them have dominating international or diocesan-level organizations. No matter how much more organizationally involved Catholic laity become, they will be doing so in an already established international organization of great sophistication. The emergent result will be something new, as will the professional-lay relationship.

A series of norms has been established and expectations raised that will be hard to put aside. Change has been initiated as a way of life in an organization noted for its historical resistance to change. Conflicting forces have been set in motion to produce a continual process not before encountered.

CONCLUSIONS: THE ORGANIZATION OF CHANGE

The inherent contradictions generated within the Church have been brought to the surface. The Church is now going through a period when a series of overt pressures is moving it in different directions. Even among those aspects that characterize its clergy as professionals, there are conflicting movements. It is thus set upon a course of inevitable, though uncertain, change.

The clergy, for example, are involved in a series of conflicting pressures about their assignments. On the one hand, they are attempting to bureaucratize the procedures for transfer and promotion and to gain colleague control over these procedures. On the other hand, many of these same priests—especially the younger ones—urge that the laity through parish councils be given a voice in Church procedures. In addition, they emphasize that the most important criterion for promotion should be the interpersonal competence of the priest—the most immeasurable and unbureaucratic criterion. Decentralization to their level gives them more power and is, in fact, more professional than even doctors in hospitals. But decentralization to the level of the laity removes some of the power.

Democratizing the Church means more stress and conflict, because it raises the necessity of mobilizing forces and supporters for various positions. Democratizing it means politicizing it, which means more conflict and continual change.

Differences from one part of the Catholic Church to another have existed side by side for centuries. Whatever uniformity or coordination had to exist was taken care of at the center, whether it be at a diocesan level or in Rome. The differences existed side by side with unity because there was no need for them to confront each other. But unity and subsidiarity at the same time is not an easy thing to achieve. As the priests form associations which must come to some kinds of agreements among themselves, then these differences will come into the open.

The Church as profession and the Church as community have always been in a state of tension. Now the potential for conflict which had always been present will be realized. The forums and mechanisms are there. The inclusion of the laity within existing Church decision-making units will further confuse our attempts to understand the nature of this "profession as organization." Nevertheless, it is clear that questions of organizational decision-making processes will become an increasing part of professionalism. And, in this profession, the struggles over questions of hierarchical authority, to which we have referred above, may give way to struggles over issues of general Church policy and practice.[11]

There should be no surprise that there are pressures which conflict with each other, although there may now be a discernible trend toward decentralization and liberalism. What is interesting is that different groups are able to use the ideologies associated with the priestly role and with religion to justify each one of these conflicting pressures. Appeals for each of the changes or arguments against them are based on prevailing ideologies. For example, as the priests help support the rise of lay influence, they threaten the present organizational structure of the Church. But they are able to do so based in ideologies of Christian community. The history of the Church is long enough to permit the claim that any ideology is based on traditions from the past. At the same time, greater lay voice may permit the priest greater autonomy vis-à-vis his bishop. Yet the laity will remain suspect in light of the more advanced position of the clergy on social issues.[1][2]

All of these ideologies exist at the same time, to be dredged up whenever any one of them supports a position. It is thus interesting that conflicting ideologies can exist at the same time and not really be brought up unless a fight takes place. The creation of new forums and avenues of dissent within the Church now makes it more likely that such ideologies will be brought forth and that fights will be fought. Even when the fight does occur, there is not necessarily a specific and open confrontation among these ideas. They may be cited and ignored respectively.

Any structural social entity, whether a religion or a profession, carries within it a series of beliefs and ideas which answer to an assorted number of problems. They usually do not get called all at once, but sequentially. None of us is individually consistent, for our principles are organized around a set of problems and can never be absolute. They are not applied or translated to other areas where they are not considered appropriate—but it may be possible for someone to translate them so as to cause embarrassment. Organizational changes and shifts in professional-client arrangements provide occasions for the confrontation of such ideologies. The Church and the profession of priest are now in such a state.

If we again consider the Church as "profession as organization," it then serves as a model for other professions characterized by organized practices. Accounting and law firms, in their relationships of the professional to the organization, resemble the Church of the past; though the persons who made all the decisions were also professionals, they made these decisions by right of their hierarchical position. The Church is now trying to move to a collegial authority structure after centuries of hierarchy. If it happens, it will serve as a model for other professional organizations.

NOTES

1. For an account of the occupation and career of priests, see Fichter (1966).

2. For literature about professionals in organizations, see Vollmer and Mills (1966: sec. 8). For an opposing point of view, see Goldner and Ritti (1967).

3. See Etzioni (1969) for accounts of social work agencies and schools. Also see Rogers (1969) for schools.

4. For an account of the historical relationship between popes and bishops, see Bassett (1969).

5. See Rynne (1968) for an example of this. It is especially noteworthy that his book first appeared as a series of articles in a popular magazine—*The New Yorker*. It should also be noted that the author's name is a pseudonym. The *National Catholic Reporter*, a newspaper originated after Vatican II, has also played a large role in this country in continuing to disseminate information about changes and conflicts in the Church.

6. See Freidson (1970) for an account of the use of this and other autonomy maintenance mechanisms among physicians.

7. See Rogers (1969) for an account of this phenomenon in the schools.

8. The laity's influence on the Church is but one example of the many pressures for change from outside the priesthood. We deal with these in more detail in a forthcoming work.

9. There have been a number of lay organizations throughout recent Church history. However, these organizations, such as the Knights of Malta and the Knights of Columbus, are service or social organizations and have not played a political role in the Church.

10. One of the authors has attended priest senate meetings. The authors have been jointly engaged in a study of the priesthood utilizing interviews, observations, and survey data.

11. An assertion that engineers are similarly engaged in such struggles over technical policies in industrial organizations is contained in Ritti and Goldner (1969).

12. For an account of a similar relationship in Protestantism, see Hadden (1970).

REFERENCES

BASSETT, W. (1969) "Subsidiarity, order and freedom in the Church." Presented at the Canon Law Society of America Symposium on Unity and Subsidiarity in the Church, Dayton, Ohio.

ETZIONI, A. [ed.] (1969) The Semi-professions and Their Organization. New York: Free Press.

––– (1964) Modern Organizations. Englewood Cliffs, N.J.: Prentice-Hall.

FICHTER, J. H. (1966) Religion as an Occupation. Notre Dame, Ind.: Univ. of Notre Dame Press.

FREIDSON, E. (1970) Professional Dominance. New York: Atherton.

GOLDNER, F. H. and R. R. RITTI (1967) "Professionalization as career immobility." Amer. J. of Sociology (March): 489-502.

HADDEN, J. K. (1970) The Gathering Storm in the Churches. New York: Doubleday Anchor.

MORRIS, J. D. (1968) "Priests widen dispute with O'Boyle." New York Times (October 3).

New York Times (1970) "Catholic laymen score 23 dioceses." (November 16): 1, 41.

––– (1968) "Catholics in poll back birth curbs." (September 1): 46.

O'DEA, T. F. (1968) The Catholic Crisis. Boston: Beacon.

RITTI, R. R. and F. H. GOLDNER (1969) "Professional pluralism in an industrial organization." Management Sci. 16 (December): B233-B246.

ROGERS, D. (1969) 110 Livingston Street. New York: Vintage.

RYNNE, X. (1968) Vatican Council II. New York: Farrar, Strauss & Giroux.

SCHURMANN, F. (1968) Ideology and Organization in Communist China. Berkeley: Univ. of California Press.

THOMPSON, V. A. (1961) Modern Organization. New York: Alfred A. Knopf.

VOLLMER, H. M. and D. L. MILLS (1966) Professionalization. Englewood Cliffs, N.J.: Prentice-Hall.

WILENSKY, H. (1964) "The professionalization of everyone?" Amer. J. of Sociology (September): 137-158.

Chapter 11

SCHOOLTEACHERS
AND MILITANT CONSERVATISM

PHILIP M. MARCUS

INTRODUCTION

Any discussion about professionals, or subprofessionals, must include teachers as an example of a group being denied full rights and privileges, full entry into the exalted circle of true professionals.[1] But the very size of their group and its expenditures command attention. Teachers comprise the largest group of all professionals as classified by the census. They have retained this rather envious state over a long period of time, comprising 40% of all professionals in 1900. By 1960, teachers were still the largest single group of professionals, their numbers having tripled, but their proportion of the total professional group had declined to only 28.5% (Folger and Nam, 1967: 78). The decreasing proportion can be accounted for in terms of the tremendous increase in the service sector of the economy, especially among professionals.

Teaching is important to understand because it is traditionally a woman's profession and can provide many insights into the unique problems women encounter and the techniques they employ for handling their career difficulties. Teachers comprise the largest group of all women professionals, although the proportion had declined from 85% in 1900 to approximately one-half by 1950. In 1966, 90% of all elementary school teachers were female

(Silverman and Metz, 1970: 26). The study of teachers will help also in understanding changes in other occupations as increasing numbers of women enter them. For example, as more women enter university teaching, medicine, and law, we can anticipate, to some extent, their impact upon these male-dominated occupations.

It is ironic that teaching, although denied full professional status at present, will probably become the prototype for most professional groups and organizations in the future. Of all professionals, teachers have been considered the most conservative, fearful, quiescent, submissive, and docile; yet, in the past two decades, as their work settings have changed, they have emerged as an extremely visible, militant group demanding rapid salary increments, tenured security, autonomy in and control over classroom working conditions, and the establishment of criteria for membership admission. Research on teachers, sadly neglected by sociologists, can provide important insights about the possible reactions other professionals will have as their work settings become similar to that of teachers.

Teachers will be the prototype of the new and emerging professional because the changes they have undergone and the problems they have confronted in the past two decades are just now beginning to be experienced by other professionals. The impact of increasing bureaucratization, large size, external intervention, specialization among members, and societal demands for accountability even with the absence of performance criteria have all been felt in the school systems; they are just now reaching medicine and law, universities and social work. No longer is there an assumed conflict between serving the client and being a good organization member; in the modern professional organization, to serve the client is to meet organizational goals. In a school, the illiterate child is a failed mission, just as in a hospital a sick person is an incompleted task.

This paper examines some of the changes which have occurred in the teaching profession over the past two decades, showing how increased size of organization, bureaucratization of school districts, specialization of teachers, and societal demands for education have all contributed to an increased militancy among teachers for professionalization and community recognition. However, it will be argued, teacher militancy and power have given rise to increased constraints exerted by the community. In the future, these constraints will provide additional professional self-awareness to teachers, while placing them in a most conservative mold. Thus, the strength utilized as an impetus for change will be transformed rapidly into a wall of stability. Throughout this paper, the primary focus will be upon the social structural bases of professional behavior, rather than upon the social-psychological variables which so often accompany, and rationalize, change. However, to provide a well-balanced perspective, teacher characteristics will be examined briefly.

WHO ARE TEACHERS?

There are almost two million teachers in the public schools today, concentrated primarily in large urban areas: 2% of the school systems employ over 40% of the teachers. It has already been mentioned that teachers comprise the largest single group of all professionals, almost 30% in 1960; 50% of all professional women are teachers. It has sometimes been argued that the increasing number of male secondary school teachers has given rise to teacher militancy. However, since 1900, male teachers have comprised approximately 15% of all male professionals; approximately 50% of all secondary school teachers and 10% of the elementary are males. While the proportion of male secondary school teachers has remained relatively constant (dropping sharply only in 1920), the proportion of males at the elementary level has never returned to its high of 30% at the turn of the century.[2] While these figures would not indicate any major shifts toward militancy, it is possible that those males now entering teaching differ from those working prior to 1950. On this point, it should be noted that, among secondary school teachers, almost 40% of the males had fathers who were manual workers, compared to 23% of the females. In contrast, twice as many female as male teachers had fathers who were professional or semi-professional workers, 22% versus 11% (National Education Association, 1963: 84-85). Thus, one might expect male secondary school teachers to be more socially mobile than females as well as more amenable to unionization and collective negotiations by their professional associations. Such expectations are entirely consistent with Cole's study of New York City and Boston schools where males were found to be more militant than females (Cole, 1968, 1969; Rosenthal, 1966).

In 1970, of the $35.2 billion expended on public school education, $19 billion were spent on classroom teacher salaries. This figure represents a cost of $364 per pupil, over twice as much spent ($170) in 1957-1959. Of all education costs, teacher salaries have risen the most rapidly.[3] Teacher income, however, reflects the structural bases of deprivation which might be felt by male teachers. As a proportion of all professional income, teacher income was 83% for males but 112% for females. Between 1949 and 1959, the percent increase was greater for females than for males. And, finally, the percent increase for male teachers was less than for all male professionals, while the percent increase for female teachers was greater than for female professionals (Folger and Nam, 1967: 88).

In 1900, 90% of the female and 53% of the male teachers were single but, by 1960, the proportion had dropped to approximately 30% for females and 16% for males. The greater proportion of married males, experiencing financial responsibility for a family and deprivation of income, easily leads them to become discontented with their chosen occupation. In 1965, 17% of male secondary school teachers surveyed reported they would not become teachers if able to start over again, as compared to only 7% of the female teachers (Silverman and Metz, 1970: 26).

Male teachers handle some of their teaching problems by supplementing their earnings with outside jobs: the NEA study reported 50% of the male (versus 9% of the female) teachers had summer jobs, while 38% of the male (versus 5% of the female) teachers also held outside jobs during the 1960-1961 school year (National Education Association, 1963: 85).[4] Other males move out of teaching into administration: over 66% of elementary school principals are male and the proportion in secondary schools is even higher (Clark, 1964: 754).

There is some indication that males have different expectations of remaining in teaching than females. Clark reports that 65% of all women teachers expected to leave the occupation within five years, but over 80% of these hoped to return to teaching. While only 30% of the beginning male teachers expected to remain in teaching, the remaining group indicated they planned to obtain nonteaching jobs (Clark, 1964: 754). Clearly, then, the initial expectation for males is to leave teaching while for females it is to leave teaching with eventual return. Thus, one would conclude that males remaining in teaching, suffering from relative deprivation, would also feel like failures because they did not, or could not, move into another job. The median years of service for secondary school teachers in 1965-1966 were about the same for both sexes, 7.0 for males and 7.2 for females. However, almost twice as many females as males have twenty or more years of experience. The difference in median years of experience between the two groups has continually narrowed as the secondary school female teachers decreased from a median of 12.4 years in 1960-1961 to 7.2 years in 1965-1966 (Silverman and Metz, 1970: 26).[5]

In general, male teachers earn more than their female counterparts. In 1965, the median wage differential among secondary teachers was $600 (Silverman and Metz, 1970: 26). One reason for this is they have less discontinuity in their teaching. An NEA study reported that 44% of all teachers had at least one break in their service and 8.3 was the mean years of absence. Males averaged 4.3 years of absence, and only 24% had a break in service; females were double their male counterparts, but, interestingly, single females had virtually the same statistics as males (National Education Association, 1963: 40).[6] Thus, clearly, it is the married female teachers whose discontinuity partially affects the salary differential between the sexes. (Salary discrimination based directly on sex criteria is relatively unimportant in teaching.)

Another factor affecting the wage differential between male and female teachers is that the latter have less education. Thirty-seven percent of secondary school males had more than a bachelor's degree in 1965 while only 26% of the female teachers had that level of education. (Among all elementary school teachers, 16% had more than a bachelor's degree while 13% still had *less* than a bachelor's degree [Silverman and Metz, 1970: 26].) Part-time teaching is also much higher among females than males and this tends to decrease annual earnings.

Salaries, then, may be higher for male than for female teachers but, as indicated above, males undoubtedly will feel a sense of deprivation because they are in a female occupation, they have many males around them who consider themselves failures because of an inability to leave teaching as originally planned, they receive lower salaries than males in other professions and think it necessary to supplement their earnings with additional jobs outside of education.

The above discussion provides the social characteristics of teachers, telling us something about the factors which could lead to an increased susceptibility to unionization and/or collective action when structural changes and upheavals occur in the schools themselves. Thus, it was not merely the psychological predisposition to act which gave impetus to unionization, but rather a combination and interaction of personal and structural variables.

STRUCTURAL CHANGES IN SOCIETY

First we must examine the increasing size of school districts and the number of employed personnel in school buildings. Between 1910 and 1960, enrollment in the public schools increased 23.6 million. more than one-half this growth taking place between 1950 and 1960. Two-thirds of this increase can be attributed merely to population increase but the other one-third has to be attributed to enrollment increase. For example, in 1960, even among the sixteen- and seventeen-year-olds, over 85% of the group were enrolled in school. Among younger children, the proportion was over 95% (Folger and Nam, 1967: 41).

Since 1957, the consolidation of school districts has increased at a rapid rate. The number of school districts in the United States has been reduced 50% since 1957 (Corwin, 1965: 41). One-quarter of the nation's school systems educate nearly 80% of the U.S. school-age population, although the large school districts have made it virtually impossible for the local areas to provide sufficient funds through property taxation, and approximately 40% of education funds today come from the state or federal government.

Consolidation of school districts has occurred even though the local community school was considered the most desirable form of organization. Parents felt they paid taxes to have their children trained in jobs which would serve the local community after graduation. However, the changing occupational structure made it virtually impossible for parents to have their children adequately educated without the aid of specialists. Complex courses were needed and more equipment required to teach children the skills beyond simple literacy. Small districts could not afford these specialties and it became necessary to combine. Improved systems of transportation and construction of elaborate road networks made it relatively easy to bus children from one area to another. Therefore, consolidation of school districts has been achieved even though some local groups opposed it.

The consolidated, larger districts employing specialists who had advanced training made it difficult for the lay school boards and local citizens to evaluate the material which was being introduced into the school system. It became expected that a teacher, in the secondary, and even the elementary schools, would have received a bachelor's degree, or more, reflecting some specialized training. Central administrators acquired increasing delegated power as lay boards withdrew to oversee the library purchases and argue over the merits of teaching about communism or the virtues of the United Nations.[7]

Small school districts could not obtain the necessary resources because their populations were declining. Younger persons, especially, were migrating to large metropolitan areas. Twenty million people left the farm between 1945 and 1965. The children themselves began to receive more education than their parents and larger numbers stayed in school in order to obtain the necessary education for their later occupations. The economic depression of the 1930s and the second world war were periods of lowered birth rate, decreasing the availability of teachers in the early 1950s; this shortage also encouraged consolidation.

The population explosion after the second world war gave rise to a demand for more elementary schools and teachers. Increased education of the population as a whole, due to the large number of people who attended college after World War II, coupled with the complexity of jobs, also gave rise to demands upon the secondary school system. This is the period of time which saw the rapid decrease in rural jobs as more technology was introduced on the farms and a rapid increase in the service segment of the economy occurred.

The migration to cities, often by people with many children, required education in relatively concentrated areas. While it is true that the drop-out rate declined over the past twenty-five years, the visibility of teenagers was increased because of their concentration in the urban areas. This visibility became a threat as one learned of the zooming crime rate among adolescents, heard about gang fights, drug addiction, and theft. The teacher became important as an alternative source of influence to keep children in schools, off the streets and channeled into respectable occupations.

The educated population, with their relatively small families living in suburbs, also demanded specialists to train their children for college and prestigious occupations. The inability of the family to place their children in the occupational structure rapidly increased the need and dependence upon noneducation specialists, such as psychologists, guidance counselors, and trainers for courses in human adjustment. The school rapidly became the parent surrogate in the suburb.

There were additional reasons for the increased social demand upon teachers other than the teacher shortage and the inability of parents to prepare their children for the occupational structure. Competition with the Russians and their engineering feats were considered threatening to our national security. Demands for mathematics and science were supported by federal grants to help improve the quality of teaching. The increasing proportion of women in the labor force required baby sitters for that part of the day they worked. The importance of the school as a baby sitter should not be minimized (Goslin, 1965: 11-13).

In short, there were many social demands placed upon the school systems in the fifties and sixties from the urban areas with their increasing ethnic demands, from the decreasing power of the suburban family to place and educate their children, from the rural areas with their inability to adequately support or train their children, from the national demand for education to fill the high-skilled jobs, and from competition with foreign governments. The surfeit of children and the teacher shortage aggravated the situation.

STRUCTURAL CHANGES WITHIN THE SCHOOLS

While American society was undergoing rapid changes demanding increased education in quantity and quality, the internal structure of the schools also underwent a series of dramatic shifts. Perhaps the most obvious change within schools has been the increased specialization of the teaching staff. Teachers have increased the level of their own education during the past two decades. Much of this additional college and graduate work has been concentrated in specialized areas such as mathematics, social science, reading, physical or natural science.

Specialization has occurred because of the explosion and wide dissemination of knowledge, requiring teachers to educate students who have easy access to mass media as well as exposure to and training by relatively well-educated parents. Teachers must also learn to utilize equipment designed to incorporate new learning theories. The latter made the teacher vulnerable to accept university and commercial innovations which compete with their own skills. In order to protect their classroom domain, additional specialized training was often sought.

Increased teacher specialization has made it exceedingly difficult for principals or other administrators to supervise work or judge performance. Assessment of teacher skills has passed from the superordinate to other specialists in the school system. Obviously, the process has moved most rapidly in high schools and least rapidly in elementary schools.

The principal is one who has received advanced training in administration and whose forte lies primarily in the ability to coordinate and motivate teachers and to negotiate with the central district administration for the resources teachers need. As such, the principal's ability to assess teacher performance rapidly decreases as the specialization and expertise of each increases. The entire problem is compounded because the teacher performs in a relatively sheltered, nonvisible environment where norms of classroom autonomy and sanctity prevail.

If the principal was one who primarily coordinated activities, negotiated with the central administration, and acquired little knowledge about teachers' performance because of problems sampling their work, then it also became difficult for him to provide useful information for their daily problems and activities. In order to obtain solutions to problems, teachers would seek peers and other specialists who were readily accessible during coffee breaks, lunch hours, and other informal get-togethers. Avoiding the principal prevented the exposure of one's own ignorance, precluding a somewhat depreciating and self-defeating act because of the inability to make independent judgments or solve one's own problems. Seeking help from a principal or, for that matter, any superior often threatened the superordinate because his own directives were being questioned or found inadequate to handle the subordinate's difficulty. Thus, superordinates rejected communication, attempting to find the subordinate emotionally or intellectually incompetent for the task rather than questioning seriously the organization structure or the directives he himself had given.[8] In short, for one reason or another, teachers often obtained relatively little technical help from their principals.

Peers, on the other hand, tend to be more supportive because they are flattered when asked questions and, during the ensuing discussion, are challenged to discover new ideas about doing their own jobs. Competition for attention among the peers is stimulating as they vie for prestige and attraction from colleagues. Group cohesion is developed by ridiculing and depreciating those who caused the initial problems. Thus, laughter at clients helps develop internal group solidarity while simultaneously releasing anxiety and hostility. The repertoire of problem-solving devices is expanded and group norms are established. Peer relationships, then, when utilized in lieu of supervisory contacts, support horizontal coalitions and identifications. These would not ordinarily arise in organizations where participants are traditionally docile and conservative, where the female sex of most workers tends to make them predominantly identified with the male administrators who direct and control the schools. Specialization is the initial locus around which the coalitions form.

Another factor inhibiting close supervision in schools has been the teacher shortage, coupled with good roads, which permits disgruntled persons to move easily to more desirable, and often competing, districts. In addition, it must also be remembered that during the late 1950s and early 1960s, within American society as a whole, there has been the civil rights movement. Although the impact of this movement has yet to be assessed for persons beyond the minority groups themselves, it is probably safe to speculate that one derivative result has been the reevaluation of criteria for excellence throughout the society. Not only was it necessary to admit groups whose external symbols were once considered inferior, but we have come to realize that many of the established and venerated criteria are no longer adequate for the selection and evaluation of personnel. We have learned that tests devised by experts over generations often possess inherent biases and discriminate unwittingly against certain groups of people. We have learned that many forms of subtle discrimination against skin color, sex and ethnic groups appear to an extent beyond our rational powers of assessment. We have been forced to modify our standards of competency. For example, in schools we have found that merely teaching children to perform well on certain standardized examinations is not the only sign of a good teacher; we may now consider the good teacher as one who is capable of keeping the children in school and motivated to perform well at nonacademic tasks. High competency in vocational training may be equal to or more important for some students than doing well in college preparatory courses. Teachers whose friendship is accepted by distrustful and suspicious minority groups may be a more valuable asset than those who produce a high level of adequacy in certain foreign languages. And, finally, we have learned to admit certain types of subject matter which were never considered appropriate: for example, courses in black history, psychology of women, urban affairs, poverty. If it was difficult to evaluate those who taught writing, mathematics, reading or any other well-established subject in the schools, it has become impossible to assess the specialized material for which we have no standards whatsoever.

Principals, having difficulty assessing teachers' work, are forced to issue directives or superimpose measures to gather data for administrative decisions. Not only does the central district administration require information from local school buildings to develop policy and coordinate programs, but each individual principal requires information to obtain resources and protect his staff from community pressures and ideological incursions. Lacking direct access to teachers because he cannot easily solve daily job problems, a principal must make decisions and try to implement them without sufficient data. It is no wonder that he often becomes rejected by his staff who find his directives inadequate for their tasks, resent his interference with their self-image of professional autonomy and feel his measures of their competencies are inappropriate. Thus, resentments are frequently intensified in schools because the hierarchical structure lacks sets of alternatives and resources for assisting teachers, the reward structure of prestige and financial remuneration seems arbitrary and particularistic, and superordinate directives appear constraining and depriving of professional self-images.

Peer groups, which supposedly exert authority for professionals, cannot function adequately as alternatives to the hierarchy in large-scale organizations. Most work performed is not observable and there are poor measures of assessment. (Autopsies can reveal flagrant violations of medical technique but lack of reading skill is usually attributed to low pupil motivation or parental concern.) Peer groups, being composed of equals, cannot muster coordinative skills to divide the labor and integrate the specialties. Nor can they adjudicate conflicts among the specialists themselves and impose sanctions for continued normative violations. In short, there is a lack of structure in schools, most notably in the secondary, which contributes to teacher unrest, anxiety and discontent. Males experience the lack of structure more than females, complaining that they have a heavy or extremely heavy load or that they work under considerable strain and tension.[9]

Theoretically, group norms might develop to stabilize the school setting, standardizing procedures and allocating responsibilities. Unfortunately, as we have seen, social changes affecting the school have occurred so rapidly in the past few years, and the organization has been so totally incapable of buffering the changes, that norms could not develop. The problem is intensified by the turnover of teachers, perhaps as high as 14%. New teachers, whether they be of the 175,000 to 200,000 yearly graduates or of the 45,000 to 50,000 returning to teaching from the labor reserve, require more socialization as well as more technical assistance than those already on the job. They require relatively more social support to execute their duties and handle anxiety-provoking and guilt-laden situations with both students and parents. Social relations on the job, how to treat peers, and how to compete for student favors all require norms for guidance. When norms are well established and supported by peer sanctions, relatively little formal socialization is required. However, when high turnover exists, norms do not congeal and persons must spend much of their time working out social relationships, personal standards and expectations. Student turnover and mobility is also relatively high, thereby depriving staff of stability from these social relationships. No longer can teachers obtain clues from their classes as to student expectations, e.g., amount of reading assignments, testing and grading procedures, utilization of media, punishments and privileges. Once again, a strong organizational hierarchy could provide the functional alternative to group norms but, as we have seen, such a stabilized structure is absent in most schools today.

In summary, then, the past two decades have seen a rapid transformation in the teaching occupation. Societal demands, coupled with an organizational structure that could not adjust fast enough to keep pace with external changes, have created a vacuum in the work setting of teachers. They lacked sufficient tradition and stable colleague groups to develop norms and guidelines as functional alternatives to the weak organizational structure. Spurred by a successful contract after a threatened strike in New York City, teachers began to join unions to bargain for money to handle problems of deprivation and work rules to meet their needs for structure. An administrator-controlled National Education Association was reorganized to give teachers more policy influence and resuscitated to compete with the American Federation of Teachers for membership. Although the two organizations differed greatly in the past, since 1965 there has been a merger of tactical procedures and goals. Membership in the AFT is approximately 150,000 and heavily concentrated in a few large cities; NEA membership is about six times as great and has affiliates throughout the country.[10]

THE EMERGENCE OF TEACHER NEGOTIATING ORGANIZATIONS

It is our contention that professional associations, that is, militant teacher collective negotiating organizations, have emerged during the past two decades primarily as alternative mechanisms to stabilize the weak hierarchical structure found within school systems. Although teachers may have joined unions or professional associations for a wide variety of psychological reasons, without the lack of structure as a catalyst, there would be little support for contracts which establish rates of remuneration and specify minimum performance requirements.

Teachers were probably induced to join unions in a manner similar to other workers. Given the relatively deprived and disgruntled males in secondary schools, given the tentative and weak normative peer structures surrounding the specialized coalitions, and given the inability of superordinates to direct and assist teachers, those most prone to collective negotiations enjoined their friends to employ common tactics to solve problems.

Lipset and his colleagues have argued that, among typographers, small friendship groups operating in relatively large shops tend to be most prone to political activity. Friendship allows for the partially interested person to be drawn into the political action in order to preserve his relationship with the activists (Lipset et al., 1956: 150-175). Similarly, in schools where male teachers felt deprived, they could meet with persons involved in teacher unions during lunch, staff meetings or visits. Complaints about salary or administration which seemed perennial and disturbing could be discussed in terms of organizing for collective negotiations and settlements.

The first and most obvious issue negotiated collectively has been money, a primary concern of the relatively deprived males who are usually breadwinners within their families. Money is one of the most important commodities for school teachers because it allows them to purchase many symbols of middle-class life. Money is of little value intrinsically, but it is a medium of exchange for symbols of social position and social status. These symbols can then be used in social relationships outside of the school setting in exchange for friendship, obtaining social deference and acquiring entree into desirable social circles. In a highly developed industrialized society where roles are segmentalized, a job is usually performed before an audience which evaluates and bestows rewards. In the case of teachers, however, performance is before a somewhat unwilling audience, and one virtually incapable of evaluating their abilities. Demands for higher pay compel the local community and the broader society to acknowledge their social contributions. In 1970, almost 63% of the median school districts' budget went for teacher pay. Those teachers in smaller districts earned less than those in the larger ones (Furno and Doherty, 1970: 47-49).

The second major demand of teachers is a form of job control or job structuring. In fact, female teachers place more emphasis upon job control, especially size of the class, as a negotiating objective than do their male counterparts; they place more emphasis upon it than money. Perhaps one reason for demanding reduced class size has to do with the desire of most professionals to have a one-to-one relationship with their clients. It becomes extremely difficult for a teacher to maintain a professional self-image when forced to talk to a large number of persons, often not knowing their names or much about their personal lives. Part of the professional self-image is rationalized with a set of values, emphasizing personal client service along with quality performance. Most teachers thoroughly subscribe to the shibboleth that to teach the whole child, to motivate and provide social-emotional support to students, one-to-one relationships are necessary. Teachers will depreciate the value of mechanical instructional devices and/or large classes because it deprives them of personal contact.

The data on the impact of class size and student learning have been extremely consistent for almost thirty-five years: they show that, with but a few minor exceptions, class size has almost no impact upon learning (Rossi, 1966: 129; Janowitz, 1969: 17-19). However, there is little doubt that increasing the size of the class increases the long anathematized aspect of the teacher role, such as administrative work, and decreases the possibility of the one-to-one stereotypic professional image. Over the past sixty years, average class size has decreased; in 1970, the median district had 44.6 teachers per 1000 students. Concurrently, over the past few years expenses for and the number of paraprofessional instructional personnel has increased rapidly (4.35 per 1000 students in 1970).

Other matters which have been negotiated, usually with great success, by teacher collective negotiating organizations have been in the area of autonomy and independent decision-making. For example, the employment of nonprofessionals to supervise lunchroom activity, the release of teaching time to attend professional meetings, the specification of frequency of meetings with the principal or other administrators, or parent-teacher conferences, the amount of free time to prepare classroom assignments during the day, the selection of course material, etc., have all been negotiated. In each case, the negotiating organizations have pressed for more traditional or stereotypic symbols of professionalization rather than focusing upon which groups within the school system might be able to perform the task most competently. For example, if teachers were concerned about the opportunity to work with their students personally in a relatively informal setting, one would think that a most felicitous technique would be social contact during lunch with students who were relatively withdrawn and taciturn. However, we can find no record of any teacher organization demanding that teachers should have the time to work with students in the cafeterias during the lunch hours. The NEA study of 1960 showed that 77% of secondary school teachers reported they did not eat lunch with students; only 13% of the elementary group said they did so by preference (National Education Association, 1963: 94).[11]

Another item which has been negotiated is freedom from supervision, such as the right not to have principals make unannounced visits to the classroom and observe teaching. In schools with elaborate intercom systems, it has been possible for principals to hear what was going on in the classrooms without the teachers knowing it. In many school systems, this technique of monitoring classrooms has been removed from the principal's power.[12] (There are other questions of civil liberties involved in this issue which go beyond principals' sampling teacher performance.)

CONSTRAINTS ON TEACHER PROFESSIONALIZATION

Although a few states forbid school boards to bargain, teacher militancy has been given impetus by the enactment of many state laws recognizing the right to organize and collectively negotiate. While there is great disparity among the states, some actually require local school boards to negotiate. Most state labor relations statutes do prohibit teacher strikes, although this is seldom, if ever enforced.

There is little question that successful contract negotiations with or without a strike heightened the awareness of professional identity, facilitated recruitment, and encouraged teacher organization loyalty. While the society as a whole may be reluctant to accord full professional status, the teachers themselves have claimed it and continually try to enforce the acquisition of symbols and perquisites. The entire movement has been given additional impetus by the civil rights movement which draws attention to militant action for redress of grievances and inequity. Picketing, sit-ins and strikes are no longer the monopoly of the working class. Fighting for minority group rights as a student helps to break down some of the psychic barriers to picketing for a new contract when later employed as a teacher. Women have probably been affected by the focus upon sex discrimination and may see in teacher militancy a mechanism for redress of multiple grievances and inequities. In short, not only has there been pressure for teacher action, but some of the barriers have been surmounted.

As teachers gained momentum to demand professional working conditions, salaries and community recognition for services rendered, constraints began to emerge demanding limitations upon their potential power. Perhaps the most obvious example of constraint has arisen in New York City, the symbolic birthplace of the emergent teacher organization. Civil rights groups began to demand control over the local schools, pressuring for community determination of teacher hiring and firing, administrator responsibility, curricula development, etc. (Mayer, 1969). Thus, it was ironic that the vanguard of the teacher movement became the first to strike for professional control while under attack from a newly awakened deprived community. One would expect that other groups, middle and lower class, white and black, male and female, will demand that teachers provide some specialized services in the future. Just as some doctors and lawyers have had to recognize the existence of the poor and the rights of the deprived, so teachers will find that their school buildings are not in social vacuums. In order to counteract the local social vicissitudes, teacher organizations will undoubtedly press for state and/or federal standards of education. These will free teachers, to some extent, from local harassment because they, as individuals, can disclaim much of the responsibility for the formulation of standards.

Another constraint upon teacher power has been the youth or student movement which has moved from the colleges to the secondary (and even elementary) schools. Starting as an offshoot of the white middle-class student support of black civil rights in the South, other grievances emerged in the early 1960s to demand redress. These causes gained great respect and support among many college undergraduates. Utilizing new symbols to differentiate themselves from an older generation, imbued with feelings of social injustice to be righted, students became involved with or sympathetic to those who picketed, sat-in, marched, held mass meetings, attended teach-ins or even destroyed property. After college graduation, many of these same persons became teachers and developed sympathy for or, at times, instigated student social change in the school systems. Dress codes and rules for social dancing, hair length, course subject-matter and student participation, all became concerns among those faculty who pushed and helped the students, and those who fought them. It was in the suburbs, among the white middle class, that one found the most student pressure for realistic courses on drugs, on sex and abortion, on poverty and race, on pollution, war and other sensitive subjects. The students, stimulated by the mass media as well as their active political friends and older siblings, placed faculty on the defensive when platitudes were not supported by facts, when moralisms outweighed logic. Those teachers who became threatened by student activism tried to curb the superficial symbols of independence (e.g., dress styles, hair length, beards), often stirring other community and adult organizations to defend the young: the American Civil Liberties Union has won a number of court cases defending the rights of secondary school students against the teacher's rules.

In lower-class schools, crime and militancy have been added to teacher problems of professional power. The lack of discipline often found in lower-class schools depreciated the teacher's self-image. But the new militancy among blacks, Puerto Ricans, and Chicanos often justified attacks, physical and verbal, against middle-class teachers of *all* groups.

Teacher organizations, just gaining recognition and legitimacy as collective negotiating mechanisms, were not prepared to meet these onslaughts. Their reaction has been, typically, to establish contract clauses protecting teachers and enjoining administration to provide a buffer between teachers, their students and the community. Thus, the contract becomes reinforced as a mechanism for establishing stability under circumstances of little structure and uncertainty. Teacher's power in the schools, then, becomes curtailed because of an inability to set and enforce rules and an unwillingness to confront parents. In contrast to doctors who control the hospitals, teachers often miss the opportunity to assert their position, preferring to retreat into a delimited specialist role. Contracts, then, have become defensive tools, protecting teachers, stabilizing their jobs, but not advancing their profession. The clauses specify what teachers will not do, while little is said about what they will do.

Other factors which limit teacher power are the leveling off of the birthrate and the national economy. Schools of education have produced between 175,000 to 200,000 new teachers per year. Even though many graduates never teach, by 1970 there was a surfeit which constrained contract negotiators to focus more on the protection of those with jobs as opposed to a concern with furthering professional status. Thus, salaries, tenure and decreasing class size once again became considerations rather than the establishment of criteria for adequate performance and the specification of minimal levels of competency. One might expect that the greater the pressure for nonability criteria as a basis for hiring, firing, salary increments, the greater the community pressure for alternatives to teachers.

Each alternative mechanism, whether it be Sesame Street-type television programs, teaching machines, contracts with commercial organizations guaranteeing reading and/or mathematics results, all depreciate the skills of teachers, forcing them to become handmaidens, midwives or technicians. High salaries and professional recognition are unlikely to be forthcoming when teachers act only as motivators and have little as a concrete product.

One consequence of community demands for improved performance from teachers will be the pressure, through the negotiating organizations, to standardize wages and working conditions throughout a state and even region. This will permit greater movements across districts as there will be relatively little discrepancy among them. (Social backgrounds of students, of course, will still remain a variable, although cross-district busing may affect standardizing this too.) The pressure to standardize will also place demands upon the state legislators to change the tax base of education away from property levies. More state contributions to school finances will result in further decreasing local control and the virtual extinction of school boards whose functions, even now, are anachronistic and moribund. In their place, civilian review boards will probably emerge to oversee all aspects of school behavior, including the protection of teacher and student civil liberties, the enforcement of universalistic achievement standards, and the representation of community interests in curricula developments.

Standardized tests will place teachers under great constraint to adopt new teaching techniques in order that their students perform adequately. The conflict will emerge as to the control over these techniques. Teachers have resented the outsiders' invasions of the classroom; it remains to be seen whether or not defense against new techniques and machinery can prevail. Given the importance of education in American society, the high social cost for failure and the great financial investment, it is extremely unlikely that teaching will be left completely to teachers.

As community incursions and demands increase in severity, as performance criteria become developed, utilized and legitimated, rivalry between the two negotiating organizations will decrease and consolidation will occur. One would expect a rise in strikes in the immediate future as contract negotiations become intensified. Such an intensification will probably politicize teachers as they look to state officials for favorable budgetary allocations and legislation. Should the enforcement of antistrike laws become common against teachers, it would not be surprising to see enlarged coalitions of state and local employees, including welfare workers, nurses and other semi-professionals.

We have examined the curtailment of teacher power and some of the limits placed upon their professionalism. Teachers themselves have unwittingly encouraged some of these constraints because their collective actions for structure have been primarily defensive against administration and community.[13] They have been unable to develop a constructive role which provides the community with a needed service that is controllable by the teachers themselves. The competitors for education resources have frequently exploited community needs for their own gain, often demonstrating greater competency than the teachers themselves. While educators have fought among themselves about trivial, sloganized techniques (e.g., Do we educate the whole child? Do we educate or do we train? Do we search our souls and sensitively train our personalities or do we depreciate and condemn the bedeviled bureaucracy?), complex community needs have risen along with the rate of expenditures. Few groups of teachers have seriously examined the possibility of strengthening the organizational structures in which they work as a feasible alternative for obtaining professional status.[14] As a result, the teaching profession today emerges as a conservative force in the community, hostile to administration, resistant to change and incapable of providing service to meet social needs. As one reads the attacks on doctors' and lawyers' unwillingness to serve the public, one can only wonder if teachers will come to share full professional status by eliciting similar condemnation and obloquy.

Perhaps the major hope for teacher professionalization is the contract, because it requires periodic revision and renegotiation. In this manner, social change is required as new provisions are added, old ones clarified or strengthened, and others deleted. If provisions can be negotiated and supported by the teachers which will state mechanisms for the enforcement of high performance, then community suspicion will be allayed and teachers will receive the recognition they claim they deserve. At present, few semi-professions have such an opportunity for advancing the social standing of their group.

NOTES

1. Thus, two of the major sociological theorists imply that teachers will never be admitted to full professional status (Wilensky, 1964: 137-158; Goode, 1969).

2. To be precise, the percent of male secondary teachers did rise from 44% to 57% between 1950 and 1960. However, in 1965, the percent of males had dropped to 54%. We do not consider these variations as important as some writers assume (Folger and Nam, 1967: 80; Silverman and Metz, 1970: 26).

3. The figures are from Furno and Doherty, 1970: 41-43.

4. The mean percent of total income from sources other than teaching salary was 12.5% for males in secondary schools and 3.8% for the female counterparts (National Education Association, 1963: 88).

5. The median number of years experience for elementary school teachers, most of whom are women, was 13.3 years in 1960-1961 and 10.0 years in 1965-1966. Thus, teacher experience, in general, is decreasing but the male level remains constant. As might be expected, median age of male teachers has remained relatively constant from 1930-1960, whereas for females it rose from twenty-nine in 1930 to forty-five in 1960 (Folger and Nam, 1967: 84). In 1965, the median age for secondary school males was thirty-two and for females, thirty-five. Elementary school teachers tend to be older than those in the secondary (Silverman and Metz, 1970: 26).

6. The labor reserve of teachers in 1960 was made up almost entirely of women. Eighty percent of all teachers between the ages of twenty-five to thirty-four were in the labor reserve, although this figure dropped to 30% for females age thirty-five to forty-four, and 12% for females age forty-five to fifty-four. In contrast, less than 2% of the male teachers up to age fifty-four were ever in the labor reserve, as a proportion of the number in the labor force (Folger and Nam, 1967: 104-106).

7. For examples of community conflict between lay boards and citizens aligned against the emerging power of professional teachers, see Coleman, 1957; Minar, 1966.

8. This discussion of communication problems follows the theoretical work of Blau and Scott, 1962: 130-134.

9. Data for these statements are available in National Education Association, 1963: 77.

10. Membership growth had been increasing in the 1950s for both organizations: between 1950 and 1960, the AFT grew by 43% and the NEA by 57%. However, competition to organize teachers and secure improved contracts took a sharp upswing after the AFT won representation rights over the NEA affiliate in New York City in 1961 (Wildman, 1971: 134).

11. We make no pleas for personal contact between teacher and pupil outside of the classroom. Our only concern is the hypocrisy level that teachers share with all professionals.

12. This is not the appropriate place for a thorough discussion of issues and collective negotiations in education. The few items selected are merely illustrative of attempts to gain and retain status as well as structure the school organization and work setting. The interested reader is referred to Moskow and Doherty, 1969; Wildman, 1971; Lieberman and Moskow, 1966.

13. Selden notes that "two-thirds, at least, of the collective bargaining contract clauses other than those conferring added salaries and fringe benefits are designed to stop management from doing something" (Selden, 1968).

14. It is interesting to note in this connection that Corwin reports "that, in practice, 'bureaucratization' has not meant more centralized control; but on the contrary, it has meant more autonomy of groups within the system. The immediate problem, then, is not how to preserve control but how to harness the potential of the autonomy" (Corwin, 1969: 247).

REFERENCES

BECKER, H. S. (1957) "Social class and teacher-pupil relationships," in B. E. Mercer and E. R. Carr (eds.) Education and the Social Order. New York: Rinehart & Co.

BIDWELL, C. E. (1965) "The school as a formal organization," pp. 972-1022 in J. G. March (ed.) Handbook of Organizations. Chicago: Rand McNally.

BLAU, P. M. and W. R. SCOTT (1962) Formal Organizations. San Francisco: Chandler.

BRIM, O. G., Jr. (1958) Sociology and the Field of Education. New York: Russell Sage Foundation.

BROOKOVER, W. B. and E. L. ERICKSON (1969) Society, Schools and Learning. Boston: Allyn & Bacon.

CICOUREL, A. V. and J. I. KITSUSE (1963) The Educational Decision Makers. Indianapolis: Bobbs-Merrill.

CLARK, B. R. (1964) "The sociology of education," pp. 734-769 in R.E.L. Faris (ed.) Handbook of Modern Sociology. Chicago: Rand McNally.

COLE, S. (1969a) "Teacher's strike: a study of the conversion of predisposition into action," Amer. J. of Sociology 74 (March): 506-520.

––– (1969b) The Unionization of Teachers: A Study of the UFT. New York: Praeger.

––– (1968) "The unionization of teachers: determinants of rank and file support." Sociology of Education 41 (Winter): 66-87.

COLEMAN, J. S. (1961) The Adolescent Society. New York: Free Press.

––– (1957) Community Conflict. New York: Free Press.

––– et al. (1966) Equality of Educational Opportunity. Washington, D.C.: U.S. Government Printing Office.

CORWIN, R. G. (1970) Militant Professionalism: A Study of Organizational Conflict in High Schools. New York: Appleton-Century-Crofts.

––– (1969a) "Patterns of organizational conflict." Administrative Sci. Q. 14 (December): 507-520.

––– (1969b) "The anatomy of militant professionalization," pp. 237-248 in P. W. Carlton and H. I. Goodwin (eds.) The Collective Dilemma: Negotiations in Education. Worthington, Ohio: Wadsworth.

––– (1965) A Sociology of Education. New York: Appleton-Century-Crofts.

FOLGER, J. K. and C. B. NAM (1967) Education of the American Population. Washington, D.C.: Bureau of the Census.

FURNO, O. F. and J. E. DOHERTY (1970) "Cost of education index 1969-1970." School Management 14 (January): 35-98.

GOODE, W. J. (1969) "The theoretical limits of professionalization," pp. 266-308 in A. Etzioni (ed.) The Semi-Professions and Their Organization. New York: Free Press.

GOSLIN, D. A. (1965) The School in Contemporary Society. Glenview, Ill.: Scott, Foresman.

GROSS, N. et al. (1958a) Explorations in Role Analysis: Studies of the School Superintendency Role. New York: John Wiley.

––– (1958b) Who Runs Our Schools? New York: John Wiley.

––– and J. A. FISHMAN (1967) "The management of educational establishments," pp. 304-358 in P. F. Lazarsfeld, W. H. Sewell and H. L. Wilensky (eds.) The Uses of Sociology. New York: Basic Books.

HALSEY, A. G., J. FLOUD and C. A. ANDERSON [eds.] (1961) Education, Economy, and Society. New York: Free Press.

JANOWITZ, M. (1969) Institution Building in Urban Education. Hartford, Conn.: Russell Sage Foundation.

KATZ, F. E. (1964) "The school as a complex social organization." Harvard Ed. Rev. 34 (Summer): 428-455.

LANE, W. R., R. G. CORWIN, and W. G. MONAHAN (1967) Foundations of Educational Administration: A Behavioral Analysis. New York: Macmillan.

LIEBERMAN, M. and M. H. MOSKOW (1966) Collective Negotiations for Teachers. Chicago: Rand McNally.

LIPSET, S. M., M. A. TROW, and J. S. COLEMAN (1956) Union Democracy. New York: Free Press.

LITWAK, E. and H. J. MEYER (1967) "The school and the family: linking organizations and external primary groups," pp. 522-543 in P. F. Lazarsfeld, W. H. Sewell and H. L. Wilensky (eds.) The Uses of Sociology. New York: Basic Books.

LORTIE, D. C. (1969) "The balance of control and autonomy in elementary school teaching," pp. 1-53 in A. Etzioni (ed.) The Semi-Professions and Their Organization. New York: Free Press.

MASON, W. S. (1961) The Beginning School Teacher: Status and Career Orientations. Washington, D.C.: U.S. Government Printing Office.

MAYER, M. (1969) The Teacher Strike: New York, 1968. New York: Harper & Row.

MINAR, D. W. (1966) "The community basis of conflict in school system politics." Amer. Soc. Rev. 31 (December): 822-835.

MOELLER, G. H. and W. W. CHARTERS (1966) "Relation of bureaucratization to sense of power among teachers," Administrative Sci. Q. 10 (March): 444-465.

MOSKOW, M. H. and R. E. DOHERTY (1969) "United States," pp. 295-332 in A. A. Blum (ed.) Teacher Unions and Associations: A Comparative Study. Urbana, Ill.: Univ. of Illinois Press.

National Education Association (1963) The American Public School Teacher 1960-1961. Washington, D.C.: National Education Association.

REISS, A. J., Jr. [ed.] (1965) Schools in a Changing Society. New York: Free Press.

ROSENTHAL, A. (1966) "The strength of teacher organizations." Sociology of Education 39 (Fall): 359-380.

ROSSI, P. H. (1966) "Boobytraps and pitfalls in the evaluation of social action programs." Proceedings of the American Statistical Association.

SELDEN, D. (1968) "Professionalism," pp. 66-70 in P. C. Sexton (ed.) Readings on the School in Society. Englewood Cliffs, N.J.: Prentice-Hall.

SILVERMAN, L. J. and S. METZ (1970) Selected Statistics on Educational Personnel. Washington, D.C.: Department of Health, Education and Welfare.

TROW, M. (1961) "The second transformation of American secondary education," International J. of Comparative Sociology 2 (Summer): 144-167.

WARREN, D. I.(1969) "The effects of power bases and peer groups on conformity in formal organizations." Administrative Sci. Q. 14 (December): 544-556.

--- (1968) "Power, visibility and conformity in formal organizations." Amer. Soc. Rev. 33 (December): 951-970.

--- (1966) "Social relations of peers in a formal organization setting." Administrative Sci. Q. 11 (December): 440-478.

WILDMAN, W. A. (1971) "Teachers and collective negotiation," pp. 126-164 in A. A. Blum et al. (eds.) White-Collar Workers. New York: Random House.

WILENSKY, H. L. (1964) "The professionalization of everyone?" Amer. J. of Sociology 70 (September): 137-158.

Chapter 12

MAKING SOCIAL WORK
ACCOUNTABLE

SHERYL K. RUZEK

Social work is a paradoxical profession beset by many dilemmas. While social workers see themselves as "helping professionals" or "enablers," neither their clients nor the public generally hold this view. Clients often regard social workers primarily as "gatekeepers" who control access to a variety of desired advantages. To adopt or give up a child, receive financial assistance, or secure release from a correctional institution, the client generally must see a social worker who will certify or approve requests. The social worker sees such gatekeeping as

Author's Note: *This paper developed out of a study of social change and social control in psychiatry, certified public accounting, and social work—principal investigator Arlene Kaplan Daniels—supported by NIH grant HD 02776-02. The interviews relevant to this study were conducted with 66 social workers in private practice, child welfare and probation services. Thanks are due to Morris J. Daniels for his help as co-investigator in the initial formulation of the larger study and his supervision of the data collection in social work. They are also due to his wife, Rochelle Kern Daniels, and to David Gauss who did the interviewing. I am especially indebted to Dorothy Miller, Director of Scientific Analysis Corporation, whose theoretical insights and empirical knowledge of social work enabled me to review the literature and analyze the data which had been collected. I should also like to thank Arlene Kaplan Daniels, Rachel Kahn-Hut, and Shirley Cartwright for invaluable editorial criticisms.*

secondary; he sees his responsibility as proferring advice, counseling, and helping the client to "clarify his problems." But the client is seldom interested in these additional services (Miller et al., 1969). The public is likely to view the social worker as a meddler, busybody, or "bleeding heart" dedicated to bankrupting the taxpayer. The therapeutic or enabling role is seldom recognized or appreciated. (Meyerson, 1959; Padula and Munro, 1959).

In addition to the image trouble created by this discrepancy between the social worker's, clients' and public's view of the service offered, the image of the profession is tarnished by its association with welfare. The public does not usually differentiate between the public assistance worker (a technician or clerk of sorts) and the "professional" worker with a master's degree in social welfare; both are identified as tenders of the welfare state. Thus the social worker seldom is accorded the professional status which he feels he deserves.

Social workers also face the dilemma of being professionals trapped in powerful bureaucracies controlled by lay boards and elected officials who seldom share the values, goals, or perspectives of the professional social worker. Their employee status has curtailed their autonomy and control over their work, and has limited their professional prerogatives. At the same time their bureaucratic location has insulated them from client pressures and has hindered the emergence of a system of professional accountability to protect the client from incompetent, unethical, or unscrupulous practitioners.

This issue of professional accountability is a growing concern in social work for several reasons. As social workers continue to professionalize, there is increasing dissatisfaction within the profession about traditional forms of bureaucratic control over practice. At the same time social workers are moving into new areas of practice where there are neither professional nor bureaucratic accountability structures. As client dissatisfaction and demand for a say in the action increases, social workers must face the problem of ensuring high standards of service. This will not be easy because of the cross pressures from the profession itself, employing organizations, "competing" professionals in related fields, and clients—all wishing to impose their standards of service upon the practitioner.

To appreciate the situation which social workers face and to assess the meaning of accountability for professional performance, we must first consider the origins and nature of the social work profession, for social workers have not come into their troubles overnight; their dilemmas have been inherent in their profession since social work began. We shall first consider the emergence of the predominant areas of practice—casework, group work, and community organization. Then we shall examine how the social worker's traditional and changing clientele and location of practice are related to his mixed mandate for advice and control over his clientele. Finally we shall consider how all of these factors have affected the accountability structure in the profession.

THE EMERGENCE OF SOCIAL SERVICES

Early social services were a voluntary response to a perceived need, and were generally provided outside of formal welfare organizations by private individuals or religious groups. As the problems of poverty, delinquency and social disorder increased in the process of nineteenth-century industrialization, various public and private groups arose to assist the poor and downtrodden. Private philanthropy and social workers emerged to serve the "worthy poor"; township employees and almshouse workers provided public assistance to the less acceptable or "disreputable" poor.

While social control had been implicit in individual charity, it became explicit as full-time paid social workers appeared with the founding of the Charity Organization Society (COS) in 1877. The organizers of the COS deplored "relief," and argued that it encouraged pauperism. They hired women as social workers to make investigations of the poor for the well-to-do contributors. On the basis of the social workers' reports, the "most worthy poor" were singled out. The wealthy volunteers then carried out the more prestigious tasks of determining what was needed in each case and soliciting contributions. A volunteer "visitor" dispensed the aid and offered herself as a moral model for the destitute (Lubove, 1965: 1-18; Pumphrey and Pumphrey, 1961: 168-191).

Actually, the rich did not step forward quite as quickly as had often been assumed to fulfill the roles of visitors. Because of the failure of the COS to attract volunteers, visiting as well as investigation fell into the hands of the paid agent (Coll, 1969: 44-45). But while social workers gained ascendency as purveyors of aid, they became handmaidens of the rich who had no intention of turning over decision-making or control of services to their hirelings. Social workers merely carried out their tasks of "identifying" the "worthy poor," then cutting off and excluding the "unworthy" as their superiors bid them do.

Although agencies such as the COS served the needs of many of the "worthy poor," many others required assistance. Public aid was provided by state and local employees in the form of "Indoor" (almshouse) and "Outdoor (community) Relief" prior to the Civil War (Coll, 1969: 17-35). In 1863 the states began developing welfare programs to coordinate and supervise existing programs. State welfare boards later developed standards for private agencies such as orphanages and homes for the aged, and supervised those which received public as well as private funds. There was considerable opposition from social workers whose close association with powerful lay contributors led them to share the ideology of the era of free enterprise, laissez-faire and private control (Kidneigh, 1965: 6).

The turn of the century was marked by rapid expansion, immigration, and industrialization, and these processes created social problems which caught the attention of the public. In the style of the era, the demand for social services resulted in a proliferation of fragmented and highly specialized programs. As community awareness became focused on particular social problems, community leaders created a program or agency to deal specifically with it. As a consequence, one family might find it necessary to go to three or four separate agencies to receive needed services (Kidneigh, 1965: 7).

The Social Security Act of 1935 substantially followed the pattern of social services in the private sector. No comprehensive program or agency was established to provide social services; instead various separate uncoordinated agencies were created. The Act also incorporated and institutionalized the view of the "worthy" and "unworthy" poor. While services such as old-age security pension programs, aid to widows and orphans, and unemployment insurance were disbursed by clerks in a rational bureaucratic value-free manner, other services came to be administered by social workers and defined as "welfare doles" (Kallen et al., 1968).

Modern social workers still provide many of the same functions as their predecessors—the genteel visitors and the almshouse workers. But today these functions are organized around the social work techniques of casework, group work, and community organization. Yet regardless of the techniques which they employ, social workers are forced to come to terms with their mixed advice-control mandate implicit in the history and development of their specialty.

Social workers have emphasized their advice and counseling function while at the same time accepting a controlling role in a variety of settings. While the worker's first ethical obligation is expected to be his client, the social worker is expected also to uphold the welfare of the community at all times. In upholding the general welfare, he has been expected to inform juvenile authorities, police, health authorities, and immigration officials of the existence of conditions which fall within their authority. In the process of investigating situations which require social services, he in essence has become an agent of public social control (Pumphrey and Pumphrey, 1961: 313-315; Scott, 1969: 110-112).

The situation has become critical as the recipients of "advice" are beginning openly to challenge the control which the advice givers exert in the extension of services (Haug and Sussman, 1969). Other clients deny any desire for advice (Miller et al., 1969). And within some social work circles and among academics, the covert control exerted through providing "advice" to unwilling recipients has been called into question. While it was once argued that social and legal control was in the "best interest of the clients," it has recently been suggested that this control was in reality in the best interests of only certain segments of society, including the professionals offering the service (Berube and Gittell, 1970).

With these overriding features of social work in mind, let us turn to an examination of the main types of practice, the emergence of patterns of service, and the development of a mandate for advice and/or control in each.

THE DEVELOPMENT OF CASEWORK

The casework technique itself is regarded as a problem-solving process intended to help people cope more effectively with the difficulties which beset them. Caseworkers primarily try to provide help in such a way that the client's own problem-solving capacities and resources are strengthened or enhanced. An essential part of the helping process is the establishment and maintenance of a good working relationship between the caseworker and the client. Descriptions of this relationship vary somewhat, but a typical description is offered by Perlman (1960: 536):

> [The relationship is] characterized by the caseworker's warmth, compassion, helpful intent, and objectivity, and on the client's part by trust and some readiness to carry his share of the work to be done. Within this relationship, acceptance and expectation combine to make for a working partnership which is focused toward changes in the person and/or interaction.

While this ideal-typical relationship is clearly patterned after the voluntary client-practitioner relationship in which the client is a willing participant, social workers do not generally enjoy this type of relationship with their clients. The client is most typically captive in such environs as prisons, reformatories, homes for unwed mothers, and public mental hospitals. Even in less obviously coercive situations, the client is not exactly a willing participant. In schools, public welfare programs, and family treatment centers, the client may come not only under pressure from family members, but also under pressures from public officials, or law enforcement agents. In these situations, the relationship is clearly not characterized by trust and mutual desire to alter behavior. Indeed, as Zimmerman has suggested, it would be more accurate to characterize some of these relationships as ones of mutual distrust (Zimmerman, 1966). Despite the clear discrepancies between the typical social worker-client relationship and the "ideal" therapeutic professional-client relationship after which casework is modeled, little attention has been given to describing or ameliorating the contradictions.

The casework emphasis on the nature of the client-practitioner relationship and on therapy raises other serious questions as well. What are the similarities or differences between this model of social work and psychotherapy? While social workers have often tended to sidestep the issue of what differentiates casework from other types of therapy, professionals in related fields have not been so willing to do this. Some professionals in psychiatry and psychology have felt that casework is not quite so distinctive, and that social workers have encroached on *their* territory. While some reject the idea of having social workers engaging in the treatment process at all, others generally are willing to accept them in a subordinate role (Singer, 1969; Strauss et al., 1964: 77-79, 146-153; Zander et al., 1966).

Although there is pressure to more clearly define the boundaries of practice, the problem is exacerbated by equally vague conceptions of the boundaries of psychiatry and psychology. Furthermore, social workers do not have a clear battleground on which to fight their rivals nor do they have a clear motivation to do so; for these more prestigious professionals have been accepted as their mentors.

THE DEVELOPMENT OF GROUP WORK

During the first two decades of the twentieth century, youth organizations, settlements, and churches initiated a variety of programs to help people collectively. While the general goal was the improvement of society, the focus was squarely on the individual (Pumphrey and Pumphrey, 1961: 361-370).

Group workers have practiced in agencies such as settlement houses, YMCAs, Boys' Clubs, denominational youth organizations, and 4-H clubs. Traditional practice in these settings, however, often is indistinguishable from nonprofessional volunteer services. As nonprofessionals have served ably as "group workers," social workers in this field have not always been afforded professional status despite their claims of possessing special knowledge and skills (Cogan, 1960; Levy, 1958). Given their style of practice, group workers have been less prone than caseworkers to adopt a strictly "therapeutic role." Instead they seem to hold a rather ambiguous role with few if any clear professional prerogatives (Roth and Eddy, 1967: 75-77).

Group workers have not only lacked a clear role; they have had an ambiguous mandate either to control or advise their clients. In traditional settings control has been extended only through personal influence of "setting a good example" of acceptable behavior. But as group workers are increasingly employed in correctional institutions, residential and day care centers for children, and in psychiatric and medical facilities, they no longer serve only as role-models for their clients. They are increasingly vested with the responsibility of making fateful evaluations or decisions (Cogan, 1966; Solomon, 1968).

COMMUNITY ORGANIZATION

As casework and group work became established as standard spheres of professional social work activity, concern developed in the field over the fragmentation of social services and the failure of social workers to serve the larger community. As an outgrowth of these concerns, attempts were made to form federated agencies (as the United Crusade Agencies) which social service organizations such as family service agencies, sectarian settlements, and youth organizations could join to plan and coordinate services and from which they could launch joint fund-raising campaigns (Pumphrey and Pumphrey, 1961: 371-373).

Prior to the 1940s, community organization primarily consisted of fund raising, administrative, and coordinative social welfare planning. But during the late 1930s distinct and different definitions of community organization began to emerge. In the past two decades these new tendencies have been firmly established. Some organizers have continued to participate in community groups in the traditional roles as coordinators, consultants, and advisors. But others have become directly involved in specific community affairs; block workers, rural workers, civil rights and neighborhood workers have all become actively involved with their clients. Today, reform, planning, and participation are all recognized spheres of activity in community organization (Chatterjee and Koleski, 1970; Murphy, 1960).

While community organization has traditionally been regarded as an "advice" activity, it has always involved a degree of social control. For as militant social workers point out, employing organizations have often expected practitioners to channel discontent into established channels of social action; they have revoked support of practitioners who sought to organize for radical social change. Social workers have recently begun to question the appropriateness of acting as controlling agents of established institutions and some have suggested that to serve their advisory (and "reform") function best, they must become advocates for their clients and eschew traditional organizational commitments (Brager, 1968; Funnye, 1970; Rein, 1970; Terrell, 1967; Thursz, 1966).

A CHANGING CLIENTELE AND SETTING

The clients of the caseworker, group worker, and community organizer traditionally have been the poor, downtrodden, or delinquent; they have been "welfare recipients," runaways, unwed mothers, and underprivileged ethnic minorities. In the past the public (and many clients as well) shared the social worker's belief that it was the individual (by choice or chance) who was to blame for personal misfortunes—not the society. Thus, social services were viewed only as stopgap measures to help the individual back into the "system" (Wilensky and Lebeaux, 1958: 138-140). Furthermore the client was expected to be grateful for the "help" and appreciative of the worker's attention.

But in recent years, clients have come to regard social welfare services as a right, not a privilege. They see as a right the chance to have adequate income, health care, education, and other necessities of life in an industrial society (Marshall, 1965). Simultaneously social welfare services are being expanded to serve middle-class clients, suburban schools, adoption agencies, family service agencies, and private clinics. Through the combination of these changes, social workers, along with other professionals, are being forced into awareness of the resistance of clients to control and coercion (Haug and Sussman, 1969; Paull, 1967). As the demand for client control over service becomes stronger, social workers must grapple with defining an appropriate role for themselves in their new situation.

But regardless of the clientele, social workers are almost always employees of social service agencies. The great majority work in public or private welfare agencies, public custodial institutions, or community service organizations which are generally administered by professional social workers, although controlled at the top by lay boards and public officials. Some social workers, however, are beginning to move into large organizations dominated by other professions where teachers, physicians, lawyers, and non-social work administrators are subordinates in the hierarchy. Other social workers, particularly those in community work, are practicing in collaboration with practitioners from other professions in loosely structured new organizations. A tiny minority have recently moved into private practice or "fee for service" casework in private agencies and clinics. While this resembles "free professional" practice somewhat, social workers typically work in close association with other social workers, psychiatrists, or psychologists.

AN ADVICE-CONTROL FUNCTION

The shift in clientele and organizational location for social work has been accompanied by an increasing awareness of the control aspects of social work practice and a growing emphasis on the advice function of social workers. In this profession, control and coercion can be overt or covert (Taylor, 1958). For example, in corrections, the social worker may activate the force of the state (through the court and police) to impose social expectations (e.g., reporting to the parole officer at regular intervals). Similarly the child welfare worker may use the force of the court and police to separate children from their parents. One social worker described the situation in this manner:

> As a child welfare worker . . . you do have the force of law behind you and so if you get into a situation where there is say child abuse, you have the power of the court and you can actually . . . remove the child from the home whether [the parents] want it or not. Coming into the situation you have enough ability at least initially to work with a family in a positive sense because [the family] is so apprehensive about the fact that [failure to cooperate] will entail a legal action.

In many agencies social workers are expected to channel client discontent into "acceptable" modes of social action and thereby "control" or "contain" more militant dissent (Rein, 1970). In educational institutions social workers may assess students' potentialities and file reports which affect their life chances (Cicourel and Kitsuse, 1963). In many casework situations the client is to be "helped" to conform to more "socially acceptable" behavior (Taylor, 1958). For example, social workers may convince unwed mothers to place their children for adoption so the children will have "normal" homes and the mother will not be stigmatized by rearing illegitimate children; practitioners may persuade children that it is in their interest to conform to school officials' behavioral expectations.

Social workers, as other professionals, prefer to see themselves as advisors or enablers rather than as controllers. For example caseworkers have shown a decided preference for engaging in casework with "voluntary" clients in clinics and private agencies. For these clients are not only more prestigious; they may be motivated to alter their behavior and tend to share the values and orientations of the social worker. In addition, the voluntary client tends to reinforce the social worker's definition of himself as an enabler or helper whose services are valued (Scott, 1969: 9-92; Miller and Ashmore, 1967). One practitioner in our study described this type of practice as follows:

> In private practice ... you don't have to go out and get them. They come to you. ... They're asking for help and they assume that you are a person who can help [them] with [their] particular problem or they wouldn't have come.

In community organizations where social workers are employed by indigenous community groups or autonomous social action groups (e.g., civil rights groups, labor unions), the practitioner can take a clearly advisory role. He may even function as an advocate of his constituents against other institutions (e.g., welfare departments, courts, employers). And as he generally shares the goals and values of his clients, he can secure their cooperation in carrying out his work. The support of his clients also reinforces his definition of himself as a reformer who provides a valuable service.

But not all social workers are able to assume strictly advisory roles. Private and clinical casework positions which attract voluntary clients are scarce, and few community groups can afford to employ professional social workers free from government funds—and control. Therefore most social workers practice within established agency frameworks and serve captive or quasi-voluntary clients. But despite the structural differences between clearly advisory practice and other types of practice, social workers attempt to define their function as advisory at least in part.

Thus corrections workers emphasize their "counseling" or therapeutic" role with delinquent youths and play down their controlling function (Brennan and Khinduka, 1970; Ohlin et al., 1965). For example one practitioner that we interviewed in a correctional institution viewed her role in the following manner:

> I don't see this position as corrections as much [as a] social work role . . . I accept my role as a probation officer for my girls. I'm the admission worker so I go to the various [juvenile] halls and interview the girls who may be coming here. I accept the fact that my decision [is important] in whether [or not] a girl comes to this locked setting which she sees as a punishment. I can accept that it is a form of protection for the community and for the girl. But I see [the correctional institution] as being very treatment-oriented and not just a closed placement.

The shifting emphasis in social work toward advisory roles has been viewed with consternation by many within the profession, for various reasons. Some view the emphasis on therapeutic services, psychiatric social work, and particularly private practice as a step in the wrong direction. While they do not decry the loss of the control function, they argue that social workers are straying from their traditional "reform" function and responsibility to the poor and underpriviledged (who can seldom afford "advisors"), (Briar, 1968; Cloward and Epstein, 1965; Varley, 1966).

As one practitioner in our study put it:

> [Agency work] is where social work is—with the neediest clients. This is where social work has its real identity. . . . [In private practice] you lose the sense of what social work is all about.

Some practitioners object to their colleagues who enter into other advisory roles, but for different reasons. Social workers sometimes criticize their colleagues in community organization as being irresponsible and unprofessional in adopting a "radical" or "advocate" role. They argue that social workers should adopt a more neutral, apolitical (and hence professional) stance (Epstein, 1968; Rothenberg, 1968). One of our respondents expressed this view as follows:

> I am concerned that we're becoming a bunch of social activists. I don't like it. . . . I can't see mobilization and marching around. I really don't.

That's the rebellious way to do it, where I believe in the evolution of . . . the individual himself. . . . We used to be content to treat the individual or the family, or perhaps a community. Now we are beginning to treat the United States government, and I don't see it. That's a political thing, not a social work thing.

Thus, while social workers may prefer to serve as advisors, in doing so they may be accused of failing to meet traditional responsibilities or meeting them so well that established practitioners and institutions feel threatened. In some ways the situation is similar to the circumstances which existed in the early days of social work. The wealthy ladies preferred the honorific and genteel task of carrying calves-foot jelly to the "worthy poor." The less honorific task of providing subsistence to the destitute "riffraff" was left to low-status hirelings. But social workers may serve both of these categories of clientele today. In consequence they are faced with mediating their conflicting desires for prestige and position within the status hierarchy by finding "better" clients and their fear of abdicating their professional obligation to provide a needed service, the cornerstone of professionalism.

Thus far we have noted the mixed mandate for advice and control which social workers have both received and helped develop. Another question, beyond that of the social worker's mandate, is that of his accountability for his actions, particularly those which are fateful for his client. Does his profession set certain standards and do its authorities sanction practitioners who are lax? If he is the agent of a third party (as are most social workers), are his primary responsibilities defined as client service, meeting bureaucratic regulations, or both? Let us now examine the different systems of control imposed on social workers to ensure that the client's welfare is protected.

THE POWER OF THE PROFESSION

Although social workers have attempted to emulate autonomous professionals, they are captive professionals. In the final analysis it has been the employing organization, not the social work profession, which has had the power to define goals, set limits of discretionary action, select and define "qualifications" for practitioners, and sanction those who go astray.

Partially ignoring this, social workers speak of "professional control," and maintenance of high standards. As evidence of professional control, social workers sometimes point to the fact that as members of the National Association of Social Workers (NASW) they adhere to a code of ethics. But there is nothing in the code which specifies what the social worker is expected to do in any concrete situation. Furthermore its actual effectiveness in regulating behavior is problematic and social workers themselves (like other professionals) do not always take this type of "professional control" too seriously (Daniels, 1973). The following comments regarding ethics and professional sanctioning power are illustrative of the little importance some of our respondents attached to this type of control:

> I think that ethical standards have been formulated, but [although] principles are formulated . . . [there is] a lack of implementation.

> Well, certainly we have a code of ethics with the NASW. But I don't think we really implement it that much . . . I have been very frustrated with the association by not really doing anything. Very token gestures and all this. Perhaps we do need more clear implementation of the ethics of the profession.

The NASW recognizes the ambiguity of the status and admits that criteria for determining whether an alleged violation is serious enough to warrant investigation are not clear (NASW, 1963: 167). Even where sanctions are imposed, they are rather ineffectual since most employment is based upon the possession of educational certificates which are not affected by standing in the association. Furthermore, NASW sanctions only effect member social workers and only about one-third of all employed social workers are NASW members (Toren, 1969: 147). Thus control by the professional association is indeed limited.

Although social workers have sought greater control over their profession through legal license to practice, they have not been successful. Social workers are not licensed or certified in any state except California, where use of the titles "registered social worker" and "licensed clinical social worker" are restricted to those who are state certified. In the interim while seeking licensure, the NASW has developed a voluntary certification scheme—membership in the Academy of Certified Social Workers (Kidneigh, 1965: 16-17).

Actually, since few social workers have practiced outside of bureaucratically controlled organizations until recently, there has been little impetus for the development of separate professional, as opposed to bureaucratic accountability structures. And so a prime concern is to consider the relationship of the social worker vis-á-vis his employer. Then we shall assess the power of the employer to hold the practitioner accountable for his professional activities.

THE POWER OF THE EMPLOYING ORGANIZATION

The social worker has traditionally been the middle-man between the powerful rich and the powerless poor. He has not been able to determine the services to be provided, nor has he provided the funds. And despite appearance of "shared authority" between professionals and board members, authorization and evaluation of services have ultimately rested with lay boards and public officials; the actual power of the social worker is therefore quite ambiguous.

Furthermore, the social worker's attempts to relieve starvation, eliminate truancy, rehabilitate criminals, or contain the least prestigious of the mentally ill are not viewed as heoric acts by the public or his employers because of the embedded notion that to some extent the recipients of his services are morally responsible for their condition. Thus rather than being a hero he may be regarded as a "do-gooder" or "meddler" who is interfering with the laws of retribution, or one who is destroying the "natural order." Because the social worker's task is not considered prestigious, he may share to some extent the stigma of his lowly clients.

In an effort to turn degradation by association into status by association, social work has traditionally placed great emphasis on the values upheld by the lay controllers. Thus, "professional" social workers are those who claim allegiance to the goals and values of the organizations which employ them. They demonstrate their allegiance by arguing that agency rules and procedures are in the best interest of both the clients and the public and that the social worker is filling all his obligations by enforcing agency regulations. There is no necessary conflict of interest caused by employee status. The social worker's alliance with establishment employers has been further buttressed by the ideology that the "mature worker" accepts the regulations and limitations of agency practice (Brager, 1968; Scott, 1969: 115-123).

The bureaucracies in which social workers are employed use the typical (or standard) organizational methods of supervision to provide accountability. Supervision, however, has been provided by "colleagues" turned administrators. This system of authority is a compromise which both recognizes and denies the estoeric nature of the professional activity. It denies the claim that the task is too esoteric, sacred, or private to be evaluated by anyone but the practitioner, while at the same time, it is an acknowledgment that the task is not so routine as to be judged by "just anyone." It should be emphasized, however, that supervisory colleagues are not just "colleagues." They tend to take on the views and policies of the employing organizations to a greater extent than do nonsupervisory professionals (Scott, 1969: 97-98). For as in any organization, it is those who adhere to agency views and enforce official regulations who are promoted. Conformity to official views is particularly important in social work, for there are few avenues for career advancement other than moving up in agencies. Thus social work administrators and supervisors judge and evaluate their "colleagues" on the basis of agency, rather than purely professional, goals (and these sets of goals may or may not be consonant).

Regardless of the service involved, individuals and agencies negotiate standards on which to base evaluations of whether or not professional and/or bureaucratic standards of service are maintained. As agencies in which social workers are employed vary in the extent to which organizational goals are consonant with professional goals of service, it is difficult to generalize on the degree of accountability structures may be expected to reinforce professional standards. However, bureaucratic and professional goals are often different, and accountability systems in these settings may focus primarily on assuring practitioner adherence to bureaucratic regulations.

The extent to which the social worker's activities can be evaluated and assessed on either basis is related to the degree of observability of the professional activity, the clarity of the goals, and the clarity of the techniques which are utilized to meet goals.

The degree of observability of an activity is dependent upon the way in which the activity is defined by the professional and the organization. Professional activities may be defined as (1) public, or open to all interested parties, (2) open only to the client and other professionals, or (3) private, and open only to the practitioner and the client. It should be emphasized that the relative openness of the activity is not determined by its inherent characteristics, but rather by the social definition—which is open to negotiation. For example, the professional one-to-one therapy session may be made "private" by forbidding direct observation and keeping only perfunctory notes; it may be made "public" by recording and transcribing (or even videotaping) the event and making the "reproduction" available to students in training, a child's parents, or teachers.

In settings where most practitioners are either fully trained or committed to social work as a profession, severe clashes may arise between practitioners and employers over the "appropriateness" of observability. For example, in adoptions and corrections, social workers may claim that in order to carry out their responsibilities to their clients effectively, confidentiality between social worker and client must be maintained. The agency, however, may weigh the value of confidentiality against the need to meet either legal or agency requirements, such as matching prospective parents and children on the basis of race or religion in adoptions, or in notifying police or other authorities of "illegal" activities in corrections.

Whereas agencies can enforce observability quite easily, it is more difficult to impose organizational goals or specify techniques. This difficulty is partly related to the vagueness of bureaucratic goals and techniques in social work; but it is also due to professionals' attempts to control these aspects of practice. Where professional definitions are weak or organizational definitions are exceedingly strong and reinforced by a public mandate, the agency may be able to impose its goals (as in public assistance). Where the agency's legitimacy to define goals is weaker and the profession claims ascendency, professionals and agency officials must negotiate and accomodate to each other (as in family service agencies). Where the agency and the professionals claim clear but disparate goals and mandates, supervision and regulation may remain problematic; each may attempt to control the situation in accord with its own definition of what is appropriate (as often happens in juvenile correctional agencies).

Generally, where professional definitions of goals and techniques have been accepted by the bureaucracy, there will be little control of work on a day-to-day basis. In family counseling, for example, bureaucracies support the social worker's right to private interaction with the client although routine case review and consultation may be required. Furthermore, professional goals of counseling are so vague (e.g., adjustment, acceptance) and the techniques are so difficult to evaluate (e.g., the "warmth" or "strength" of the "relationship"), that these activities are difficult to control bureaucratically. And as the agency is seldom pressured by any powerful segments of society to set alternative goals, the agency has little impetus to delineate relatively objective standards by which to judge performance. In these settings professionals have fairly wide latitude in their practice.

In some settings there may be agreement on the goals, but disagreement over the appropriateness of techniques. For example, when social workers engage in casework with wayward or delinquent children, they may share the agency goal of keeping children "out of trouble." But professionals and officials often disagree over the appropriateness of certain techniques for attaining the goal. The "relationship" which the professional develops with the child is very difficult to evaluate, yet bureaucratic officials attempt to set standards of tone and style. Workers resist by claiming that "relationships" are exceedingly personal and individual, and only they can judge what is appropriate in a given case. The social workers that we interviewed suggested that they sometimes clash with supervisors (and colleagues as well) over the appropriateness of "talking tough," being a "pal," being "too soft," and taking children home with them or on outings. In these situations it is difficult to assure adherence either to professionally or bureaucratically approved techniques of service. For although crude bureaucratic measures of social worker performance, such as number of runaways or parole violations, may be utilized, the worker may argue that his clients (who are already discredited) are at fault; it is not his poor performance, but the number of "hard core" delinquents in his caseload which accounts for the high rate of runaways or recidivists. As the agency is seldom able to demonstrate clearly what techniques *do* yield "success," agency officials and professionals may continuously battle at the parameters of acceptable practice.

A related problem is conflicting notions about professional prerogatives. The more "professionally" oriented workers sometimes argue that circumvention of rules based on "professional discretion" allows greater flexibility and increases the quality and quantity of services to the client (Blau and Scott, 1962: 60-74; Hanlon, 1967; Scott, 1969: 136 n. 13; Stein, 1961). But while rigid or "ritualistic" adherence to all bureaucratic formalities may in fact impair service the social workers that we interviewed recounted injuries which social workers caused their clients by circumventing agency regulations. For example, in public assistance if the worker fails to report the presence of a man in the home "acting as spouse," and allows the female client illegally to receive maximum financial assistance, the woman may later be tried for "welfare fraud" and sentenced to jail. Children placed for adoption by workers who disregard the natural parents' religious preference may be removed from the home when the "oversight" is discovered. And the social worker who checks on foster children via telephone instead of making home visits as required by the agency may suddenly discover blatant child abuse or serious behavior problems which should have been prevented. Thus while agency regulations may be unworkable or unreasonable, merely ignoring them does *not* insure client welfare.

ORGANIZATIONAL SANCTIONS

As we have shown, the employing organization may attempt to define the goals which are to be honored, and the techniques which are appropriate for reaching the goals. In addition, the agency may impose a degree of observability which facilitates determining whether or not practitioners have met organizational (and/or professional) standards. But when a practitioner goes astray, how is he brought back into line? Or if the worker fails to "reform," what sanctions can the agency impose?

In social work, initial violations generally are handled "therapeutically" at the supervisor-subordinate level. Advice, counsel, and "discussion" are expected to bring the worker into line (Scott, 1969: 102-103; 108-110; Toren, 1969: 169-177). If the social worker's performance does not improve, the supervisor may submit negative work evaluations which are reviewed by higher level administrators; the worker may then be transferred to another work group, demoted, or even fired. For major violations of professional ethics, agencies may charge the social worker with unethical conduct through the NASW if he is a member.

But while the employing organization may effectively insure adherence to some bureaucratic regulations, the client may still not be protected from biased, incompetent, or unscrupulous practitioners. For organizational accountability structures are primarily designed to protect the *agency* from the practitioner; they are designed to assure adherence to *agency* goals and policies. For example, in adoptions, the emphasis is on finding "suitable homes" for children; there is little interest in seeing that prospective parents are not denied a child because of the personal biases or prejudices of the social worker.

In social work, then, neither the professional association, the state, nor the employing agency effectively holds the social worker accountable for some of the fateful decisions which the practitioner makes for his clients. Given this situation, only the client is left to question the social worker's actions.

THE POWER OF THE CLIENT

The actual power of the client to hold the social worker accountable for his actions is seldom great enough to seriously alter the social worker's practice. The private client has the greatest direct control over what the practitioner may do to him, but he has little power to discredit or sanction him. He cannot rely on the professional association to sanction the errant member; for, as we have already shown, the NASW is unable to control incompetent or unethical practitioners. That clients have even pursued this means of adjudicating grievances is questionable. For example, one social worker, who is a member of a local NASW ethics committee, reported in interview that to his knowledge a complaint had never been made by a client or social worker against another social worker on either the national level or in his chapter. As formal channels for sanctioning practitioners are ineffective, the client's actual control over the practitioner is limited to "taking his business elsewhere." While this may prevent further harm to the individual, it does nothing to protect other clients from straying into the unscrupulous practitioner's hands.

But in most social work settings, the dissatisfied client cannot "go elsewhere." Even in private adoption agencies, where prospective parents are not captive clients, they may have few alternatives if dissatisfied; they may in fact be forced into the "black market." For in states where adoption agencies are state licensed, a "bad report" becomes part of the central file. If the rejected applicant seeks a child at another agency (either public or private), the damaging report follows him. The following case is illustrative of the "free client's" situation:

In an "adoptions workup" the social worker asserted that the prospective mother sat with her dress up and her legs apart, indicating either latent lesbian tendencies or immature sexuality; she was, therefore, unfit to adopt a child. Because the agency is state licensed, this report will be sent to any agency where she applied for a child.

The complaining client in a public agency is often ignored. For most clients complain to the worker's direct supervisor if they complain at all. And these supervisors tend to support their subordinates' actions on the grounds that the decisions were based on "professional evaluations" or that the clients "always have a lot of gripes." The client may then take his problems upward "through channels," but here again, officials may be more committed to "managing discontent" than sanctioning errant practitioners. In fact when clients complain to "higher-ups," routine procedures often exist for turning the matter back to the practitioner involved. Our respondents provided the following examples of how client complaints are handled:

> There have been complaints to my supervisor about something that I have done . . . . Frequently [clients] are paranoid, so . . . they complain . . . and we try to handle this in as non-hurtful a way as it is possible. What usually happens is they send a letter to the governor's office and the governor sends the letter to the chief probation officer and then it goes to the area director and then right back down to the supervisor and right back to you. Then you usually have to write a report and then it goes on back up and that's it.

> The client was unhappy about what I had put into [an adoption] report. It was a negative report, and [the client] was rejected. I was supported by the supervisor.

Where agencies such as welfare rights organizations do exist or there are well developed bureaus for adjudicating client grievances, the client may have a greater opportunity to seek redress (Tenbroek, 1956). His success, however, may depend upon the values and attitudes abroad in both his community and the larger society. For example, in one public welfare department, an informant reported that workers were very hostile towards their agency. When clients objected to service, many workers encouraged their clients to press for a State Welfare Board review; and they instructed their clients on how to make the formal complaint. At the time, the state political climate was sympathetic towards welfare recipients, and the Board often ruled in the client's favor. But in welfare departments where workers are not hostile to their agencies, the client may receive less assistance in making complaints. And when the political climate is less favorable to the welfare recipient, the Board may be less likely to rule in the client's favor.

Thus, the power of the client to hold the practitioner accountable for the fateful decisions that he makes is extremely limited. The client is restricted not only by the limits of his own persistence and determination to voice his dissatisfaction, but also by the structures which exist to allow him to process his complaints. Some may adjudicate their grievances through proper channels, but for others, there is no redress.

As we have shown, social workers are being forced to recognize their mixed mandate for advice and control. As awareness of the incompatibility of these mandates grows both within the profession and among client groups, social workers must grapple with the problems of defining and delineating appropriate types of services and developing standards to insure client welfare. While agency workers bridle against bureaucratic control, they have not come to terms with the core issue of accountability for their actions any more than have their colleagues in private practice. For simply throwing off traditional accountability systems will by no means assure high standards of service or protect clients from incompetent or unscrupulous practitioners.

But should social workers simply attempt to develop an accountability system resembling the accountability systems in the established professions such as law and medicine? We think not. For such systems are seldom effective from the client's perspective (Daniels, 1972; Freidson, 1970a, 1970b). In fact, they serve to insulate the professionals and protect them from their clients rather than to protect clients from professionals. And there is no reason to believe that such a system would be any more effective in social work.

Instead, we would suggest that any effective accountability system in social work would have to develop specific standards of professionally appropriate and inappropriate behavior so that precedents could be established and clients could expect a formal system of review. Such a system is not likely to develop easily or without conflict. For the social work profession, employing organizations, related professionals, and clients are all clamoring to impose their own standards with varying degrees of success and differential power. Nonetheless, new systems of accountability will have to be developed as social work moves into new areas and faces mounting pressures on all sides.

REFERENCES

BERUBE, M. R. and M. GITTELL (1970) "In whose interest is 'the public interest'?" Social Policy (May/June): 5-9.

BLAU, P. and R. SCOTT (1962) Formal Organizations: A Comparative Approach. San Francisco: Chandler.

BRAGER, G. (1968a) "Advocacy and political behavior." Social Work 13 (April): 5-15.

——— (1968b) "Comments on currents: our organization man syndrome." Social Work 13 (October): 101.

BRENNAN, W. C. and S. K. KHINDUKA (1970) "Role discrepancies and professional socialization: the case of the juvenile probation officer." Social Work 15 (April): 87-94.

BRIAR, S. (1968) "The casework predicament." Social Work 13 (January): 5-11.

CHATTERJEE, P. and R. KOLESKI (1970) "The concepts of community and community organization: a review." Social Work 15 (July): 82-92.

CICOUREL, A. V. and J. I. KITSUSE (1963) The Educational Decision-Makers. Indianapolis: Bobbs-Merrill.

COGAN, J. L. (1960) "Social group work," pp. 540-549 in Social Work Yearbook. R. Kurtz (ed.) 1960: New York: National Association of Social Workers.

COLL, B. D. (1969) Perspectives in Public Welfare in United States. Department of Health, Education and Welfare, Social and Rehabilitation Service. Washington, D.C.: U.S. Government Printing Office.

CLOWARD, R. A. and I. EPSTEIN (1965) "Private social welfare's disengagement from the poor: the case of family adjustment agencies," pp. 623-664 in M. N. Zald (ed.) Social Welfare Institutions. New York: John Wiley.

DANIELS, A. K. (1973) "How free should professions be?" in this volume.

EPSTEIN, I. (1968) "Social workers and social action: attitudes towards social action strategies." Social Work 13 (April): 101-108.

FREIDSON, E. (1970a) Profession of Medicine. New York: Dodd, Mead.

——— (1970b) Professional Dominance. New York: Atherton Press.

FUNNYE, C. (1970) "The militant black social worker and the urban hustle." Social Work 15 (April): 5-12.

HANLON, A. C. (1967) "Counteracting problems of bureaucracy in public welfare." Social Work 12 (July): 88-94.

HAUG, M. and M. SUSSMAN (1969) "Professional autonomy and the revolt of the client." Social Problems 17 (Fall): 153-161.

HUGHES, E. C. (1958) Men and Their Work. New York: Free Press.

KALLEN, D. J., D. MILLER and A. DANIELS (1968) "Sociology, social work, and social problems." American Sociologist 3 (August): 235-240.

KIDNEIGH, J. C. (1965) "History of American social work," pp. 3-19 in H. Lurie (ed.) Encyclopedia of Social Work 1965. New York: National Association of Social Workers.

LEVENSTEIN, S. (1965) "Private practice of social work," pp. 566-569 in H. L. Lurie (ed.) Encyclopedia of Social Work. New York: National Association of Social Workers.

LEVY, C. S. (1958) "Is social group work practice standing still?" Social Work (January): 50-55.

LUBOVE, R. (1965) The Professional Altruist—The Emergence of Social Work as a Career 1880-1930. Cambridge: Harvard University Press.

MARSHALL, T. H. (1965) Class, Citizenship, and Social Development. Garden City: Doubleday.

MEYERSON, E. T. (1959) "The social work image or self-image?" Social Work 4 (July): 67-71.

MILLER, D., W. T. VAUGHAN, and D. E. MILLER (1969) "Effectiveness of social services to AFDC recipients: Appendix A in California Welfare: a legislative program for reform." Sacramento: Assembly Office of Research and Assembly Committee on Social Welfare.

MILLER, D. H. and D. L. ASHMORE (1967) "The ethology of social work." Social Work 12 (April): 60-68.

MILLER, H. (1968) "Value dilemmas in social casework." Social Work 13 (January): 27-33.

MURPHY, C. G. (1960) "Community organization for social welfare," pp. 186-191 in R. Kurtz (ed.) Social Work Yearbook. 1960. New York: National Association of Social Workers.

National Association of Social Workers (1963) NASW Personnel Standards and Adjudication Procedures. New York: NASW.

OHLIN, L. E., H. PIVEN, and D. M. PAPPENFORT (1956) "Major dilemmas of the social worker in probation and parole," pp. 523-538 in M. N. Zald (ed.) Social Welfare Institutions. New York: John Wiley.

PADULA, H. and M. MUNRO (1959) "Thoughts on the nature of the social work profession." Social Work 4 (October): 98-104.

PAULL, J. E. (1967) "Recipients aroused: the new welfare rights movement." Social Work 12 (April): 101-106.

PERLMAN, H. H. (1960) "Social casework," pp. 535-540 in R. Kurtz (ed.) New York: National Association of Social Workers.

PUMPHREY, R. E. and M. W. PUMPHREY [eds.] (1961) The Heritage of American Social Work. New York: Columbia University Press.

REIN, M. (1970) "Social work in search of a radical profession." Social Work 15 (April): 13-28.

ROTH, J. A. and E. M. EDDY (1967) Rehabilitation for The Unwanted. New York: Atherton Press.

ROTHENBERG, E. (1968) "Points and viewpoints: professional purity and manipulation." Social Work 13 (July): 3-5.

SCOTT, W. R. (1969) "Professional employees in a bureaucratic structure: social work," pp. 82-140 in A. Etzioni (ed.) The Semi-Professions and Their Organization. New York: Free Press.

SINGER, P. R. (1969) "A psychologist takes issues." Social Work 14 (January): 143-144.

SOLOMON, B. B. (1968) "Social groupwork in the adult outpatient clinic." Social Work 13 (October): 56-61.

STEIN, H. (1961) "Administrative implications of bureaucratic theory." Social Work 6 (July): 14-21.

STRAUSS, A., L. SCHATZMAN, R. BUCHER, D. EHRLICH, and M. SABSHIN (1964) Psychiatric Ideologies and Institutions. New York: Free Press.

TAYLOR, R. K. (1958) "The social control function in casework." Social Casework 39 (January): 17-21.

TENBROECK, J. (1956) "Operations partially subject to the APA: public welfare administration." California Law Rev. 44 (May): 242-261.

TERRELL, P. (1967) "The social worker as radical: roles of advocacy." New Perspectives: Berkeley J. of Social Welfare 1 (September): 83-88.

THURSZ, D. (1966) "Social action as a professional responsibility." Social Work 11 (July): 12-21.

TOREN, N. (1969) "Semi-professionalism and social work: a theoretical perspective," pp. 141-195 in A. Etzioni (ed.) The Semi-Professions and Their Organization. New York: Free Press.

VARLEY, B. K. (1966) "Are social workers dedicated to service?" Social Work 11 (April): 84-91.

WILENSKY, H. L. and C. N. LEBEAUX (1958) Industrial Society and Social Welfare. New York: Free Press.

ZANDER, A., A. COHEN, and E. STOTLAND (1966) "Psychiatry, clinical psychology, social work," pp. 237-243 in H. M. Vollmer and D. L. Mills (eds.) Professionalization. Englewood Cliffs: Prentice-Hall.

ZIMMERMAN, D. H. (1966) Paperwork and Peoplework: A Study of a Public Assistance Agency. Ph.D. dissertation, University of California, Los Angeles.

Chapter 13

LAWYERS VERSUS INDIGENTS
Conflict of Interest in Professional-Client
Relations in the Legal Profession

CAROLYN F. ETHERIDGE

The legal profession conforms closely to the traditional model of professions in sociology. It is a long-established profession which performs a client-centered service, based on the ideology of equal justice and the due process of law. That service involves the application of the vast body of law to particular cases. Those areas of the profession that function within the court system operate under the rhetoric of the adversary system—the ideal of hearing both sides of a question strongly argued before an impartial judge.

Characteristically, the profession controls recruitment and training, operates through referral systems and informal sponsorships, with an internal sanctioning system governed by the professional association and its subsidiaries. The American Bar Association is one of the strongest professional associations, exercising considerable influence over its members through affiliated state and city associations.

Law as an occupation confers high prestige, typically falling in the first bracket of any occupational stratification scale, and it tends to recruit primarily from its own class—from the sons of professionals, and a few daughters. There is a highly systematic code of ethics defining the client-counsel relationship and the duties of the lawyer in the service of his clients. This includes a firm commitment to the idea of a single lawyer serving a single client, placing all his or her skills at the latter's disposal. The financial reward for this service is not supposed to be the main motivator.

But in law, as in other professions, there is a peculiar circularity in the conception of client service. Professionals, and the public, tend to assume that practice is governed by the "best interests of the client." The idea of service legitimates the exercise of professional discretion. It is the automatic explanation given in response to any questions concerning existing practices, or proposed changes. The logic of the argument forms an unbreakable circle which states that professionals make decisions about practice because of their expertise; the power that this gives will not be abused because it is always exercised in the client's best interest; the interest of the client, however, can only be judged by the professional. Obviously such an argument leaves much room for discretionary interpretations of the client's interests.

In this paper I shall examine one specific change in the practice of the legal profession—the method of defending indigents in the criminal law courts—and show that while client service is indeed assumed to be the guiding basis for professional decisions in this area, the actual content of professional argument centers on issues which protect the lawyer's autonomy and privilege by focusing on the maintenance of "professionalism."

LEGAL SERVICE AND THE INDIGENT CLIENT

As a practice, indigent defense creates a potential conflict of interest for the professional. While lawyers, like everyone else, are concerned with making a living, the official ideology clearly implies that inability to pay should make no difference to treatment, and that money is an unprofessional criterion for defining service. With indigent defense, however, the client is by definition poor, and financial reimbursement becomes a significant question. Further, these clients are involved in the criminal courts. Partly perhaps because of its "unprofessional money-grubbing" features, criminal law practice has low status within the profession (Carlin, 1966). Thus these clients neither pay financially for services rendered nor does serving them confer prestige. In the absence of such rewards, how does the profession approach "client service" in this area?

There is no professional dispute over the principle that all people are entitled to defense against charges in the courts, and further, that they require defense by a lawyer. Clearly the complexities of the law and the court system produce a need for specialized counsel during trial if a fair defense for anyone is to be given. However, the application of this principle to indigent defense has not been automatic. It recently became a source of considerable dispute within the profession—a dispute which does not primarily appear to be concerned with the clients. As will be shown, the legal profession has concerned itself in the past with indigents. However, the recent extension of concern did not come from those practitioners directly involved, nor from the internal power centers of state and local bar associations concerned with improving service. It was as a result of U.S. Supreme Court rulings that the profession was forced to review its services and to confront the issue of providing legal defense for increasing numbers of indigent clients.

THE UNITED STATES SUPREME COURT: DEFENSE–WHO NEEDS IT?

The debate over defense of indigents accused of crimes has intensified in the last decade, due to the landmark U.S. Supreme Court decision in 1963. In Gideon versus Wainwright (372 U.S. 335; Sup. Ct. 792) the Court ruled that all felons must be provided with the option of defense counsel, at public expense if they could not afford a lawyer. The rulings of the Court on this issue involve the application of the Bill of Rights of the U.S. Constitution to court practice—federal and state. The history of the rulings reflects the movement from decentralized states' independence to the expanding powers of federal government, and contain violent debate over the question of states' rights to self-government.

The first eight amendments to the Constitution contain of course the guarantees of individual liberty: freedom of speech, press, religion and assembly; protection for the privacy of the home; assurance against double jeopardy and compulsory self-incrimination; the right to counsel and to trial by jury; freedom from cruel and unusual punishments. In 1833 in Barrow v. Baltimore (7 Peters, 243) Chief Justice Marshall wrote into law the specific decision that these rights did *not* apply in state courts. This clarification was lost in 1868 through the Fourteenth Amendment. Section 1 provides that:

> No State shall make or enforce any law which shall abridge the privileges or immunities of citizens of the United States; nor shall any State deprive any person of life, liberty or property without due process of law; nor deny to any person within its jurisdiction the equal protection of laws.

Ever since, the argument has raged over whether this means the total incorporation of the provisions of the first eight amendments into the state court system. Indigent defense is just one element in this controversy.

The 1960s saw several landmark decisions extending guarantees to state courts. Thus in 1966, Miranda v. Arizona (384 U.S. 456, 86 Sup. Ct. 1602) ruled to protect the individual against physical coercion and extorted confessions; since 1956, Griffin v. Illinois (351 U.S. 12), the state must provide a free trial transcript for indigents to facilitate appeals; in 1961 Mapp v. Ohio (367 U.S. 643) ruled the Fourth Amendment applicable to state courts—no illegally seized evidence could be admitted at state trials. (The argument over what constitutes illegal evidence—search and seizure, wiretapping and so forth—continues to rage, of course.) The trend was clear: a move towards implementing national guarantees of due process, and uniform court procedures at all levels of the system.

On what basis did the Supreme Court expand the right-to-counsel to all felons, with every expectation in the profession that it will shortly include misdemeanants too? Obviously in a basic sense this is a question of client service. But, as will be shown, the expansion of the demand for counsel is caused by an ever-widening definition of the incapacity of laymen to deal with the courts. The justification for legal defense by a lawyer, rather than simply the right to argue one's case before the bar, is based in the emphasis on special expertise. Thus the expanding demand is accomplished through increasing reinforcement of the idea that professionals alone are capable of performing professional tasks. As noted, this is also the basis of professional autonomy and power. Thus the Supreme Court in no way challenges the basic power of the legal profession; they support it. But this series of decisions forced a reevaluation of the use of that power in one specific area of practice.

The first major ruling on this question, Powell v. Alabama in 1932 (287 U.S. 45) places a heavy emphasis on esoteric knowledge, expertise and professional competence:

The right to be heard would be, in many cases, of little avail if it did not comprehend the right to be heard by counsel. *Even the intelligent and educated layman has small and sometimes no skill in the science of law. He lacks both the skill and knowledge adequately to prepare his defense even though he have a perfect one. He requires the guiding hand of counsel at every step in the proceedings* against him. Without it, though he be not guilty, he faces the danger of conviction because he does not know how to establish his innocence. *If that be true of men of intelligence, how much more true it is of the ignorant and illiterate, or those of feeble intellect* [287 U.S. 45, 68-69, italics added].

However, although for the first time the Supreme Court held that the Constitution entitles the accused to a defense lawyer, it carefully limited the holding of the case to specific circumstances

in a capital case, where the defendant is incapable adequately of making his own defense because of ignorance, feeblemindedness, illiteracy or the like [287 U.S. 45, 71].

This introduces the second dimension—that specific characteristics of the client should condition the application of the rulings: the "exceptional circumstances" approach.

In Johnson v. Zerbst, 1938 (304 U.S. 458) this changed at the federal level, stressing that

> The *average* defendant does not have the professional legal skill to protect himself when brought before a tribunal with power to take his life or liberty [304 U.S. 458, 462-463; italics added].

Counsel were to be provided in all federal cases. At the state level the special circumstances approach continued and operated with increasing confusion after Betts v. Brady in 1942 (316 U.S. 455) when the application of the Sixth Amendment to state courts was denied, since Betts had "ordinary intelligence" and was familiar with court procedure, having been tried before for earlier crimes. In 1948 Uveges v. Pennsylvania added to the confusion by detailing

> the gravity of the crime and other factors such as the age and education of the defendant, the conduct of the court or prosecuting officials and the complicated nature of the offense charged and the possible defenses thereto [335 U.S. 457, 441]

as other possible considerations.

These were hardly clear guidelines and in the decade from 1950 to 1960 increasing hostility mounted towards attempting to apply the "formula." Finally the U.S. Supreme Court agreed to hear what was initially Gideon v. Cochran, which became the famous Gideon v. Wainwright decision of 1963 (372, U.S. 335). The exceptional circumstances approach was the focus of one major argument:

> Here is *a trial in which the defendant was skillful and the judge made every effort to protect his rights.* Yet *even here close examination* of the law and the facts *reveals that the defendant was repeatedly hurt by lack of counsel.* If such prejudice occurred in this trial, it would seem that *there is no trial in which counsel is unnecessary.* Thus the rule of Betts is based upon a false assumption [372 U.S. 335; italics added].

An Amicus Curiae brief was filed for the defense with the support of twenty-two states. The decision handed down overruled Betts, making defense counsel mandatory in all felony cases at the state level. Justice Black in reading the majority opinion concluded:

> reason and reflection require us to recognise that in our adversary system of criminal justice any person hailed into court, who is too poor to hire a lawyer, cannot be assured a fair trial unless counsel is provided for him. This seems to us to be an obvious truth [572 U.S. 335, 344].

Thus, based on the claim of esoteric expertise found only among lawyers, the Supreme Court rulings set the limiting conditions for provision of counsel. While supporting professional control, they created a demand for the expansion of services. Prior to the ruling most states had been providing counsel for capital cases; its immediate impact however was to make the adequate provision of counsel mandatory for all felonies in all courts. Thus in this arena of client service, the pressure initially came from outside, not from the immediate practitioners or the central policy makers of the traditional bar. And every extension of due process, moving from the notion of limited characteristics to the premise that no layman can adequately defend himself, underscored and extended the basic theme of professional expertise, which in turn validates professional autonomy and control.

Once the pressure was exerted however, was the "best interest of the client" the main factor in the decision over how to provide service? I suggest that client service is a taken-for-granted credo and that no matter what method of providing service is discussed the real dispute is over control.

THE LEGAL PROFESSION: DEFENSE—WHO GIVES IT?

There are essentially two methods used in the United States to provide counsel for indigents: the assigned counsel system and the public defender system. The assigned counsel system is the traditional and still dominant form. Once financial need is established, the court judge appoints a lawyer to serve. Appointment is made on a case-by-case basis, from a list of attorneys in private practice. In principle the assigned counsel is "expected to represent his client with the same professional standards as if he had been retained" (Silverstein 1965: 15).

The system is thus formally very simply operated. The way it actually functions varies between states and counties along several dimensions.

The most common practice in the selection and compensation of lawyers is for the presiding judge to have a list of local attorneys who will serve. The composition of this list varies greatly. In some jurisdictions there is heavy emphasis on younger inexperienced members of the bar; in others assigned cases may form a strong income base for a small number of lawyers. At all events, assigned counsel for felony cases vary widely in ability and experience and the criteria for assignment depends on a variety of factors: the county, the judge involved and the seriousness of the crime. (It is frequently noted that serious homicide cases invariably attract good counsel since these crimes can involve considerable exposure and prestige.) Payment for these services also varies tremendously—ranging from no payment, through standard reimbursement and moderate compensation, to full reimbursement of all costs plus compensation. This affects the preparation of cases, hiring investigators, bringing in witnesses, and so forth. However, under the court-assigned procedure the only major difference from normal court operations is the way in which the client obtains his attorney—through judge's allocation instead of private retainer.

This procedure changes when defender offices are introduced— whether funded privately or publicly. The basic concept of defender systems involves

> salaried lawyers [who] devote all or a substantial part of their time to the specialized practice of representing indigent defendants [Silverstein, 1965: 39].

Public defender offices are funded from public sources initiated by state statute or local ordinance. The selection of attorneys can be by judicial appointment, popular election or by some agency specifically established for the purpose. Private defender offices are funded from private gifts and individual contributions and may be run privately by the local bar association or some nonprofit-making legal aid defender association. The selection of counsel is then usually made by the bar or governing board of the corporation. A private-public system combines the two as a private organization using combined funding sources.

In this type of defense system, variations are found in salary scales, investigation costs provided, tests for indigency, major kinds of cases handled and efficiency of records. However, in general conception the main difference between the two systems is the change in the client-counsel relationship. Under the assigned counsel system the traditional formal relationship of an individual lawyer providing services for a specific client is in principle retained. The institution of a defender office replaces this with personnel who are paid a regular salary for their work (not case-by-case reimbursement), which is to defend all clients in the court system who are charged with felonies and happen to be indigent. They are salaried officials of the system, not individual attorneys to individual clients.

The debate over defense systems escalated in the profession in the early 1960s and after Gideon, when it was essential that some effective system for meeting the increased demand for counsel should be established. The debate was conducted in the profession's journals, bar association reports, judicial seminars and so forth during this period. In the law reviews, several major symposia connected with this issue appeared. The Minnesota Law Review published a symposium in 1961 on the right to counsel (45 Minnesota Law Review 693-896). In 1964 the Missouri Law Review produced a symposium on indigent defendants (29 Missouri Law Review 328-353) and in the same year the Texas Law Review produced a special issue on criminal law (Texas Law Review 43: 271-399). These reviews included the viewpoints of public defenders, superior court judges, court-appointed counsel and public prosecutors.

The Silverstein report, published in 1965, was initiated by the American Bar Association itself, funded by the National Legal Aid and Defender Association (NLADA), and remains the definitive study within the profession. (Earlier classic works include Beaney, 1955, and the Association of the Bar of the City of New York study, 1959.) Silverstein (1965) includes a general survey of statutory requirements and the existing offices in all states in 1963. An extensive field investigation of a sample of 297 counties in fifty states, together with intensive studies of court dockets in 194 counties were conducted, from which comparative information on the details of different existing systems was obtained.

In 1963, of the 297 counties studied, 247 were using some kind of assigned counsel system and 37 had public defender systems. (The remainder had public-private systems or some combination of the various alternatives.) Thus, as noted, the assigned counsel system was and still is the most common traditional method of providing counsel to indigents.

In examining all of these sources several central questions are raised. Two of them produce complete unanimity: no one in the profession questions the premise of internal control. Not even the most public spirited defender suggests that control of the office should come from outside the profession itself. Neither is there any argument over the need for financial reimbursement. As the argument over systems was conducted, reform of the assigned counsel system always included the creation of adequate compensation for the individual attorney; and an adequate salary for the defenders was always part of any plan for a defender office. In the first case this means bringing reimbursement into line with average retainer compensation; in the latter, a salary commensurate with the public prosecutor. On both of these issues the argument is made that the *client* must have an adequately paid attorney; and that losing professional control of the system is against the interests of the client.

What then was the focus of the controversy? At center is the traditional establishment bar making an ideological argument for the individual client-counsel relationship. This legitimates the assigned counsel system, which also provides an income for certain members of the profession, and more particularly is under the control of the bar itself. In contrast the public defender office can create an independent, salaried office, potentially free from ongoing local bar supervision. Part of the central argument is phrased in terms of whether the abdication of the assigned counsel system would involve a decrease in professionalism and weaken professional autonomy. The two positions taken on this are exemplified by the following statements. On the one hand,

> The public defender is just as much a product of the twentieth century as the doctor who works for a public hospital or clinic. Each may have lost something of his traditional autonomy but neither needs to compromise his standards of professional competence [Silverstein, 1965: 5].

On the other hand, the defender office

> departs from our adversary system. It forces the accused to accept a lawyer appointed and paid by his opponent. It involves invasion of the lawyer's duty to represent the poor [Minnesota Law Review, 45: 43].

Both sides recognize that

> the public defender concept is an institutional and ideological break from the traditional notion of the private lawyer serving his individual clients [Silverstein, 1965: 52].

The Silverstein report, written essentially by and for the profession itself, in fact summarizes most of the arguments about the two alternatives, while indicating a final preference for public defender systems.

Thus the advantages of the assigned counsel system, apart from preserving the traditional role of the lawyer, are that it

> affords wide participation of the bar . . . provides valuable experience for young attorneys. . . is simple to operate . . . costs little or nothing to operate . . . [and on the other hand] . . . In counties where assigned counsel are compensated, the system provides income to many members of the bar.

The disadvantages are that

> assigned attorneys are often young . . . or others who lack experience in criminal law . . . they are more likely to advise their clients to plead

guilty (or on the other hand) in order to gain trial experience . . . are more likely to advise their clients to plead not guilty. [Further] . . . whatever may be said about the effectiveness of an assigned counsel system in rural and medium-sized counties, it is not suitable for counties of 400,000 or more people. Assigned counsel are not reimbursed for out-of-pocket expenses for investigation and preparation . . . the methods of selecting attorneys . . . are not fair . . . [they] are not appointed early enough [and] . . . are paid little or nothing [Silverstein 1965: 18-32].

The public defender system by contrast

provides experienced competent counsel. . . assures continuity and consistency . . . is a better screen for eligibility . . . is more economical to operate in metropolitan areas . . . eliminates the likelihood of the undesirable practice . . . whereby the attorney attempts to get a fee from the defendant or his family. . . [and lastly] the defender and prosecution have a continuing relationship, thus assuring better cooperation between them [Silverstein 1965: 45-48].

The disadvantages focus on the issue of political independence from any government funding source and of course the client-counsel relationship.

These then are the arguments exchanged among professionals themselves. And examining them, the only direct ideological statement is in fact the client-counsel relationship doctrine which attempts to defend the traditional system against invasion by external control. With a few exceptions, the rest of the arguments are much more concerned with commentary on actual or proposed practice. And these, on the whole, tend to deal with consequences for lawyers and attorneys—rather than clients.

It might be possible from the literature to develop a simple conspiracy notion that the establishment bar, to protect its traditional interests, is fighting public-spirited lawyers who want to see an efficient office, independent of bar control, set up. Certainly the defender office supporters stress the practicality and efficiency of the system—especially for large metropolitan areas. This, together with attacks on existing practices, forms the heart of the formal attack on the assigned counsel system.

I suggest however that something else was occurring. There is little systematic work on the internal operations and practices of the legal profession as such (exceptions include Blumberg, 1967; Carlin, 1962, 1966; Carlin and Howard, 1965; Freund, 1963; Ladinsky, 1963; Lortie, 1959; Smigel, 1960, 1964; Thielens, 1957. For a more journalistic account see Mayer, 1966). Despite the absence of detailed studies, during recent years some basic changes do seem to have been taking place. Specifically, the emergence of civil liberties as a major issue of concern for some lawyers (represented by the legal counsel affiliated with the American Civil Liberties Union and by the creation of Committees on Civil Liberties in many local bar associations), the development of conspiracy laws and trials (from Spock to Chicago, New Haven, New York and onwards), and the emergence of a new style of legal aid lawyer who works out of "store-front" offices for "radical causes"—collective and individual—all of this suggests that there is a new collective orientation in a subsegment of the profession that is unlikely to accept the traditional rules of conduct of the establishment bar. It suggests that perhaps, to some segments of the profession, freedom from bar control is at least as important as efficient service, and perhaps seen as a prerequisite of it.

This suggestion was certainly born out in an intensive case study of the debate over a public defender office in one large metropolitan area (Etheridge, 1970). All of the rational efficiency arguments were made, but beyond that a fight over control was indeed going on. Specifically, the local bar was unwilling to loose any control over practice and it became clear that main defender office supporters included local "rebels" who had already been in trouble with the bar for trying to take on "public issue" cases (such as preventing a freeway from being run through the central downtown ghetto area), and who frankly viewed the bar as a hostile reactionary force which would never show real concern for poor people in the courts. In this case, during the process of negotiation, it became clear that the actual focus for violent hostility had little to do with the nature of the service to be provided and a great deal to do with intra-professional battles over jurisdiction at the local level. Let me stress again however, that neither side ever suggested that the system could be run at any level—administrative or legal—without lawyers, although laymen might help at the official policy board level.

Returning to the general debate, in the entire process it seems that the focus on "client service" gets lost in general issues of practicalities and professional problems. It is always assumed that clients will finally be best served by professional decisions. Taking that for granted, the profession conducts its debates. Whatever the nature or main focus of internal debate though, if it is true that ultimately clients get served, is the emphasis on professional concerns important? Obviously it becomes important as it affects service. And thus becomes important in any evaluation of the relationship between professional autonomy and client service. Is there then any evidence that one method of indigent defense rather than the other represents superior client service?

THE CLIENTS: DEFENSE—WHO GETS IT AND WHAT IS IT?

From the point of view of the profession the argument concerns service to some collectivity that has one common feature: poverty. All that is stressed is that the clients are poor, and by virtue of that fact alone should not be denied counsel.

Does it make any difference to these clients whether they are serviced by retained, assigned or public defender counsel? The Silverstein (1965) data, on close examination, produce two major findings. First, the only area in which data locate clear difference is in cost. Whether measured by public expenditure or cost per capita, in high density population areas the defender office is cheaper, the break-off point being 400,000 people.

The second major finding is that on all substantive questions, there is little difference between assigned counsel or public defender systems in practical consequences for the accused. The real difference emerges between the experience of indigent defendants with any kind of provided counsel, and the experience of nonindigents. In percent of defendants pleading guilty, in defender office counties the mean for retained counsel is 59.0

TABLE 1

COMPARATIVE COSTS OF ASSIGNED COUNSEL AND DEFENDER SYSTEMS BY SIZE OF JURISDICTION[a]

County Population in Thousands	Median cost as public expenditure in thousands of dollars		Median cost per capita by county in thousands of dollars	
	Assigned Counsel	Defender	Assigned Counsel	Defender
less than 50	0.7	3.6	0.031	0.093
50-99	2.7	4.4	0.035	0.057
100-399	7.5	9.4	0.037	0.045
400-999	34.0	29.1	0.059	0.044
1000 or more	88.7	77.3	0.081	0.041

a. Abstracted from Etheridge, 1970: 97 Table 2.

versus 71.8 for defenders; in assigned counsel counties the mean for retained counsel is 52.2 versus 69.5 (Etheridge, 1970: 98). In percent receiving prison versus probation sentences, defenders achieved 73.9% prison and 26.1% probation, while retained counsel in those counties achieved 51.4 versus 48.6%. The assigned counsel systems were similar: 69.6% prison versus 30.4% probation, against retained counsels' record of 48.0% prison and 52.9% probation (Etheridge, 1970: 99). In all cases, the retained counsel data differ more from either appointive system than they do from each other. Regardless of other factors, such as nature of the crime and prior record, it remains true that all the data conclusively demonstrate is that nonindigents and indigents are treated differently, and that in larger population centers public defender offices are cheaper.

The absence of any concrete evidence of difference between defenders and assigned counsel in terms of service suggests that professional arguments over these alternatives are not solely geared to the question of client service.

Turning to what actually happens to indigent defendants, a further question can be raised. What is the relevance of the entire professional argument, couched in the language of standards, protecting client-counsel relationships, providing best possible service and so forth, to a process which does not seem to involve much actual legal defense work?

The consequences of the operating court system are that the indigent defendant is unlikely to be released on bail, unlikely to be released on personal recognizance, and likely to be in jail waiting pretrial hearing and its consequences for some time. At some point some counsel, whether defender or assigned, will see him (or her) and probably urge a guilty plea—either to the charge set by the District Attorney on the basis of his acts, or to some lesser charge involved in a "negotiated plea" (Sudnow, 1967; Schaeffer Committee, 1967). For the courts, this expedites the clearance of a backlog of cases. The advocated "consistency of service" and the fact of the defender and prosecutor having a "continuing relationship" tends to mean simply the expedition of plea-bargaining.

The overload on the court system has recently been well documented by the first federal census of city and county jails, taken on March 15th, 1970. Of the 160,863 inmates, 52% had not been convicted on any crime. Of these, 35% had been arraigned and were waiting trial; 17% had not been arraigned. Concern for this situation has made itself more immediately evident through the massive New York City prison riots of 1971—a city with the second largest jail population in the U.S.: 17,399 prisoners in 75 jails on census day. The relationship of plea-bargaining to client load is clear: the court system, as a complex administrative machine rather than a center for the ideals of justice and trial by jury, can handle more people more rapidly if it can simply assign penalties to a series of guilty pleas, rather than going through the lengthy process of jury selection and full trial. Plea-bargaining as a fact of life was recognized by the legal profession in 1967, when the Schaeffer Committee of the American Bar Association's Project on Minimum Standards for the Administration of Criminal Justice called for recognition of such pleas as a legitimate legal practice, and urged the attempt to find ways in which judges could promote and control negotiated justice.

Members of the profession directly involved in the area of criminal law are clearly aware of the facts of daily practice. And there is genuine concern among certain members of the bar to improve the provision of legal services to the poor. Evidence for this includes the rise of poverty-oriented law, as already mentioned, and the emergence of the Manhatten Bail Project and the Vera Institute, which works to release indigents on personal recognizance. It also includes the fact that although initially forced, the ABA did conduct a massive survey into the question of indigent defense (Silverstein, 1965) and has held numerous conferences to discuss it, and that the NLADA exists, and instituted a drive for experimental projects in indigent defense systems in 1965. Beyond this, my own subjective experience in interviewing lawyers concerned with the problem, indicates a genuine concern to apply legal protection where it is due. This does not imply a "noble savage" view of the client. It is part of professional occupational life to be concerned with the application of one's skills and to be concerned with practice.

But given the reality of court life, and the internal concerns of the profession, does the evidence support the continued acceptance of the idea that the arbitrary discretion facilitated by professional autonomy is constrained in practice by concern for "client service?"

AN EQUATION REASSESSED

The equation under review states that because the main basis for professional decisions over practice is the "best interests of the client," total professional autonomy, based on special knowledge, is legitimate. The client simply receives the consequences of these decisions.

This paper questions the assumption that client service is the main criterion for decision-making. It also questions whether the main criteria actually used—centering on issues of "professionalism"—are relevant to client service, as illustrated by this case. I suggest that client service is taken for granted by professionals themselves as they argue through a series of conflicts concerning questions of professional protection.

Thus, indigent defense became a major issue only when the profession received strong external pressure. It may be argued that the U.S. Supreme Court is part of the profession. But its truly supreme function in interpreting constitutional law is far removed from the practicalities of the administration of criminal law by local professional associations and practitioners. The latter did not institute the issue. They did not generate the demand for service. Once the demand was made, I have suggested that a close examination of the argument over alternative systems of service indicates far more concern for the consequences for professionals and traditional ideals of professional relationships, than for the real practicalities of life for the indigent in the criminal court. Further, that under all of this was a question of internal segmentation (Bucher and Strauss, 1961) and conflict. I further suggest that much of the content of the argument is in fact irrelevant to client experience under the current court system. The profession is however eminently practical in dealing with financial issues, and in major population centers public defender offices will probably become the norm.

In sum, professional interests in professionalism and client interests in experience do not necessarily coincide. Professionals have solidly based self-interest in preserving their autonomy and privilege—which play a part, indeed a significant part, in professional behavior. At the same time, these occupations are not formally supposed to base decisions on such premises. Thus we have a case where a set of internal battles focusing on control, financial rewards and the protection of practitioners is periodically justified in the terminology of client interest.

There are some practical and some general questions raised by this example. The argument that the professionalism debate is irrelevant to the client comes from the fact that the court system is increasingly functioning as an administrative organization with salaried officials and nontrial procedures. If it is largely a people-processing machine, using predetermined procedures of arrest-guilty plea-sentencing, then the question of required professional competence as a defense attorney-advocate comes under review. If this is a bureaucratic machine, perhaps it should be acknowledged as such—which could suggest a total redesign of the court procedure with an increase in largely administratively trained personnel, with some knowledge of law, rather than fully qualified defense attorneys. The fact that the procedure might run counter to dominant cultural values in handling the "scales of justice" can be treated either as some unavoidable "cultural lag," or perhaps lead to some attempt to totally redefine the court process.

Perhaps a dual system exists. For those cases which do not plead guilty and which demand trial by jury, the arguments concerning "professionalism" and remuneration of counsel could be relevant. The extension of full and speedy due process to all those arrested under the current system is recognized as impossible. Neither is it the norm. Where it occurs the expertise of counsel is clearly needed. But if it only occurs in a minority of cases is it in fact in the best interests of the clients as a whole to use this model to determine their experience?

It is clearly in the interests of the profession to preserve the model: it justifies their existence. If the long-run preservation of the advocacy system of justice is an objective, it may be in the interests of the social system to pursue that model. But is it in the interests of the clients? If asked, would they agree that the full protection of due process, however long it took, was most important—or a procedure that would process them quickly through the consequences of their actions? If they find themselves in jail longer when they demand a trial than when they do not, of what particular benefit are lawyers to them? At the same time, of course, every increase in the bureaucratization of the courts decreases the professional control of the lawyer. The substitution of rules of procedure removes the mystique of professional expertise. There is a well-recognized tension between bureaucratic principles and professional principles of work.

Practically then, this particular issue raises some familiar questions about the court system. Beyond that however, the basic question remains: how does the assumed reciprocity of client service as an ideology and professional autonomy as a decision-making base function? The ambiguity of the term "client service" becomes crucial. Professionals decide what that is, in the process of making decisions. They do not have a conception of what it is on which they then base decisions. Insofar as it is only the profession that defines the terms of service, no external agent can evaluate what it means, except in terms of practical consequence. To the profession it means the application of traditional perspectives to particular areas of practice. At present there are no external controls, there is no formal system for the collective definition by clients or other laymen of what client interests might be taken to mean. The idea that professionals should be subject to external review is contrary to all traditional norms of professional occupations. University professors are still recovering from the shock of "client control" in the demand for services on many campuses.

The conclusion implied here, however, cannot be that the *necessary* alternative to professional autonomy is some form of client control or external review—although it leads to speculation of that kind. It does say that the current basis for granting the right to define client service to professionals themselves is based on a faulty assumption: that there is a natural coincidence of client and professional interests. An alternative response to this unequal equation would be a straightforward recognition of its inequality and an attempt to identify under what circumstances client and professional interests do conflict. The acceptance or rejection of professional autonomy in making decisions in such cases could then be based on recognition of that reality.

REFERENCES

Association of the Bar of the City of New York (1959) Equal Justice for the Accused. Garden City, N.Y.: Doubleday.

BEANEY, W. M. (1955) The Right to Counsel in American Courts. Ann Arbor: University of Michigan Press.

BLUMBERG, A. S. (1967) "The practice of law as a confidence game: organizational cooperation of a profession." Law and Society Review (June): 15-59.

CARLIN, J. (1966) Lawyers' Ethics, A Survey of the New York City Bar. New York: Russell Sage Foundation.

――― (1962) Lawyers on Their Own: A Study of Individual Practitioners in Chicago. New Brunswick: Rutgers University Press.

ETHERIDGE, C. F. (1970) Conflict and Negotiation Processes: The Emergence of a Public Defender Office within the Legal Profession. Ph.D. dissertation, University of Washington.

FREUND, P. A. (1963) "The legal profession." Daedalus (Fall): 689-700.

LADINSKY, J. (1963) "Careers of lawyers, law practice and legal institutions." American Sociological Review (February): 47-54.

LEWIS, A. (1964) Gideon's Trumpet. New York: Vintage.

LORTIE, D. C. (1959) "Laymen to lawmen: law school, careers and professional socialization." Harvard Education Review 29 (Fall): 352-369.

MAYER, M. (1966) The Lawyers. New York: Harper & Row.

SILVERSTEIN, L. (1965) Defense of the Poor In Criminal Cases in American State Courts. American Bar Foundation.

Schaeffer Committee (1967) American Bar Association, Project on Minimum Standards for the Administration of Criminal Justice.

SMIGEL, E. O. (1964) The Wall Street Lawyer. New York: Free Press.

――― (1960) "The impact of recruitment on the organization of the large law firm." American Sociological Review 25 (February): 56-65.

SUDNOW, D. (1965) "Normal crimes: sociological features of the penal code in a public defender office." Social Problems 12 (Winter): 255-276.

THIELENS, W. Jr. (1957) "Some comparisons of entrants to medical and law school," in Merton et al., The Student Physician. Harvard University Press.

Chapter 14

THE UNIVERSITY AND THE
PROFESSIONAL MODEL
Amplification on a Magnification

LIONEL S. LEWIS

Ever since Americans in large numbers began believing that
universities were essential to the American Dream, the lot of the
professor has greatly improved. Some professors are counselors to
public and private men of influence (Lewis, 1969a), many do
research that is sponsored and presumably utilized by government
and business, and most now make enough to afford a sizable
mortgage. Clearly, the days when the popular image of the
professor was that of an impractical, absent-minded eccentric are
long past (Lewis, 1968). Today, as everyone well knows, a great
deal of serious work goes on in the university.

Given this airy view, it is not surprising that most people, both
within and outside the university, are pretty well convinced that in
the crunch academic men are guided by professional norms. In the
last two decades, the proportion of the population who would
agree with Jencks and Riesman's (1968: 529) contention that
individuals in the university community are judged "almost
entirely on the basis of the one set of standards almost all its
members accept: professional performance" has grown significantly.

Author's Note: *The research reported here was assisted by a grant awarded by
the Committee of Faculty Research Grants of the Social Science Research
Council.*

"Professional" is a complex concept, and there is no precise way of telling what might be meant when it is used with reference to one or another aspect of the university—some may be suggesting that professional norms are omnipresent, while others may be suggesting something less. In any case, it is certain that, regardless of what is conveyed in one or another context, any usage would encompass the basic elements of professional behavior, e.g., disinterestedness, service, commitment to task, excellence, responsibility, rationality. And, more central to the theme of this paper, all would include the notion of technical competence, which Parsons has described as "one of the principal defining characteristics of the professional status and rôle" (1939: 460). Surely, who would deny that the valuation accorded an academic man derives from his expertise?

Thus, while it is generally recognized that from time to time favoritism, pettiness, ideology, or old school ties taint purely academic matters, there is widespread agreement that professional principles are a vital force at least among professionally active scholars. For one thing, it is commonly believed that academic men adhere to a puritan ethic founded on self-discipline, austerity, and hard work. It is said that the best way for an academic man to advance his career is to advance his discipline. And the shorthand formula for this assumption, *publish or perish,* has been granted the status of an inviolable law that, we are told, hangs heavy over the academic marketplace (Lewis, 1967).

This somewhat fanciful characterization of academic life is hardly ever questioned: it is unlikely that the professoriat itself would readily acknowledge the invalidity of a formulation which had them hard at work, manfully struggling for and ultimately deserving their moderate rewards. To attribute many of the evils of university life to excess zeal instead of what might actually be indolence is indeed a nice trick. The belief that a department adheres to objective standards in hiring or promoting colleagues does a great deal to bolster the self-images of its members: it supports the notion that they have it tough, in that they have been and must be productive, and that what they have they should have.

It would be indeed more than what one could reasonably hope for if a less idealized and more balanced description of what goes on behind the ivy-covered façade, were abroad. After all, virtually everything written about the university is written by academics themselves, so that the popular image of university culture has been molded and is continually reinforced by what amounts to a special interest group—the interest here being to sustain a flattering caricature. And, as a consequence, the stereotype of the scientist as a practical, skillful, active, effective, diligent servant of truth (Lewis, 1968; Yamamoto, 1968: 300-302) is akin to Tawney's (1926: 201) portrait of the archetypal puritan: "He disciplines, rationalizes, systematizes, his life; 'method' was a Puritan catchword a century before the world had heard of Methodists. He makes his very business a travail of the spirit."

The result of all this romantic thinking is that although one could easily spend every working day reading the glut of books and journals concerned with academic life, one would encounter little that was truly objective. This is not simply a reference to, on the one hand, sour-grapes exposés by the disenchanted; it is actually not necessary to set up such straw men. The truth of the matter is that the premise that professional norms are central to academic culture has been accepted without qualification by practically everyone who has thought that he had something original, intelligent, or interesting to say about higher learning (that is, nearly everyone). Typically, Jencks and Riesman (1968) and Parsons and Platt (1968) have advanced the notions of meritocratic advancement, universalism, and cognitive rationality in their analyses and descriptions of university life, and even the critic Jacques Barzun (1960: 70) in lamenting "the invidious system of academic promotion, the perversion of the under-graduate curriculum, and (most recent) the professional teacher's contempt of teaching," has attributed this condition to the "mania for research."

Given the overwhelming and unquestioning acceptance of the really questionable supposition that at bottom academic men are professional, one could foretell with a degree of certainty that Caplow and McGee, who ostensibly laid bare the seamy underlife of academia, would also be taken in. Not only do they accept this proposition as valid, without so much as a smirk, shudder, or grimace, but actually reiterate it, loudly and clearly.

> The data leave us with a strong impression ... that although the scholar's judgment of his colleagues is often blind and biased, and occasionally downright crazy, it *is* professional. Men are not judged by their tempers or their table manners, unless either of these is unspeakably bad. The judgment made is based on performance and is as equitable as conflicts of viewpoint permit. Although the judge may not be impartial, he does seem to confine his judgment to what is relevant—and to succeed remarkably well in keeping nonprofessional factors out of his consideration [Caplow and McGee, 1958: 93].

It all sounds irrefutable.

Granted the tenacity of myths and the propensity for self-delusion, anyone still not convinced in the face of common sense or experience that Caplow and McGee's assertion is pure whimsy need only examine the roster of tenured faculty in one, two or three departments in any major university. In spite of a variety of opportunities for support of research projects and publications that accrue to those located at prestige institutions, one would have to fall back on "nonprofessional factors" to explain the composition of the faculty of these departments—and also the composition of faculty in many departments in less conspicuous institutions.

THE USE OF LETTERS OF RECOMMENDATION

To assess the potency of professional principles in one facet of academic life, an examination of letters of recommendation written by sociologists for sociologists seeking an academic position was undertaken, and the analysis of these letters revealed that particularism, nonprofessional and, perhaps, irrational factors were as much a part of the evaluation of these social scientists, as were criteria usually thought to be germane to the research and teaching functions. To graciously and smoothly accommodate various social arrangements, for instance, was a quality worthy of praise. Those who were amiable, docile, and of sound mind received special approbation. The possession of characteristics usually not associated with professional behavior seemed to be a positive end in itself (Lewis, 1969b).

It cannot be concluded on the basis of these findings that academic men are not concerned with the professional dimensions of their colleagues. Obviously, they are: every letter made some reference to a candidate's teaching or research ability, and in some the detail about these aspects of a candidate indicates considerable thought on the part of the writer. In fact, even if such letters should reflect little interest in a man's professional qualities, it would be as foolish to deny that academics were unconcerned about these matters as it is to assert that this is all that they care about. Recruitment is only a small part of academic life, and there is more to recruitment than letters of recommendation, which might actually at some later date be shown to have a minor effect on the process as a whole. It is not a question of turning things on their heads and arguing that the influence of professional norms on academic matters is nil or minuscule, but only of putting reality in perspective by directing some attention to the issue of how basic they apparently are (or are not). The research reported here was undertaken with the hope of doing precisely this.

Among other things, there is the additional problem of not knowing whether it is possible to generalize safely from one of the newer and self-conscious social sciences to "established" disciplines in the humanities and hard sciences, where, it is said, people know what they are about. This uncertainty is increased by the fact that many of the sociologists for whom letters were written were seeking their first academic appointment and had too few professional accomplishments about which a professional evaluation could be made.

As vital as qualifications and reservations are in discussing any topic, they are not as valuable in moving one in the direction of the truth as is supplemental research. With this disclaimer in mind, it was felt that an examination of additional letters written by clearly professional academics and concerned with the *professional* problem of academic recruitment, written for academics clearly *professional,* in *traditional* academic disciplines was in order, would be welcome, and could best advance an inquiry into the commitment to professional norms by academic men. Consequently, we will proceed prompted by the presupposition that a letter of recommendation is reflexive, in that it reveals as much about the values of a writer as about the qualities of a candidate.

After nearly ten months of continuous but mostly fruitless search, a usable sample of 110 letters of recommendation written by full and associate professors on behalf of men seeking appointments at the level of full or associate professor was obtained. Almost all of the letters originated from nationally prominent universities, although a few came from prestigious liberal arts colleges located in the East and Midwest. Half the letters were written for men seeking a position in a Department of Chemistry, and half were for men seeking a position in a Department of English Literature. In every case, the appointment under consideration was to a large, reputable university, recognized as having sound and mature graduate programs. Beyond what has been said, it is not possible to make precise statements about the nature of the sample, since before the letters were made accessible in the majority of cases, most identifying information— i.e., each mention of the candidate's name, the letterhead, the salutation, and the signature—was blocked out. Nonetheless, from the body of the letters, which were not at all altered, there is no indication that any letter ultimately used in the study did not meet the conditions explained to those who made them available for the project.

THE SOCIAL ETHIC AS A CAPITAL CONCERN

Generally, there is as much emphasis on the social ethic in letters written for chemists as there was in those written for sociologists. Just as the letters for sociologists placed considerable emphasis on how "congenial, cooperative, likeable, and/or effective in interaction" (Lewis, 1969b: 236) a candidate was, the letters for chemists emphasize that candidates "get on well," have "good relationships," are "considerate" and "cooperative," and are "liked," "respected," and "popular." Just as the letters for sociologists characterized candidates as "amiable, warm, personable, pleasant . . . patient, modest, quiet, easygoing, relaxed . . . stable, well-adjusted, balanced [and] even-tempered" (Lewis, 1969b: 238), the letters for chemists characterize candidates as "pleasant," "genial," "agreeable," "friendly," "mature," "good-humored," or, in a word, "delightful." In both sets of letters considerable space is given over to testifying that individuals are remarkably skilled in social intercourse and in outlining how closely their personalities conform to the American ideal—someone who offends no one.

> [He] is a fine person. He is considerate of others and gets along well with associates and students. I have known him well as a fellow member of the English Lutheran Church.

> [He] is a very amiable gentleman and should make an admirable colleague.

There are as many references to a man's personality in the letters of the literary scholars as in those for chemists, and being "pleasant" is without question a quality held dear. That someone is a "nice guy" is always worth mentioning; it appears that, all things being equal, without exception the man who is affable is a more desirable candidate than the man who is not.

> He has a tough, resourceful, and at the same time sensitive literary mind. In addition, he is one of the nicest people I know; this is not just an empty compliment but a real testimony to a warm and congenial personality.

> Has he a "first-rate mind?" I don't know—first enough, I'll say. He's a decent fellow, too—reachable, warm and interested in unifying his experience.

Yet there are striking differences between the letters of literary scholars and those of chemists. First, a significantly smaller proportion of the letters written for the former than for the latter raises the issue of how well a man relates to his colleagues. The literary scholars just do not seem to care about this as much as other academics. When the topic is touched upon, some literary scholars, with no embarrassment and, in fact, with some relish, detail those qualities of a candidate that could well sour departmental relationships.

> Though his manner is pleasant and he is an interesting conversationalist, [he] has proven at times to be unnecessarily tactless and aggressive in his dealings with his colleagues and with the administration.
>
> If [he] has a fault, it is that he strikes some as rather cocky; but then he has something to be cocky about. I suggest to those who interview him that they ought not to be put off by this manner, because [he] is in every respect personally as well as intellectually above reproach.

At times, the tone of the letters goes beyond simple casualness, in that some writers show a certain admiration and pride for the man who is careless in his interpersonal relations. The writers are not just making the best of a bad situation, but seem to see abrasiveness as something desirable in itself—perhaps as a mark of honesty, perhaps as a sign of what some would call creative individuality, perhaps as insurance that departmental affairs will not become too arid.

> He is not, to be sure, a man who tolerates fools gladly, and he strikes many as abrasive, but I find him a most appealing person, and a warm friend.
>
> In point of personality, [he] is a bit frenetic, not always tactful; he steps on toes, gets people angry. He is also sensitive, witty, capable of inspiring the deepest affection.
>
> [He] is younger than some of his own graduate students; he is brash, even impudent sometimes; no doubt he is in some respects immature, for instance in the fulminations he writes about departmental policies or habits. But for me there is in all his motions a saving intelligence, self-irony, and relevance that make him a most engaging and effective gadfly. Maybe I wouldn't want a whole department like him, but I do wish we had a couple more.
>
> I should add that I will strenuously oppose his leaving . . . and that a considerable number of my colleagues including some who at times have found him difficult, share my determination to do everything possible to keep him here.

Whatever their motivation, it is of particular interest that some literary scholars are on the surface not apprehensive about how a candidate might handle encounters with his colleagues. Although there is no way of telling how any department which is considering such a candidate would react to these kinds of remarks, whether or not, for instance, a clique of oligarchs would feel threatened enough to block the appointment, at least an attitude that one should either overlook the fact that a man might not get on splendidly with his colleagues or to be frank about this has been embraced as part of the subculture of literary scholars.

After reading more than two thousand letters of recommendation from a variety of disciplines written on behalf of both faculty and students over the past couple of years, one would not be overstating the case in saying that, on the whole, academics are obsessed by the desire to be surrounded by individuals marked by charm, a conforming personality, and skills in interaction. Against this, the impression that among literary scholars there is toleration for men who are not wholly engaging is indeed striking. To express delight over manifestations of nonconformity—even if the concession is only verbal and ritual—is a radical departure from what one finds among other disciplines. It might well be that along strictly academic lines literary scholars are also more flexible in cultivating and permitting diversity; surely the nature of their research, which does not require the degree of collaboration or cooperation that is necessary in complex scientific experimentation, would be conducive to this.

THE EXUBERANT PERSONALITY

Literary scholars may not, on the one hand, brood about Rotarian camaraderie, but they are, on the other, plainly preoccupied with the business of associates who are live wires—specifically the type of individual who "displays verve," "shows spontaneity," is "quite lively and stimulating," has "dynamic attitudes," "is sprightly," has "a truly vital personality," is "boundless and exciting," is "a mover and shaker," "is buoyant and personable," or "is an animated conversationalist." In only one letter is a man described as something that does not effervesce, and here the matter is broached equivocally: ("He is a quiet, somewhat sober and reserved young man . . . [yet he] proves to have unexpected intelligence, sensitiveness, and force."). It is almost as if being luminous in spirit has somehow become equated with having a brilliant mind, and vivacity is but a reflection of hidden intellectual resources. Although bubbling over may be a sure sign of cerebral ferment, there is no indication from the letters that the obverse is a tenet of the literary scholar's culture; sobriety and stupidity are never equated. To be sure, this may be because essentially everyone is blessed with lavish vitality, and there are few clues as to what might be thought about an individual somewhat more normal. For the man referred to above, we are assured that "he is unusually perceptive [and] a most promising man," but actually there is no telling if this comment is intended to offset an unfavorable reaction to the information about his restrained manner or is nothing more than supplemental data offered simply to apprize an interested reader.[1]

On the face of it, it is not so much a question of literary scholars demeaning those who are of moderate temperament as it is of their placing unusual value on those whose "style is breathtaking." The man with "zest" and "a special charm" can, if nothing else, be counted on to amuse. To anyone caught up in a tiresome academic routine, this is clearly a pleasant prospect. And it may be only natural that men in a discipline primarily concerned with that born of the lively mind would be especially taken by the idea of being surrounded by lively men. The possession of a sense of humor is the surest sign that a man can at once brighten a department both socially and intellectually. Even if it turns out that a candidate's sense of irony and wit do not truly reflect a clever mind, a department still has a refreshing diversion around. Thus, a sense of humor in a candidate is a quality that cannot help but be looked upon favorably, and it was not unexpected that reference was made to it in almost a quarter of the letters.

I am very fond of [him] as an individual. He is frequently our guest and we always enjoy and are stimulated by his incisive and witty conversations. The acuteness of his mind and the originality of his wit combine to an analytic acumen which is tempered only by his kindness and charm. He is cordial, but open; sharp, but fair . . . .

Personally he is attractively witty, by no means overbearing but quietly imposing, sometimes a little disconcerting in his blunt disagreement with unwisdom and usually right in thinking it is unwisdom.

To his wide acquaintance with English and American literature, he brings a sharp wit and a very personable manner.

[He] is a personable young man, witty, amusing, volatile.

The light touch may be especially attractive in those men who are not always tactful with others; as everyone knows, laughter is effective in dissipating tension. The candidate with a sense of humor as an extra gift might be expected to wear better than the bare-boned extrovert, who himself has considerable appeal.

Turning to the chemists, as far as dynamism is concerned, an individual need not be an extrovert nor an introvert; it is perfectly all right either to have a "personal flair" or "charisma" or to be "quiet" or "unassuming"—that is, as long as neither is in the extreme. There is an unmistakable expectation that the course one holds should not be too different from that of others; the more closely one's personality approximates the mode, the more readily one is deemed suitable. A person who is too animated or one who is too retiring might not become "a compatible member of the team."

[He] is an individualist and non-conformer, but his abilities as a thinker and planner are superb.

Personally, [he] is pleasant and voluble. At times, when under pressure, he becomes somewhat volatile . . . . In spite of his unusual abilities, I do not recommend [him] for your staff opening.

Personally, [he] is quiet, and on short acquaintance, it is not easy to converse with him. After one becomes better acquainted, however, one learns that [he] has a nice sense of humor and talks reasonably freely.

He has a somewhat reserved but pleasant personality and should prove to be a stimulating colleague.

It should be noted that it is never a question of a man being so withdrawn that he would be unable to effectively teach or discharge his other academic duties. That, of course, would be a serious problem. It is instead a matter of assuring an interested department that a candidate is not inhospitable. The possibility that a colleague might stand aloof haunts a number of chemists; for many academics in general, the need to be admired has ripened into a need to be loved, and one can never be sure about a man who lacks bonhomie. It is good to hear that, although a man is not by nature sociable, this will not necessarily have any effect on how much he might cherish his colleagues.

A ROLAND, PH.D., FOR AN OLIVER, PH.D.

To take note of dissimilarities between letters written for chemists and those written for literary scholars is by no means to suggest that there is not a considerable amount in their contents which is identical. On the contrary, in the general description of the ideal colleague, the two sets resemble each other more than they differ. To begin with, when the matter of academic performance is taken up in the introductory paragraphs, most of the letters touch the same bases. Candidates are invariably described as "competent," "diligent," "responsible," "intelligent," "creative," "conscientious," or "enthusiastic." Moreover, the format of a small, but by no means insignificant, number of letters is so standard that with little change, one surely being to add the name of the appropriate candidate where applicable, an account could well apply to a man in any academic discipline. To demonstrate this point, a letter written for a literary scholar and one written for a chemist are presented in their entireties:

Dear Professor . . .

I would be happy to write you about . . . if it were not for the fact that I would hate to think I ever had anything to do with his leaving us. (So I'll write you unhappily.)

This is a very hot property, as I gather you realize. [He] is an absolutely first-rate teacher and a most agreeable colleague. He has boundless energy, very wide but also deep interests, and an extraordinary ability to keep on learning and growing at a stage when most of us begin to narrow our horizons. I do not know many minds as good as his. It is high-powered and genuinely creative but—a rare thing—it operates with real esthetic sensitivity and perception. If I were to compile a list of people who I think are going to be big names in our profession, his would probably come to mind first. I hope you don't get him.

Otherwise, best wishes.

Yours sincerely,

Dear Professor . . .

. . . is one of my favorite characters on the contemporary organic chemistry scene, and I have recommended him several times in past years for positions of responsibility and challenge. He is a careful and imaginative investigator who always unearths something unexpected and important when he investigates a field. His quiet enthusiasm is contagious, and I suspect him of being quite influential in the good quality and quantity of research which comes out of . . . . I have not seen him in an undergraduate teaching capacity but have heard him lecture on a number of occasions and know that he is a fine speaker. He is also personally a most desirable colleague whom I should certainly be most happy to have in my own department.

I wish you success in attracting him.

Sincerely yours,

Aside from the literary scholar's greater ability to say nothing with elegance, there is little that distinguishes these letters.

It is not simply when academic qualifications are reviewed that this resemblance is evident, but it is just as apparent with reference to less professional considerations. For example, in both sets of letters substantial space is given over to the discussion of patterns of behavior that are in keeping with what most Americans would call decent, respectable, and normal, and not only do both literary scholars and chemists focus on the same themes and take the same position with regard to them, but they even express themselves in the same manner. Two cases in point would be remarks bearing on the candidates' families and appearance.

Family

Literary Scholars:

His wife is also a very alert and pleasant person.

His wife is yet more shy, but essentially pleasant; and she will become more obviously so . . . .

His wife is herself an active intellectual with a strong interest in Classics; she is also a charming person. They and their three children appear to be an uncommonly stable family group.

With all this [he] is a lively, open, direct, and exceptionally likeable person and so is his wife.

Chemists:

He is a very pleasant, hard-working, likeable fellow, with a nice wife.

He plays the clarinet with a proficiency bordering on . . . [N.B., not Caplow and McGee's recorder player]. [He] has three small children and a variety of interests.

In personality, [he] is pleasant and attractive. He is emotionally stable and mature, and has an agreeable dry wit. His coworkers like him and respect him. His wife is also pleasant and attractive.

[He] is an individual capable of working long hours at his chemistry, with the aid and encouragement of his splendid wife.

Appearance

Literary Scholars:

. . . is always nicely dressed and easy in conversation.

He is of an attractive personality and appearance, inclined perhaps at times to be a little on the frivolous side but this may be due to his ever-present sense of humor.

. . . is personable, good-looking and friendly.

Chemists:

Dr. . . . is of excellent appearance, good health, and attractive personality.

[He] is tall and well-built, has a gentle yet persuasive manner, is well-liked by his colleagues; he is cooperative and will assume responsibility.

He is a highly personable, dignified, and clean-cut young man, with a profound interest in chemistry and with truly outstanding laboratory skill and productivity.

Even on these topics, of course, the letters are not indistinguishable. Chemists and literary scholars both may place ample and equal value on a candidate's enjoying a conventional family life and appearance, but the prevalent ethos of each subculture sets the tone of other commentary. Given the literary scholar's penchant for permissiveness with regard to personal conduct, one would be making an obvious and correct assumption in guessing that the two observations cited below refer to chemists.

But I believe he has dissipated a good deal of his energy in non-scientific endeavors—including two unsuccessful and disruptive marriages and substantial business ventures.

[He] has a good personality and the only objectionable feature that I have noted is that this last semester he has raised a beard. I thought his appearance without the beard was very nice. I do not know how permanent the beard is. Otherwise I am sure you would be well pleased with him in this position.

Moreover, it should be pointed out that some motifs may be peculiar to only one set of letters. The most evident illustration of a theme that appears in one set of letters and not the other is the recurring emphasis by literary scholars on the candidates' manliness.

He is vigorous (though not at all flamboyant) in manner and appearance.

He is, that is to say, a fine person—hard-working, tough, demanding of others no more than he demands of himself, generous, witty, modestly imperious.

[He] is a man of exceptional moral fibre, a masculine, clean-living person.

The question of a candidate's masculinity is never raised by chemists.

Hopefully by now most readers would agree that there is a great deal in the letters from which to conclude that, in evaluating a man, academics are concerned with more than professional performance. Although other constructions could be put on the evidence, the intention of the foregoing analysis has been simply to demonstrate this axiomatic proposition. Since not enough is known about what letters signify both to their writers and to their readers, it would be too ambitious to imply anything more.

PROFESSIONAL ASSESSMENT

Needless to say, the majority of writers of letters of recommendation are primarily occupied with recounting a candidate's professional qualifications. It is an unhappy fact, however, that more often than not they lack specific information and do not always have much to say on such matters. To discourse on a topic from a position of ignorance presents its own special problems. As a case in point, given the tenet of academic freedom that it is somehow sinful to impinge upon a professor's autonomy while he performs in the classroom, how could one expect colleagues to know anything about each other's teaching? What of substance could anyone possibly say about this subject?

> I am not familiar with his work as a teacher.
>
> I have not had any opportunity to judge his capacity as a teacher.
>
> I have never heard him present a lecture.

The evaluation of teaching, then, is largely based on hearsay, extrapolation, and conjecture.

> The reports I have heard about his teaching have been unqualifiedly enthusiastic. He completely rejuvenated the advanced physical chemical laboratory course at Columbia and made it popular as well.
>
> . . . but I am told that he is an extremely good teacher.
>
> Except for the one lecture to my seminar (which was conducted with great verve and enthusiasm) I have no information on [his] abilities as a teacher. I should expect him to be good.

I have no direct experience, of course, on which to judge his teaching abilities, but I have heard him present an interesting seminar at Penn State.

I can speak less well to the point so far as teaching is concerned because I have had no direct contact with this aspect of his abilities. Of course, from the point of view of clarity of lecture and ability to participate in discussion, I can say that he is a clear and cogent speaker.

Although I have no direct information, I feel that he is also an excellent teacher.

I have no direct knowledge about his teaching. I assume he would be good at it.

Finally, and perhaps most important, he has an infectious enthusiasm for chemistry which made him a very stimulating member of the group here, and which should make him a stimulating teacher as well.

Dr. . . . is a personable individual who is interesting to talk to. Although I have never heard him present a lecture I feel confident in stating that he has both the ability and the desire to do an effective job in teaching.

I am not familiar with his work as a teacher, but would think he would be effective. He is a man of attractive personality.

He is very poised and self-confident and very personable . . . . He is probably a very effective teacher.

Given the chimera surrounding declarations about a man's capacity to teach, it is not difficult to understand how extraneous considerations come to infect professional assessment, and, ultimately, professional life. To fill a void in discharging the normal professional responsibility of reviewing and measuring the professional quality of a fellow professional, seemingly irrelevant criteria are embraced. But, under the circumstances, on what else might an opinion be based than, say, to cite the last few examples, on the social ethic? After all, it is not entirely unnatural for a writer who is attracted to a candidate to be persuaded that students would be of the same mind and would be more inclined to soak up his learning. An account has been made; the ritual has been acted out according to form.

To be sure, when a writer has something more substantial to relate, this material is specifically emphasized.

I have been teaching a course jointly with him for several years, and can say with confidence that he is an excellent and devoted teacher who establishes unusual rapport with students and is most stimulating for them.

He taught organic chemistry, both graduate and undergraduate . . . for four years. He also taught general chemistry and a course in chemical literature. He was an extremely good and effective teacher, an excellent lecturer, and very well versed in all phases of organic chemistry, both classical and modern. His courses were very well organized and up-to-date. His courses were also rigorous and demanding, not unreasonably so, but he assumed his students were in college to learn . . . .

But given the tenuousness of what is known, such instances are all too rare.

Many who are satisfied that they understand the dynamics of academic life might conclude at this juncture that the reason teaching is handled so superficially and casually in the letters is that no one much cares about this question, since, at bottom, all that a department is interested in is a man's research capabilities. This assumption is probably incorrect. A detailed study of the letters also reveals that a number of writers, particularly literary scholars, are almost completely in the dark about the scholarship of the men they recommend.

I gather that his research was first-class, but you'll have to rely on Cram for details.

I cannot give you a detailed evaluation since he has only been with me for five weeks. However, in this period I have been impressed by him.

. . . my knowledge of him is really quite limited. A year or two ago I visited the University of Illinois and was favorably impressed by [him] as a person. He showed a real enthusiasm . . . .

I would also disclaim competence to judge his research in anything but a very superficial way, and advise that such judgments be sought from others more qualified than I am.

I don't know his Dickens book . . . .

He has written to me occasionally since leaving Cornell, and appears to have maintained a strong interest in chemistry, and to have been successful in his research.

> This is a letter of recommendation for . . . of whom I think so highly that I hope we will be able to keep him here. No doubt others can speak more knowledgeably of his scholarship than I . . . .

> I haven't seen his new book, now in press, but I will be very surprised if it is not a first-rate and important piece of work. In general, I can't see how you can make a stronger appointment . . . .

> Though, of course, the proof of the pudding will be in the writing itself, as yet I have only seen outlines . . . .

Comments reflecting unfamiliarity with a candidate's scholarly activities are less common than those about teaching.

Naturally, when the writer is at all knowledgeable about a candidate's research, a lengthy and informative account is offered:

> I am aware that he is currently involved in some fundamental work concerned with structural alternatives to the α helix, which is beginning to be recognized as having minor importance as an element of secondary structure in many proteins. He is also in the process of developing some absolute methods for determination of the sense of polypeptide helices which do occur in the α helical conformation. It is noteworthy that [he], while sticking to a general and important problem, has not limited himself to a particular experimental approach, but rather has turned to many different physical and chemical methods to provide the answers he seeks. He has not been unmindful of the organic chemical techniques which may be of use, and I believe that he has a sufficient feeling for biochemistry so that he would employ enzymatic and other biological approaches as well if they seem desirable.

> While his efforts in the polynucleotide field have not been so extensive as in the polypeptide field, and are restricted to theoretical work, this facet of his research is of very high quality. His theoretical critique of the DNA degradation and molecular weight problem is an excellent indication of the exacting and analytical approach he takes. Such attitudes have all too often not characterized the work of others studying biomacromolecules. Thus his work has had the salutary effect of demanding rigor from the work of others. His recent theoretical treatment of the helix-coil transition of oligonucleotides of varying chain length promises to be a milestone in this field, and may equal in importance some of the very fine work of Zimm.

Such renditions are more prevalent among chemists than among literary scholars. Alternately, it is most likely that among the latter nothing will be known about either the teaching or the research of a candidate.

> I have not read anything that he has written; but if he can write as well as he speaks, he may have ahead of him a distinguished career as a scholar and critic.
>
> I have not been able to obtain a clearly defined impression of his ability as a teacher. He seldom discusses his work in the classroom with others in the department . . . .
>
> I have not read his manuscript on the French and English novel, but his talk makes it sound exciting; in any case, it looks as if he is ready to convert his prodigious learning into productive writing . . . .
>
> I've not heard him teach, but he gave a first rate talk here, and impressed everyone he met through a day of consultations. I can't imagine his *not* being a good teacher.

Such is the state of professional evaluation.

CONCLUDING REMARKS

Little needs to be said in summary. In universities, there would appear to be less emphasis on technical competence, a keystone of the professional role, than conventional wisdom would have us believe. In assessing their colleagues, academics are clearly concerned with questions beyond professional performance; moreover, this uncertain understanding is complicated and becomes more capricious by the fact that those who write letters do not always know a great deal about the professional activities of those about whom they write.

It might be worthwhile to speculate as to why the complex paradox of academic mythology persists, having nearly everyone affirming that university life is basically professional, denying this, and at the same time defending both positions. Professional criteria are objective criteria, and objectivity is ostensibly what the academic enterprise is all about. At one time or another, every scholar and scientist is taught that in the pursuit of knowledge and perhaps, ultimately, in the redemption of humankind, objectivity is imperative. To be convinced that objective standards, clear and unequivocal as they are, prevail is understandably reassuring. Not only might this minimize the anxiety that always surrounds uncertainty (Lewis, 1963), but it deceives many into supposing that the potency of other values, motives, and procedures which are generally dismissed as being alien to academic culture—e.g., paternalism, chauvinism, meanness, and myopia—are inappreciable. Since it is an article of faith that academics are limited by the rules of objectivity in their work, it is not puzzling why it is presumed that this is extended to other activities.

Being persuaded that objective criteria are primarily utilized in making a hard decision, such as conferring tenure, is, if nothing else, comforting. A judgment based on something concrete speaks with authority; certainly it sounds more convincing than to concede that procedures just sort of happen as a result of chance, whim, personal predilection, hanky-panky, and the like. For the insecure, the search for a colleague involves considerable risk—it is not easy to predict how a new man will behave after he gets caught up in departmental affairs. Based on his own experience, first-, second-, or third-hand, every academic man can recite some horror story of high hopes, a truncated honeymoon, intramural strife, the exodus of innocent victims as well as the least effective partisans, and the subsequent struggle to rebuild a department. And it is reassuring to assume that impersonal institutionalized practices operate to certify or disqualify any prospective colleague. It would be especially comforting for persons as obsessed about their social milieu as academics appear to be to have no doubts about the viability of these objective standards.

After reviewing and sorting out much of what it is said we know about the social life of man, Berelson and Steiner (1964: 663-664) concluded:

> In his quest for satisfaction, man is not just a seeker of truth, but of deceptions, of himself as well as others. (As La Rochefoucauld said, "Social life would not last long if men were not taken in by each other.") When man can come to grips with his needs by actually changing the environment, he does so. But when he cannot achieve such

"realistic" satisfaction, he tends to take the other path: to modify what he sees to be the case, what he thinks he wants, what he thinks others want.

Thus, we can end on a happy note: both the conditions of university life—such as the need to work together to assure the success of activity that is social in nature—and the cultivation of so much cant to conceal this fact affirm the basic humanity of academic men. That academics are only mortal, in itself, is worth reiterating on occasion.

NOTE

1. In two other letters written on behalf of candidates seeking instructorships while grimly entangled in the process of completing their dissertations, and which did not actually qualify to be used in this study, the spectre was raised that since one was sort of a lifeless bore and the other was being done in by his own seriousness of purpose, not much could be expected to come of their projects: unexciting men, unexciting research.

REFERENCES

BARZUN, J. (1960) "The cults of 'research' and 'creativity.' " Harper's Magazine 221 (October): 69-74.
BERELSON, B. and G. A. STEINER (1964) Human Behavior: An Inventory of Scientific Findings. New York: Harcourt, Brace & World.
CAPLOW, T. and R. J. McGEE (1958) The Academic Marketplace. New York: Basic Books.
JENCKS, C. and D. RIESMAN (1968) The Academic Revolution. New York: Doubleday.
LEWIS, L. S. (1969a) "Intellectuals and power." Educational Forum 34 (November): 50-54.
——— (1969b)"The puritan ethic in universities and some worldly concerns of sociologists." Amer. Sociologist 4 (August): 235-241.
——— (1968) "Students' images of professors." Educational Forum 32 (January): 185-190.
——— (1967) "Publish or perish: some comments on a hyperbole." J. of Higher Education 38 (February): 85-89.
———(1963) "Knowledge, danger, certainty, and the theory of magic." Amer. J. of Sociology 69 (July): 7-12.
PARSONS, T. (1939) "The professions and social structure." Social Forces 17 (May): 457-467.
——— and G. M. PLATT (1968) "The American academic profession: a pilot study." (mimeo)
TAWNEY, R. H. (1926) Religion and the Rise of Capitalism. New York: Harcourt, Brace & World.
YAMAMOTO, K. [ed.] (1968) The College Student and His Culture: An Analysis.

PART III

STUDYING THE
STUDENTS OF PROFESSIONS

Chapter 15

SOCIOLOGY AND THE PERSONAL
SERVICE PROFESSIONS

PAUL HALMOS

In *The Personal Service Society* (Halmos, 1970), I offered a definition of a group of professions which has acquired a significantly shared mentality in contemporary culture.

> Professions whose principal function is to bring about changes in the body or personality of the client are the *personal service professions,* whilst all other professions which are not charged with responsibilities of this sort or, at any rate, which do not set themselves such tasks as these, are the *impersonal service professions.*

The dramatic growth in the numbers and social influence of these personal service professions in modern industrial societies has not only prompted a moral renewal of leadership, but also has affected the general quality of social change in our time. Even while engaged in selfishly advancing their interests as professional groups or individuals, the culture of personal service connotes ideals which do not go very well with a laissez faire license, an unbridled system of free economy, the rapacity of penal justice, the harshness of educational discipline, and the mercenariness of marketable doctoring. At the same time, the culture inspires certain commitments to humanistic ideologies: it generally advocates the positive virtues of equity, tolerance, understanding, generosity, and sympathy. And, as a rule, the personal service professional self-consciously pretends that he sustains these values not because of an open and inspired allegiance to some creed but because of their clinical utility. These values have proved to be instrumental in the achievement of certain moral objectives, and this is why they are cherished. A nurse's kindness to a patient, a teacher's patience with a pupil, and a social worker's sympathetic understanding of a client are not only morally sanctioned *virtues*, but also professionally approved *techniques.*

Those for whom these "techniques" are occupational requisites—the "personal service professions"—are largely a product of this age. Though in medicine and in the priesthood there have been forerunners, it is only in our time that the diversification and sheer numerical growth of entirely secular personal services have spread themselves over the whole of populous, industrial societies and have affected almost every manifestation of their cultural life. The yearly accretion of wealth and income in modern industrial societies has made the constant growth of these personal services not only possible, but also inevitable. With their increasing number and market value, the moral and intellectual influence of the personnel of these services has grown and is likely to continue to grow. I have shown (Halmos, 1970) how the very leadership of society is penetrated and, in some cases, taken over by personal service professionals and how, as a consequence of this, the ideology of this personnel permeates the quality and sets the direction of social change in our time. I also sought to identify certain moral outcomes which, not surprisingly, issue from the cultivation of personal services and pointed out that these outcomes constituted "betterment" in terms of the principal moral values of modern industrial societies, whether these societies were collectivistic-irreligious or capitalistic-religious (by no means the only possible combinations).

Clearly the sociological importance of these assumptions is very great indeed, but a systematic sociological criticism of them has not yet been forthcoming. Sociology has largely ignored the progressive process of "personalization" of professional work in industrial society and has instead concerned itself, well-nigh exclusively, with problems of power, stratification, and conflict, as the major, decisive, and even exclusive agents of change. Sociology has not asked whether the expansion of the personal service professions, in fact, increasingly influences the moral-cultural quality of society. Indeed sociology seems to have mixed that question up with quite a different question—whether we should approve of any hypothesis, no matter how well-founded, which has flavors of a theory of progress. It goes without saying that the answer to the first should be given without reference to the answer to the second. Yet, strangely enough, the first is ignored because it is confused with the second. And in the case of the second, the sociologist expresses objections against conceptions of progressive improvements in life, because thoughts and imaginings of this kind convey to him a reprehensible complacency, which he feels he must combat with all his might. Unless the sociologist does his daily toilet of skepticism, he feels he is unlikely to advance his discipline. It does not sufficiently often occur to him that there is a hidden spring of optimistic bias in this his very phobia. He is like the man, who does not realize that "the bottle is 7/8 empty" is the same proposition as "the bottle is 1/8 full," and that he will be wrong if he rejects one of these propositions while affirming the other. Those who decline to follow up some implications of hypotheses on the ground that they are "too optimistic" and who subscribe only to pessimistic implications are precisely in this kind of position.

Nonetheless, it would seem that there is a small number of encouraging propositions about a "personal service society" which we may put forward without much hazard of error. One of these is that the material enrichment of humanity in the technological revolution of our time constantly widens the margin of intelligent and highly educated manpower which society can now spare for work in the personal social services. As society grows richer, more and more people can be recruited to teach, to heal, and to care for others. That this growth process is going on in industrial societies is now well established. Whereas, throughout the history of man, laboring society has been overwhelmingly taken up with the task of producing goods, material services, and reflective society—to a lesser degree—with the task of producing the symbolic reasons, rationalizations, and distractions, we are now moving in the direction of affording wider and wider margins of human time and intelligence for institutionalizing the personal services of healing, caring, and teaching. I am identifying this process and underscoring it not because I am tempted to distract from catastrophic dangers, grievous wrongs, and blatant failure, but to make possible a sociological estimate of the consequences of a process which we must take into account if we are to understand social change. This is not a matter of indulging in a misguided optimistic daydream, but one of engaging in a hard-headed calculation. This calculation is made so much the more timely and necessary as contemporary sociology has consistently recoiled from contemplating anything which may prejudge its alert attention to threatening catastrophes, manifest wrongs, and blatant failures.

The sociological premises I have in mind are simple, even naive, certainly not new; yet they are strangely neglected in the contemporary sociological theories of social change. These are that (1) continued scientific-technological growth is inevitable, and that (2) if we do not fatally cripple ourselves in global conflict, the growth will inevitably result in making available more and more human time and intelligence to serve the personal needs of man for the healing of his vulnerable and mortal body, for the instructing and consoling of his lonely soul, and for the training of his capabilities and skills. I am pointing to no utopia, only to a continuous process of change in the division of labor in an expanding industrial society. The thesis is that the process will go on, and that it is a legitimate sociological exercise to try to estimate its consequences. Whether this thesis will survive testing by the events of the coming decades, we cannot know, and here I shall not consider its prospects. The issue is how sociologists respond to it.

My present preoccupation is this: the personal service professional is usually trained in one of the social sciences—indeed, in sociology or social psychology—and, even in the absence of a formal training, he is exposed to the mode of thought evolved under the influence of the social sciences of today. On the one hand, we have a social science indoctrination of the professional; on the other hand, and conversely, the personal service professional is an operative in the context of human relations. His sociologically effected conceptions and his theoretical formulations will be tested in the context of practice, will be reported and interpreted in his professional papers, and will act back on the sociological conceptualizers and theory makers who erstwhile took a hand in his training. *My present attention is focused on this interaction:* the influence sociology exerts on the ideology of the personal service professions, and the influence of the ideology of the personal service professions on sociology.

The subject matter to which sociological concepts and theories ultimately refer is human conduct. The concepts and theories of sociology can be shown always to be based on some conception of human nature which is deemed to be responsible for human conduct. Take the concepts of social class and social status, for example. Here the notions could not even have come into view without a belief in the dominative and exploitive egotism, as well as the self-advancing competitiveness of man. On the other hand, take, for example, the concept of the socialization of the child. This idea could not have come into being without a belief in the child's native need for the love of those on whose succor he depends and whose succor he will, therefore, love. The sociological concepts presupposed an axiomatic affirmation of a native need for two things simultaneously: the experience of being loved and the experience of loving. Clearly, sociological thinking implicitly or explicitly postulates psychological categories, qualities, and potentials in man and all sociological theory-making is preceded by some psychological postulation. On the whole, I believe that these postulations tend to emphasize either an egotistic-dominative-exploitive-manipulative-hostile-aggressive orientation or an altruistic-cooperative-compliant-serving-helping-loving orientation in man. Most sociology to date, however, has stressed postulations about the first orientations, the negative, pessimistic, and combative orientations and neglected the positive, optimistic, and pacific orientations.

There are certain firmly entrenched facts in the situation which have fostered this emphasis on the part of sociology. The more the culture of the age of science imposes standards of rigor on our methods of inquiry and the more social science strives to comply with these standards, the more the sociologists will strive to be trenchant, perspicuous, and ruthlessly critical. To get at the truth, the sociologist will inevitably take up the stance of the inquirer into truth who anticipates and expects that people will try to deceive him: he will be in constant readiness to sweep aside misrepresentation, to tear off camouflage, to penetrate smoke screens. The result of this is that "the sociologist as a social critic is habitually engaged in exposing the seamy side of society" (Lazarsfeld et al., 1967). There is an almost invariable tendency to link analysis with devaluation, and to take discovery as if it were always disclosure. This negativism was cogently challenged by Nathan Glazer in the same volume:

> Thus when we say the sociology of religion, we mean the part that is not religion. When we say the sociology of industry, we mean the part that shows how people gum up productivity in the factory. When we say the sociology of health, we mean the part that shows that doctors and nurses are moved by prestige and status, rather than simply the needs of patients. The sociology of politics deals with the nonpolitical reasons why people act the way they do in political life. And the sociology of social science will emphasise ali the less pleasant reasons why people become scientists.

The gray mood and the unflattering anticipations are occupational afflictions of the searching sociological mind. Sociology is certainly not a *fröhliches Wissenschaft*. Of course, one ought to repeat that the very skepticism of this mood thus engendered is a product of a considerable intellectual scrupulousness. This is clearly a moral asset of an inspiring nature which contradicts the very skepticism it encourages. The positive moral qualities of this intellectual conscientiousness are rarely if ever given any credit in the *critical* sociological appraisal of man's conduct. This is an interesting anomaly which has always been characteristic of philosophical skepticism and which now makes contemporary sociology ideological in an unexpected yet strikingly obvious manner.

Terrified of failure in scholarly rigor or of the charge of sentimentalism and of complacent credulity, sociologists are found to be departing from the very objective standards which they have always considered the cornerstone of their functioning. It is this interpretation of methodological rigor as philosophical skepticism and pessimism which cannot but affect the training and practice of the personal service professional. In my earlier book, *The Faith of the Counsellors* (Halmos, 1966), I showed at some length how some social casework and psychotherapy theorists reacted to the positivism of social science by leaning on phenomenological, existentialist, and subjectivist notions about the nature of man and conceding in their own published work that some of the time they relied on faith and not on science; that is to say, in their professional practice they depended on certain beliefs about the nature of man, beliefs which were not derived from a scientific study of human conduct.

It is my belief that the social science thinking of the personal service professional will, of necessity, be always qualified by the personal and subjectivist interpretations of social reality, for this kind of interpretation is a sine qua non of sustained and dedicated personal service. This is not a moral prophecy, but an assessment of the technical requisites of these professions. I also further infer from this belief that sociology will continue to be tainted by this source, for to imagine the methodological rigors of sociology triumphing over the subjectivist concepts of the personal service professions is to imagine that the advancement of social science can, will, and should liquidate the personal contents and forms of this service. Here we are face to face with an intriguing paradox of our cultural history: more science leads to more technology, to more affluence, a wider margin of resources to be spared for personal services, more and more personal service professionals, and, presumably, these will encounter a more and more sophisticated, critical, and analytical sociology which the ideas and images of their actual practice will have to oppose. It would seem to me that the continued sharpening of this philosophical conflict has implications for those who are responsible for the training of the personal service professionals, as well as for those sociologists who are interested in the problems of social change.

The opposition of methodological stringencies to flights of imagination and gusts of aspirations to an unbound spiritual state of some kind is one source of discrepancy between sociology and the ideology of personal service. Another is that sociologists apply themselves to problems, breakdowns, and failures in society and are preoccupied with what's wrong with it. It may be that their preoccupation is an outcome of their motives for becoming sociologists; to make things better in society (the optimistic account) or to sell their services to society in order to enhance their status and income (the pessimistic account). Whichever explanation is favored, some sociologists—like book reviewers and theatre critics—fear that they are not earning their keep unless they can spot the blemishes, unless they are *critical*. The outcome is that, in viewing their own societies, they tend to confuse the aspiration to be courageously self-critical with an indulgence to be masochistically self-deprecatory. I am not putting forward an unqualified view that sociology is everywhere jaundiced or that its pessimism is not always provocative, but that one cannot maintain a problem-oriented discipline and allow space for optimistic prognoses without an anxiety that they may cast a veil over the sharpness of one's vivid diagnoses of ills and problems.

There are some other, less-publicized reasons for preoccupations with what is wrong. The major increments of sociological knowledge were secured in the past mainly on those occasions when there were idols to be toppled or prevaricators to be discredited. If revenge is sweet, sociological truth is gratifying if it can be hurled against the lying heads of oppressors, of the unjust, or of the deceivers. The truth of Marxism, for example, is dramatically enhanced by the discomfiture and shame of those who will have to let go of ill-gotten advantages because of a wider acceptance of this truth. Or, to cite another example, the intellectual triumph of those who defined the misrepresentations of a so-called "authoritarian personality" or a "closed mind," is dramatically enhanced by the relegation of these culprits to a clinical kind of existence instead of the politico-ideological rostrum which afforded them a certain amount of legitimacy and respectability. That "insight-giving" in psychotherapy, social casework, and education can be aggressive and even sadistic has been known widely. But now a so-called "critical sociology" seems to assume social purposes other than the institutionalized purposes of science; one could even say that sociology is refashioned into an instrument of self-righteousness for intellectuals who have come to distrust all except the legitimacy, status, and income of their own positions. One might even say that sociology has become *functional* in the sense of the theory of functionalism, that it makes possible the perpetuation and legitimation of a social class of increasing influence which can subsist in spite of its total disbelief in ideological rationalizations of the kind of advantages which it has and enjoys.

The history of sociology bears this out. In picking our way amidst the relics of Hobbesian and Spencerian ideas about social change, most sociologists seem to prefer the aggressive disillusionment of a Hobbes to the romantic complacency of a Spencer. Spencer's prophetic dictum, that "progress is not an accident, not a thing within human control, but a beneficent necessity" (Spencer, 1891) is a badly phrased statement which does not do full justice to the truth that is in it. But the truth—that in spite of disasters and errors, human life is longer and freer of physical constraints today for a much larger number of individuals than ever before—is manifestly true, and that it will be more so in the future is, to say the least, probable. Why should we not take this into prime account in our formulation of sociological theory about professionalization? Instead of which, as Robert Nisbet (1970) remarks about this Spencerian statement, "so many times has this passage been laughed at, treated with contempt, marked as the utterance of someone wholly blind to the miseries and mishaps around him." Lewis A. Coser says, about Max Weber, in the preface to Arthur Mitzman's book *The Iron Cage*, that his pessimistic and despairing vision of the future as an "iron cage" increasingly has come to replace images of the coming Golden Age of the perfectibility of man to which most social thought tended to cling ever since the enlightenment.

And Coser significantly adds, "The shadow of Weber's work lies over most serious attempts to come to terms with the fundamental issues of our day." Indeed, the so-called Frankfurt School of sociology has had leading members whose writings have been described as in the "depth of despair," such as those of Walter Benjamin and Theodor W. Adorno, and Jurgen Habermas calls upon sociologists to proclaim their disgust with social development altogether (Burisch, 1969). One is reminded of Galbraith's view that politics is a choice between the disastrous and unpalatable, except that for "politics" one would have to read "sociology." During the half-century between Weber and the Frankfurt School, if anything, the mood has become more skeptical and the attitude toward the future more nihilistic.

To understand another strain of influence exerted by the two belief systems—by the personal service ideology and by sociology—in opposition to each other's bias, we must remember that one of the cardinal characteristics of a personal service practitioner is that he aspires and strives to be personal, global, and synthesizing rather than analytical, manipulative, and fragmenting. The stress on the use of one's person is prominent in every area of training for the personal service professions. It is generally recognized that a neglect of this aspiration leads to professional failure or, at least, to inadequacy and an impoverishment of service. It is, therefore, not some pious hankering after a respectable moral stance which makes the professional subscribe to these standards, but the empirical test of their functional value. Naturally, this defense on the grounds of utility conceals some self-boosting increments of moral worth which may well be secured from this kind of explanation. The doctrine stated in its simplest form is that technique, skill, and knowledge are essential in practice, but without the rightly attuned use of the total personality of the practitioner there may still be failure or, at least, poor performance.

The sociological and social-psychological account of inter-personal relationships makes little or no provision for this kind of doctrine. Clearly, the usual sociological analysis of the personal functioning of the professional worker will not only be analytical and fragmenting, but it will not allow for the importation of mystical notions about the total and global personal entity. The interaction of the two belief systems—sociology and the personal service ideology—is that while sociology weakens the inspirational elements of professional experience and interpretation, the pro-fessional ideology of personal service weakens the positivistic authority of social science.

The most blatant variance between the two belief systems arises from the professional workers' pretense that they do not manipulate other persons. It is little realized that this implies an attempt at suspending the operation of the causal law. The personal service professional protests that what he does for a client, patient, pupil, or student is done to assist the other person to evolve in his own self-chosen direction and mode, and that his course of professional actions do not make, direct or determine—that is to say, cause—changes in the life of the other which the other would not have chosen himself. Those who administer personal help maintain a fiction of moral neutrality, the fiction that they merely lend themselves to be the means whereby the other will enable himself to follow an independently and freely chosen path. These beliefs are mostly in evidence in social casework and psychotherapy, but they have also spilled over into education and some aspects of health administration as well. The logical fallacy is quickly pointed out by the positivistic sociologi-cal mind: if the helping intervention does not effect a change, then it is useless; if it does, then it causes a result which would not otherwise have come to pass. Insofar as this is foreseen and predictable, the helping agent must be taken to proceed with the intention to effect a result and cause a result to be brought about.

Sometimes even doctors invoke the self-healing and homeostatic qualities of the organism; teachers, of course, diligently stress the "educing" and "drawing-out" function of the educator who, at his best, merely "brings out" what is best in the pupil: the nondirectiveness of the social worker and of the psychotherapist rounds out the picture of this element, the notion of a moratorium from causality. The effect of this notion on sociology is that it weakens its positivistic hold on social study; the impact of sociology on the personal service ideology is that it weakens fantasies of unsullied integrity in dealing with other inviolate persons and inviolate privacies.

Yet another and perhaps equally universal characteristic of the personal service practitioners in health, welfare, and education is that they could not function without a belief in the possibility that the condition of man can be bettered. One might advance the view that a totally stoical, let alone skeptical or even cynical, doctor, nurse, teacher, or social worker could not be conceived as a model of professional excellence. Of course, the surgeon who does not meet his patient except when the latter is unconscious may be cited as an exception. Or the behavior therapist may be quoted, for it is claimed that he manipulates and does not address his patients personally. But, clearly, no surgeon could maintain his true professional efficiency without replenishing and reinforcing his global-sympathetic attitudes to patients by periodically return-ing to personal contact with them. Nor does the behavior therapist tell us the whole truth: in his impersonal technology, he takes his personal presence for granted, and then he discounts it altogether. Indeed, a personal and intimate humanism can be observed to prevail in professional practice of this kind when that practice is working satisfactorily—that is, when it does achieve its stated objectives.

But how does sociology view this component of the inter-personal process in the personal service professions? After all, "betterment" is extraneous to a sociology which is committed to the doctrine of being *wertfrei*! A *wertfrei* ideology of personal service is a contradiction in terms, and a positivistic sociological discipline can hardly be instrumental in maintaining a belief system which makes personal professional practice possible. Yet it is also a conclusion of the positivistic sociological discipline that the continued functioning of society, especially under conditions of expanding technology and material affluence, makes the diversification and radical extension of personal service institutions of society indispensable. And even so, the categorical and logical premises of this positivistic discipline militate against the emergence and survival of a body of ideas which would make some of the vital images and assumptions of a personal service viable and credible.

The highlighting of the anomaly which concerns me here is so much the more important that it does not appear to be any less in evidence in communist countries than it is in capitalist ones. No matter what sort of economic-political-social institutions are created to incorporate the services in health, education, and welfare, at the end of the day the professional services will have to be rendered by persons to persons, and these services require the cultivation of certain preconceptions about them which social science is not equipped to furnish, but rather attuned to undermine with skepticism.

In focusing on this divergence in our cultural history, it will be objected that I have introduced a note of overoptimism about the nature of man and that I am postulating certain extravagantly favorable attributes both in the practicing professionals and in people in general. Surely, the enlightened egoism of man will suffice to regulate the ramifications of personal service. There is no need to invoke implausibly selfless principles, such as, for example, some sort of a "total personal service" to others. In pointing to the aspirations of the personal service professionals, one may ignore their ambitions, their striving for status and income. A *critical* sociology has no time for considering my rosy alternatives. One important effect of this etiquette is that sociologists will be reluctant to go back to the so-called "progress theories" of social change, or to the theories which establish the progressive realization in social change of some explicitly stated system of desired values.

To conceal their ideological negativism, such spokesmen for critical sociology declare that they accept, not reject, individual, human compassion, but what does this "acceptance" mean? Surely, it must be accepted as one of the operative principles of social change; otherwise, the "acceptance" is meaningless. But having paid lip service to the moral principle, they see no reason why as scientists of social change they should consider the implications of this acceptance. Would it not be only logical to maintain that even if the financial and economic realities do not, the social realities do *include* the reality of compassion? For if they do, then it would be no less than reasonable to object to the sociology which obstinately encourages the financial, the economic, and the power factors of social life to distract from the role of compassion in social change! At any rate, to insist that the matter be considered and included in our theory-making about professionalization and social change is not the same as to insist that compassion is a sufficient explanatory principle in these.

I have sought to draw attention to the kind of influence on sociology which issues from the rather narrower group of those who practice in the fields of health, education, and welfare in modern industrial societies, the personal service professionals. I am interested in what influence these groups can and will exert on our thinking about human relationships, and, perforce, on sociology. As will have been gathered by now, I hypothesize that this influence is not insignificant and that it is inevitably in the direction of a prelogical kind of thinking. We already have empirical evidence to support the claim that the personal service professions cannot function effectively without an aspirational imagery, which is personal. This imagery imaginatively sees the transcendence of the reality in which it operates by affirming ideals and by ennobling the hard realities of life. It seems to me that so long as personal service must transcend the positivistic philosophy which forms a basis of sociology, we must, as sociologists, face this paradoxical condition and appraise the paradox itself sociologically.

Sociology's reaction to this has been, at least so far, an overreaction. For his anxiety to ward off mystification which may come from the aspiring professional practitioners, the sociologist discounts all that may appear to him a flattering impression of civilized man. It seems axiomatic to him that the truth cannot be flattering and, therefore, what is flattering cannot be true. The sociologist has not as yet realized that this is a doctrinaire position and not a scientific one. It arises in the face of professionalization, but professionalization is not to be blamed for it: sociology is. In this area, sociology has confused skepticism with objectivity and has thus fallen short of objectivity. And so, for the time being at least, the interaction between a personal service ideology, on the one hand, and sociology, on the other, could be described as mutually inhibiting.

REFERENCES

BURISCH, W. (1969) "Jurgen Habermas and the 'Frankfurt School of critical theory of society'." Presented at the Annual Meeting of the British Sociological Association.

COSER, L. A. (1970) "Preface," pp. v-vi in Arthur Mitzman, The Iron Cage. New York: Alfred A. Knopf.

HALMOS, P. (1970) The Personal Service Society. London: Constable, New York: Schocken.

––– (1966) The Faith of the Counsellors. London: Constable, New York: Schocken.

LAZARSFELD, P. F., W. H. SEWELL, and H. L. WILENSKY [eds.] (1967) The Uses of Sociology. New York: Basic Books.

NISBET, A. R. (1970) Social Change and History. London: Oxford Univ. Press.

SPENCER, H. (1891) Essays Scientific, Political and Speculative. New York.

Chapter 16

SOCIOLOGISTS AND THEIR KNOWLEDGE
Some Critical Remarks on a Profession

DEREK L. PHILLIPS

In recent years, sociology has become increasingly more popular and more respectable as an established field of study for college students. Even high school students are being introduced to sociology. This proliferation of sociology into the colleges and high schools is assumed to be a good thing, at least insofar as it helps to develop the quality of mind that C. Wright Mills (1959: 7) termed "the sociological imagination":

> the capacity to shift from one perspective to another—from the political to the psychological; from examination of a single family to comparative assessment of the national budgets of the world; from the theological school to the military establishment; from considerations of an oil industry to studies of contemporary poetry.[1]

But it is not only students who are increasingly receptive to sociologists and sociological thought, for sociology is seen as making significant contributions to other sectors of the society as well. As is noted by Smelser and Davis (1969: 116-117):

Author's Note: *I wish to thank Eliot Freidson for his many helpful comments and criticisms on earlier drafts of this paper.*

"Sociologists are being hired in greater numbers by government agencies, businesses, hospitals, and other organizations. They are summoned more frequently on vital public issues. And they find themselves quoted more often in the public media as experts on one issue or another." Horowitz (1968: 262) observes that the social sciences "have in recent times begun to play a new and problematic role with respect to national and international policy. The problem of social policy has become acute precisely to the extent to which social science has become exact." Sociologists not only are employed by governmental and other organizations in increasing numbers, but also serve on presidential commissions (such as the President's Advisory Commission on Civil Disorders) and in other high advisory posts. Obviously, then, it is assumed that the sociologist has something important to contribute. Lazarsfeld and his associates in their book, *The Uses of Sociology* (1967: x-xi), state the following:

> The sociologist can play a variety of roles in relation to the client: he can share whatever general wisdom he has acquired; he can do a special study; he can sensitize personnel to sociological orientations. Sometimes he will assume the stance of general social critic. The sociologist has at his disposal a variety of *resources*. He has developed concepts and empirical generalizations, and sometimes theories. His techniques and experience are needed for specific studies—custom-tailored to the problem at hand. Finally, like all experts, he has encountered other situations seemingly very different from those in which the client finds himself which provide unexpected analogies—a major way to broaden the range of alternatives policy-makers perceive.

The sociologist, rather than being viewed as a cloistered scholar, is now seen as a professional, an expert whose knowledge and advice are considered sufficiently valuable to be worth soliciting and applying to contemporary social issues.

However, sociologists differ among themselves on the question of the application of sociological knowledge. Some sociologists are hostile or indifferent to the application of the field to issues of a policy nature; others feel that sociology should be applied to the benefit of one or another group in society; still others argue that sociologists should speak out as "experts" whether or not they are involved in a specific consulting or advisory capacity. Recent years have seen a whole host of articles raising questions about the relevance of sociology, its impact on the society, value-free sociology, and issues of partisanship (see, for example, Becker, 1967; Gouldner, 1962, 1968, 1970; Tumin, 1968).[2] Whatever side one takes on these issues, it seems perfectly obvious to me that sociologists will continue to become more and more involved in trying to solve a great variety of societal problems. And sociologists will come to occupy increasing positions of influence, as they continue to gain access to the corridors of power in American society

THE ROLE OF SOCIOLOGY

No matter what their position on how sociology should be used, the assumption among almost all sociologists seems to be that the profession possesses a unique and valuable body of "knowledge" or expertise. The quarrels and divisions in the field do not center around knowledge, but rather around whether or not this knowledge should be put to work, and if so, for whom. At the 1968 meetings of the American Sociological Association, Martin Nicolaus, a member of the Sociology Liberation Movement, addressed some highly critical remarks to the assembled audience of sociologists. Nicolaus described the sociological researcher as a "kind of spy," and observed (Nicolaus, 1969: 155), "The more adventurous sociologists don the disguise of the people and go out to mix with the peasants in the 'field,' returning with the books and articles that break the protective secrecy in which a subjugated population wraps itself, and make it more accessible to manipulation and control." Nicolaus, then, was accusing sociologists of taking knowledge from the people and giving it to the rulers. Nicolaus (1969: 155) went on to ask:

What if the machinery were reversed? What if the habits, problems, actions, and decision of the wealthy and powerful were daily scrutinized by a thousand systematic researchers, were hourly pried into, analyzed, and cross-referenced, tabulated, and published in a hundred mass-circulated journals and written so that even the fifteen-year-old high school drop-out could understand it and predict the actions of their [sic] parents' landlord, manipulate and control *him?*

I have no strong quarrel with Nicolaus' assertions that sociologists are the servants of the power structure, for I generally share that view. But I do differ with him in regard to his belief that sociologists actually know something important that could be used to the advantage of those in power and against what he calls the "occupied populace." That is, it is one thing to argue that sociologists (knowingly or unknowingly) serve to legitimate the decisions of some power elite, and quite another to argue that they use knowledge which actually enhances that power. I would not have expected a young radical sociologist to share with the sociological elite the belief that sociologists possess some unique body of knowledge that can be put to the use of one or another segment of the society. Reflecting on Nicolaus' remarks, however, I have come to realize that his assumption is shared by numerous other sociologists in the radical tradition: for example, C. Wright Mills, Alvin Gouldner, Irving Louis Horowitz, and Robert Lynd. More than thirty years ago, Lynd published his famous *Knowledge for What?* in which he chastised his fellow social scientists for their unwillingness to utilize their "knowledge" for the betterment of mankind. He argued that in many instances social scientists already possessed the knowledge necessary to bring about certain societal benefits. Considering the matter of war, for example, Lynd (1964: 241) asserted that "The causes of war are known and accepted by a wide group of thoughtful students." As we know, Lynd felt that there were other areas of societal concern where the social scientist had a special expertise.

By this time in the essay, it should be obvious that I do not share the views of Robert Lynd, or Martin Nicolaus, or, in fact, the vast majority of sociologists. For I see no corpus of sociological knowledge that is unique to sociology. Although the majority seem to believe that the efficacy of sociology is already established, there are some writers who have questioned this assumption. For instance, while almost all of the discussions regarding Project Camelot revolved around the propriety of the project, there were some who raised questions about the existence or creation of some body of sociological knowledge. Horowitz (1968: 298) points out that "No public document or statement contested the possibility that, given a successful completion of the data-gathering, Camelot could have, indeed, established basic criteria for measuring the level and potential for internal war in a given nation." And Tilly (1966) noted that the project was "in a field in which the most recent symposium—Harry Eckstein's *Internal War*—had displayed almost no established uniformities and no agreement whatsoever on theory, method, or likely hypotheses."

Clearly, it is not unreasonable to raise the question of how good sociological knowledge actually is. But what is the meaning of the term "knowledge"? Webster's (1964: 809) provides a number of definitions:

> 1. the act, fact, or state of knowing; specifically, a) acquaintance or familiarity (with a fact, place, etc.), b) awareness, c) understanding.
> 2. acquaintance with facts; range of information, awareness, or understanding. 3. all that has been perceived or grasped by the mind; learning; enlightenment. 4. the body of facts accumulated by mankind.

This is indeed a confusing array of definitions, but it probably reflects rather accurately the great variety of usages of the term by social scientists.

In considering this matter of "knowledge," I find myself in agreement with Meehan (1968: 15) who notes that: "At the most fundamental level, knowledge is organized experience and the search for knowledge is a search for patterns of organization." The knowledge possessed by one or another social science, then, consists of the organized experiences of men that have been assembled or accumulated so that they are publicly available. In this sense, all of the social sciences possess knowledge. It seems clear, therefore, that the only way by which sociologists can evaluate the adequacy of their knowledge is in terms of how useful it is for a specific purpose. In the social sciences, the major purpose of knowledge is taken to be the providing of *explanations* of various social phenomena. Judgments concerning the adequacy of the knowledge possessed by sociologists, consequently, have to be made on the basis of their abilities to explain the social phenomena that concern them. While most sociologists are in agreement that the goal of inquiry is explanation, there is no firm consensus as to exactly what this means. But it is possible to locate some of the ways in which sociologists speak of explanation.

THE ACCURACY OF DATA

With many of the explanations in sociology, evaluations as to their adequacy are made in terms of their providing new information or new insights about various events and situations, descriptions of what happened, or understanding regarding the relations of various social phenomena to other social phenomena. In many instances, the attempt is to "account" for an event or other social phenomenon. The goal is to provide a conceptual scheme or framework in which the phenomenon is "plausible" or "makes sense." A problem with such criteria is that we do not have any agreed-upon bases for judging whether or not various investigators have accomplished their goals. For instance, how do we determine whether or not an explanation is insightful or plausible? How do we determine whether or not studies provide "good" explanations?

Consider, for instance, the controversies surrounding Lewis' (1951) replication of Redfield's (1930) Tepoztlan study. Whereas Redfield, in his conclusions, stressed the extent of integration in the community, Lewis emphasized the strains and stresses existing there. What, then, do we "know" about Tepoztlan? Whose explanation of life in the community do we accept? And on what basis do we decide? Or consider Riesman's (1950) *The Lonely Crowd,* and the criticisms of his conclusions by other social scientists (Lipset and Lowenthal, 1961). Clearly, what constitutes a plausible explanation for one social scientist may not be persuasive to some of his brethren. It is extremely difficult, therefore, to reach any definite conclusions regarding the adequacy of many explanations in the social sciences. There are simply no agreed-upon criteria for making judgments as to whether explanations of the type just discussed are adequate or inadequate.

However, we are in a somewhat better position to locate the criteria for judging the adequacy of explanations among those sociologists who place a heavy emphasis on *explanation* (in a particular sense) and *prediction.* For instance, Smelser (1969: 13-14) asserts that: "Explanation . . . begins with the search for *independent variables* (or causes, or determinants, or factors, or conditions), to which variations in the dependent variables are referred." And Coleman (1969: 107) states that "one of the important fruits of sociological investigations should be its ability to predict."

One way of ascertaining whether those stressing explanation and prediction have accomplished their goals is to consider the amount of *variance* in their dependent variables which investigators are able to account for by their principle independent variables. The aim, of course, is to find a relatively small number of variables that will "explain" the variation in many other variables. The variance in one variable is said to be "explained" by another to the extent that the variables covary or correlate. Here we find that the evidence concerning the extent to which certain sociological variables are able to explain the variations in other variables is rather unimpressive. For example, L. K. Miller (cited in Hamblin, 1966) examined the results of all studies published in the first three issues of *American Sociological Review* in the year 1961, and found that the average "significant" relationship explained about ten percent of the variance. Psychologists have been similarly unsuccessful in their attempts to account for much variance. For instance, Robert Rosenthal (1966: 110) estimates that most behavioral research accounts for something like thirteen percent of the variance by our independent variables. Clearly, an ability to account for only ten or thirteen or even twenty percent of the variance is not very impressive and does not lead to a high degree of predictive ability.[3]

Given the difficulties and problems concerning sociological explanations, what, then, can be said about the "generalizations" which many social scientists regard as the highest product of their inquiries? Although many social scientists seem reluctant to admit it, we seem, in fact, to have been unable to provide generalizations that explain very much of the social behavior in which we are interested. While there are indeed hundreds, if not thousands, of generalizations abounding in the literature of the social sciences, the vast number are either unconfirmed in empirical research or else are of such minor magnitude in explaining any observable facts as to be of little utility. The psychologist Robert Sears (1951: 466) has noted that "an appallingly small number of the relationships that have been discovered in social psychology can be generalized . . . . With respect to attitude measurement, for example, one might ask whether *any* general principles of an antecedent-consequent nature have been found." And the sociologist William F. Whyte (1969: 22) relates that "years ago the late Louis Wirth used to terrify Ph.D. candidates by requiring them to name *one* proposition that had been reasonably well-supported by research data." In my view, contemporary sociologists (and I suspect, most social scientists) would be as hard-pressed as the students of Wirth's era to name one such proposition.

While there are many reasons for this state of affairs, one way of considering them is to look more closely at what constitutes an "explanation." We find that sociologists variously speak of having "explained" something when they have provided descriptions, insights, plausible interpretations, when they have established correlations or empirical interrelationships, or when they are able to successfully predict. Although the issues surrounding explanation are far too complex to be dealt with adequately here,[4] I think it is useful to offer some further thoughts on explanations in sociology.

Clearly a description of the phenomenon being investigated is a necessary part of any explanation; we need to know *what* happened, what are the facts to be explained. In addition to the description of a phenomenon (the *what*), we require an interpretation of it; we need to know *why* it happens or occurs. We need to account for or make sense of the phenomenon under investigation. Some sociologists argue that they have accomplished an interpretation if they can provide a set of general statements or some conceptual framework from which one can generate, or to which one can relate, a correlation or other description. Unfortunately, there is a good deal of vagueness in the sociological literature as to what is meant by a "conceptual framework" or a "set of general statements."

When both description and interpretation are combined, we have what some would regard as a "complete explanation" (DiRenzo, 1966): an explanation saying not only what happens but why it happens as well. Linking the "what" and the "why" is essential, then, if we are to have complete explanations. Obviously not all sociologists are explicitly concerned with complete explanations in the sense described above. But I think that the great majority are concerned with either the "whats" or the "whys." That is, many sociologists are concerned primarily with establishing the "facts"—descriptions of various social phenomena. This is essentially the goal of many who engage in empirical research. Although the researcher does often attempt to provide fuller explanations for some facts, frequently the "whys" are left to those who call themselves "theorists." Clearly, however, both the researcher and the theorist require that the facts to be explained (the whats) are in good order. Whether a sociologist is interested in consumer attitudes, seasonal variations in cotton prices in various parts of the world, socialization processes, the workings of the Supreme Court, the relationship between educational level and voting preferences, patterns of religious behavior, or the ideological origins of American thought, he is dependent on the *adequacy of his data.* Whether the "data" come from interviews, questionnaires, observations, records, documents, archival materials, or whatever, the sociologist must assure that his evidence is valid. Should there be serious questions about the facts to be explained, there is little reason for trying to determine how or why they came about. Therefore a necessary, but insufficient, condition for a complete explanation is that the facts be established.

Many sociologists assume that the facts have been determined and that what we need to do is account for the "whys." In my view, however, the accuracy of the facts to be explained is often subject to considerable question. For example, Price, in his book *Social Facts: Introductory Readings,* asserts that: "Facts are empirically verifiable statements about social phenomena. For example, it is a fact that the suicide rate in the United States in 1962 was 10.8 per 100,000 population" (Price, 1969: iv). If we accept Price's assertion that this is a fact, then we might want to move on to speculate (or discover) why this rate is higher or lower than the rate in some other country. But is it a fact? I think not, for as Douglas (1967), among others, has so clearly shown, the "operational definition" of a suicide differs both among and within societies. In a very real sense, various bureaucratic officials may determine who is classified as a suicide, and they do so in a variety of different ways. A recent television newscast in New York City noted that 1,100 persons in the city died within the last year as a result of overdoses of barbiturates. One-half of them were classified as "suicides." Who made the decision on suicides, on what basis, for what reasons? Need the deceased have left a note, appeared depressed, or what? Clearly, then, there is considerable reason to be skeptical about Price's fact regarding the suicide rate in the United States. Consequently, the spinning of theories to explain how or why this fact came about may be an exercise in futility.

Consider two other areas of interest to sociological investigators where attempts have been made to validate the facts (as indicated by people's responses to interviews) by examining information contained in various records: voting studies and studies of health and illness. Bell and Buchanan (1956) found that 30% of the respondents in a "general population" gave inaccurate replies to a question on voting; Parry and Crossley (1950) found that 23% of their respondents said they had voted when they actually had not done so; and Cahalan (1968) reports that 28% of the respondents in Denver exaggerated their vote in the 1947 mayoralty election. A study by Cannell and Fowler (1963), concerned with the accuracy of health information, revealed considerable discrepancies between people's reports to interviewers and the hospital records: 58% of the respondents in their study gave inaccurate reports concerning their length of stay in the hospital, 23% were inaccurate with regard to the month of discharge, 35% with regard to diagnosis, 25% with regard to type of surgery, and 10% were inaccurate in their reports as to whether or not surgery had even been performed.

Another area where sociological knowledge is based on people's reports of their behavior is that concerning birth control information and usage. Numerous surveys have been conducted to ascertain "the facts" about the use of various contraceptive devices. People's responses to inquiries about the use of these devices have generally been assumed to be valid, and widespread generalizations have been made on this basis. Recently, however, Green (1969) reported an investigation concerned with the validity of the responses given and the actual *behavior* of respondents regarding the use and knowledge of contraceptives in East Pakistan. The data included both direct and behavioral information (from the clinic and education program records) and the verbal reports of behavior from respondents. It was found that people underreported both their use and knowledge of contraceptives, although they were less reluctant to admit knowledge of family planning methods than they were to admit that they used the methods. About one out of five men and one out of four women who (according to the records) knew of contraceptives denied knowledge of them. Of all couples who had used contraceptives (again, according to the records), about one out of every five husbands and one out of every three wives denied ever having used them.[5]

Since the bulk of the sociological data used for analyzing "causes" comes from interviews and questionnaires, unrecognized inaccuracies become part of the basic facts on which explanation is based. Consider, as a possibly more widespread source of inaccuracy, the United States Census—a source of data for a large number of sociologists. Cannell and Kahn (1968: 527) remark on the U.S. Census as follows:

Perhaps the prototypical example of research interviews is provided by the national census. Most countries of the world conduct some kind of population count, and in many countries the census has been expanded to provide with regularity an inventory of social resources and problems. Census interviewers usually make only modest demands on interviewer and respondent. They are brief; they ask for *demographic data well within the respondent's knowledge and not of a kind which he is likely to regard as confidential.* Moreover, the information is requested under circumstances familiar to or expected by most respondents, and the request is backed by the legitimate power of the national government [italics added].

According to Cannell and Kahn, then, census data secured through research interviews are obtained under almost idyllic conditions. Unfortunately, though, there has been very little evidence pertaining to the extent of accuracy in census reports.

There is available, however, a recent study which sheds considerable light on this matter. Hambright (1969) reports on an investigation where a sample of death certificates was matched with the 1960 census reports, thus allowing for a comparison of response data for items asked on both records. The data on the two reports were compared for the same persons, with inconsistencies between the two resulting from errors on either death or census records, although there was no way of determining where the errors lay. Hambright (1969: 419) found a very low extent (less than 3%) of "disagreement" with regard to color and nativity. But for age and marital status, the disagreements were more considerable. Even when people's ages were compared in terms of ten-year intervals (Hambright, 1969: 417), there was disagreement for 8.1% of white males and 11.4% of white females, and 23.8% for Negro males and 30.3% for Negro females. Disagreements for marital status were even larger in magnitude. For instance, the two sets of records failed to coincide in terms of the "single" status of 9.0% of white respondents and 21.6% of Negro respondents. With the category of "divorced," the records were in disagreement with the reports of 26.5% of the whites and 42.4% of the Negroes.

It seems obvious, then, that people's reports concerning data "well within the respondent's knowledge and not of a kind which he is likely to regard as confidential" (Cannell and Kahn, 1968: 527) are subject to considerable inaccuracy.[6] This being the case, we should not be surprised to find extreme inaccuracies in reports of other social phenomena.

If inaccuracies in people's verbal reports (or any other sources of data) are disproportionately distributed in certain segments or subgroups of the population, this would raise questions about the validity of certain relationships between the social scientist's independent and dependent variables. Not only are there inaccuracies with regard to voting, health care utilization, and the like, but these may be related to the independent variables which we utilize to explain certain facts. An example of this is the often-demonstrated inverse relationship between social-class position and F-scale authoritarianism, anomia, and prejudice (e.g., McDill, 1961, Roberts and Rokeach, 1956, Srole, 1956). That is, authoritarianism, anomia, and prejudice are found to be more characteristic of the lower than of the upper classes. Christie (1954) has suggested that the apparent social-class differences in authoritarianism may be due to intelligence or acquiescence rather than to actual differences in social class. And Kirscht and Dillehay (1967: 38-39) have noted that many studies

> included potential response biases as most items were worded so that agreement indicated intolerance, anomia, or the other variables tested. Probably some of the responses were due to the tendency of relatively unsophisticated subjects to respond favorably to "high-sounding aphorisms."

It also seems likely that more sophisticated respondents may be less likely to endorse items such as those on the F-scale.[7] Similar factors affect studies of prejudice. Stember (1961: 170) points out that items which are crude in nature may bypass the educated, and perhaps this is why "results of questions expressing extreme positions ... have so often indicated a negative relationship between prejudice and education. When the issues are posed in more neutral terminology, no such relationship is evidenced."

Some of the same problems of response bias may exist in the study of mental illness (which, by the way, Szasz and others would say does not even exist as something to be explained) as it related to social class. Clancy and I (Phillips and Clancy, 1970) have presented some evidence to suggest that the association between scores on a mental health inventory and social-class position may be due partially to the class-linked influence of another kind of response set—social desirability. My point here is that the discovery of an inverse relationship between social class and authoritarianism, anomia, prejudice, or mental illness can be taken at face value only if the measures of these variables (and the results of the measurement process) are reasonably valid. If, as appears possible, these various social phenomena are not really class-related, why spend time inventing one or another explanation to deal with *how and why* these (perhaps spurious) relationships came about? In my view, sociologists spend a disproportionate amount of time and energy trying to account for what may be nonexistent "facts" and nonexistent relationships.

But what if it were possible to establish with only a small degree of error the validity of our measures? What if the facts are beyond dispute? Are we then on more solid ground? Certainly we are in a better position to proceed, but even here the problems are formidable. Imagine that we have valid measures of our independent and dependent variables and that, furthermore, we have established an extremely high (statistical) relationship between them. This does not in itself constitute an explanation. Rather a correlation is also a description—a fact to be explained. The fact itself does not serve as an explanation of anything at all. Thus, even if we have valid measures and strong associations between our variables (neither of which exists at present), the sociologist is still faced with the problem of making sense or accounting for these facts. That is, he must interpret these facts. The nature of the interpretation which he provides will, of necessity, be determined by his own (frequently hidden) models of man, experiences in society, interests, persuasions, and so on. Given this state of affairs, there might be almost as many different interpretations of some demonstrated relationships as there are sociological orientations (or even, sociologists). How, then, can we choose among varying interpretations even when we have the facts straight? Clearly, this is a difficult problem, but one we must face and one to which some sociologists (e.g., Doby, 1969) have addressed themselves.[8]

IMPLICATIONS

What I have been arguing is that much of the evidence utilized by sociologists is of questionable validity; that, furthermore, the relationships between our chief independent and dependent variables are generally quite weak; and, finally, that even if we had valid measures and strong relationships the problems of interpretation are extremely formidable. Although I may have overstated my case, let me suggest only two implications of my remarks— which, I believe, follow even if I am only partially correct.

First of all, we may be passing on to our students and colleagues a great deal of misinformation (as with the example of Price's facts concerning suicide, cited earlier) if our measures are lacking in validity. Recently, both Blalock and Hauser have remarked on measurement problems in sociology. Blalock (1969: 115) observes that "certain kinds of inadequacies in our measurement procedures may very well provide the major obstacle to be overcome if sociology is to mature in the direction of becoming a 'hard' and disciplined social science." And Hauser (1969) asserts that the problem of adequate measurement is *the* major block to progress in sociological research. Speaking specifically of survey data, Hauser (1969: 127) states: "I believe that it is at least a moot point as to whether, up to this point in the use of survey results, more misinformation than information has been gathered on many subjects." Obviously I share Hauser's view and would generalize it to other modes of data collection. Thus, we may be unwittingly generating a good deal of misinformation which eventually finds its way into the hundreds of research reports and dozens of monographs and textbooks which are forthcoming yearly from the members of the sociological profession.

Secondly, and perhaps ultimately more important to the lives of all of us, this misinformation with regard to the "what" of social life may serve to create certain "social realities" which, as we all know, may be real in their consequences. I offer an example taken from some remarks put forth by Milton Rosenberg (1967: 152) who points out:

There is now good reason to believe that a major contaminant operates in polls on matters of foreign policy. Many respondents who are essentially apathetic on foreign policy issues, who lack awareness of the very existence of some of these issues, may well characterize themselves invalidly when asked how they regard, say, the admission of Communist China into the U.N., wheat shipments to the Soviet Union, scientific cooperation with the Soviet Union, or even resumption of diplomatic relations with Cuba. More precisely, they are prone to report themselves as far more resistant than they actually are toward the mounting and execution of such conciliatory policies.

If, as Rosenberg suggests, public opinion polls show people to be more "hard-line" than they actually are, and if, as there is good reason to believe, the policy elite takes public opinion poll results into account when they formulate foreign policy, then such misinformation may have the very real consequence of leading to even harder-line positions on the part of the government.[9]

Of course, misinformation may also result in what some of us would regard as more positive consequences.[10] For example, there may sometimes be a social desirability response bias operating in opinion polls pertaining to racial prejudice, with the result that people report themselves as far *less* resistant to certain changes in legislation pertaining to racial equality than they actually are. Thus, certain changes in the law might result from such misinformation. This may, indeed, have been the case in the North in recent years, while exactly the opposite may have occurred in the South. After all, social norms operate in survey and public-opinion polls, as well as in the rest of society. That is, there may be deflection of self-characterizing attitude reports (and consequent invalidity) toward a perceived consensus. With regard to issues of foreign policy, Rosenberg (1967: 152-153) has suggested that such deflection may be "fostered by such varied factors as uncertainty and anxiety over the possibility that the public opinion interview is some kind of disguised test of loyalty; [and] embarrassment that one's basic apathy toward foreign issues will earn the interviewer's disapproval."[11]

Let me acknowledge that much of the above is conjectural and problematic, but no more so than some of the social phenomena which many sociologists regard as "facts" to be explained. Certainly I do not mean to suggest that sociologists (or other social scientists) should stop work and close up shop. What I am arguing is that perhaps we should devote a good deal less attention to issues of how and for whom we should apply our knowledge, and give greater recognition to the importance of distinguishing the various shades and levels involved in our knowledge. At present, there is much that passes for knowledge in the rhetoric of sociology, and frequently this so-called knowledge is used by privileged elites, and sometimes by radicals, to provide a façade of rationality for their actions.[1][2] We must direct our skepticism inward at ourselves as well as toward those whom we study. Berger (1963) and others have suggested that the first wisdom of sociology is that "things are not what they seem." What I have suggested is that this may be as true for the discipline of sociology as for the rest of the world which we take as our subject matter. It is our responsibility as sociologists to acknowledge that, like others, there is much that we do not know about the social world. While it is true that "you don't need a weatherman to know how the wind blows," it sometimes helps.

NOTES

1. Mills acknowledged that the term "sociological imagination" could easily be replaced by the term "anthropological" or "political" imagination, or some other term, and that he was not speaking merely of the academic discipline of sociology. Therefore, it seems to be that many of the claims made for sociology by such writers as Bierstedt (1964) are excessive and misleading. Bressler (1967) has made a similar criticism.

2. For two excellent collections of papers on these matters, see Douglas (1970a, 1970b).

3. Dunnette (1966) has reached a similar conclusion with regard to explained variance in psychological investigations.

4. Some of these issues are considered at length in the results of a symposium on the theme, "Conceptual Definitions in the Behavioral Sciences," which has been published as a collection of essays edited by DiRenzo (1966).

5. A more complete review of these studies is found in Phillips (1971).

6. An alternative explanation is that those supplying information about the deceased (next-of-kin and friends) simply do not know the details of marriage and age concerning people close to them. This probably accounts for some of the discrepancies

in the two reports, although I would think these others would have been as familiar with the marital status of the deceased as with their nativity. But even the idea that those supplying the information do not know people's ages and details of marriage has implications for some sociological research, especially that concerned with "proxy" reports by certain individuals regarding details about the characteristics and behavior of other family members (as is the case, of course, in the U.S. Census).

7. Also, see Miller and Riessman (1961).

8. I have tried to deal with these issues elsewhere (Phillips, 1971).

9. It does not, of course, stop there. There is a continuing interplay between public opinion and policy decisions.

10. The best-known instance where this may have occurred is in the Supreme Court's decision in *Brown* v. *Board of Education*. See, for instance, Garfinkel (1970).

11. Of interest in this regard is another paper by Rosenberg, where he considers several different processes thay may be involved in moving individuals toward false or exaggerated self-reports (Rosenberg, 1965). Also, see Phillips (1971).

12. As Freidson (1970) has so clearly argued, medicine and other "professions" are subject to the same charge.

REFERENCES

BECKER, H. S. (1967) "Whose side are we on?" Social Problems 14 (Winter): 239-247.

BELL, C. G. and W. BUCHANAN (1956) "Reliable and unreliable respondents: party registration and prestige pressure." Western Pol. Q. 29 (Spring): 37-43.

BERGER, P. L. (1963) Invitation to Sociology: A Humanistic Perspective. New York: Doubleday Anchor.

BIERSTEDT, R. (1964) "Sociology and general education," in C. H. Page (ed.) Sociology and Contemporary Education. New York: Random House.

BLALOCK, H. M. (1969) "Comments on Coleman's paper," in R. Bierstedt (ed.) A Design for Sociology: Scope, Objectives, and Methods. Philadelphia: American Academy of Political and Social Science.

BRESSLER, M. (1967) "Sociology and collegiate general education," in P. F. Lazarsfeld et al. (eds.) The Uses of Sociology. New York: Basic Books.

CAHALAN, D. (1968) "Correlates of respondent accuracy in the Denver validity survey." Public Opinion Q. 32 (Winter): 607-621.

CANNELL, C. F. and F. J. FOWLER (1963) "Comparison of a self-enumerative procedure and a personal interview: a validity study." Public Opinion Q. 27 (Summer): 250-264.

CANNELL, C. F. and R. L. KAHN (1968) "Interviewing," in G. Lindzey and E. Aronson (eds.) The Handbook of Social Psychology. Volume II. Reading, Mass.: Addison-Wesley.

CHRISTIE, R. (1954) "Authoritarianism re-examined," in R. Christie and M. Jahoda (eds.) Studies in the Scope and Method of "The Authoritarian Personality." Glencoe, Ill.: Free Press.

COLEMAN, J. S. (1969) "The methods of sociology," in R. Bierstedt (ed.) A Design for Sociology: Scope, Objectives, and Methods. Philadelphia: American Academy of Political and Social Science.

DiRENZO, G. J [ed.] (1966) Concepts, Theory and Explanation in the Behavioral Sciences. New York: Random House.

DOBY, J. T. (1969) "Logic and levels of scientific explanation," in E. F. Borgotta (ed.) Sociological Methodology. San Francisco: Jossey-Boss.

DOUGLAS, J. D. [ed.] (1970a) The Impact of Sociology. New York: Appleton-Century-Crofts.

––– [ed.] (1970b) The Relevance of Sociology. New York: Appleton-Century-Crofts.

––– (1967) The Social Meaning of Suicide. Princeton: Princeton Univ. Press.

DUNNETTE, M. D. (1966) "Fads, fashions, and folderol in psychology." Amer. Psychologist 21 (April): 343-352.

FREIDSON, E. (1970) Profession of Medicine. New York: Dodd, Mead.

GARFINKEL, H. (1970) "Social science evidence and the school segregation cases," in J. D. Douglas (ed.) The Impact of Sociology. New York: Appleton-Century-Crofts.

GOULDNER, A. W. (1970) The Coming Crisis of Western Sociology. New York: Basic Books.

––– (1968) "The sociologist as partisan: sociology and the welfare state." Amer. Sociologist 3 (May): 103-166.

––– (1962) "Anti-minotaur: the myth of a value-free sociology." Social Problems 9 (Winter): 199-213.

GREEN, L. W. (1969) "East Pakistan: knowledge and use of contraceptives." Studies in Family Planning 39 (March): 9-14.

HAMBLIN, R. L. (1966) "Ratio measurement and sociological theory." Department of Sociology, Washington University, St. Louis. (mimeo)

HAMBRIGHT, T. Z. (1969) "Comparison of information on death certificates and matching 1960 census records: age, marital status, race, nativity, and country of origin." Demography 6 (November): 413-423.

HAUSER, P. (1969) "Comments on Coleman's paper," in R. Bierstedt (ed.) A Design for Sociology: Scope, Objectives, and Methods. Philadelphia: American Academy of Political and Social Science.

HOROWITZ, I. L. (1968) Professing Sociology: Studies in the Life Cycle of Social Science. Chicago: Aldine.

KIRSCHT, J. P. and R. C. DILLEHAY (1967) Dimensions of Authoritarianism: A Review of Research and Theory. Lexington: Univ. of Kentucky Press.

LAZARSFELD, P. F., W. H. SEWELL, and H. L. WILENSKY [eds.] (1967) The Uses of Sociology. New York: Basic Books.

LEWIS, O. (1951) Life in a Mexican Village: Tepoztlan Restudied. Urbana: Univ. of Illinois Press.

LIPSET, S. M. and L. LOWENTHAL [eds.] (1961) Culture and Social Character. New York: Free Press.

LYND, R. S. (1964) Knowledge for What? New York: Grove Press.

McDILL, E. L. (1961) "Anomie, authoritarianism, prejudice, and socio-economic status: an attempt at clarification." Social Forces 39 (December): 239-245.

MEEHAN, E. J. (1968) Explanation in Social Science: A System Paradigm. Homewood, Ill.: Dorsey.

MILLER, S. M. and F. RIESSMAN (1961) " 'Working class authoritarianism': a critique of Lipset." British J. of Sociology 12 (December): 263-276.

MILLS, C. W. (1959) The Sociological Imagination. New York: Oxford Univ. Press.

NICOLAUS, M. (1969) "Remarks at ASA convention." Amer. Sociologist 4 (May): 154-156.

PARRY, H. and H. M. CROSSLEY (1950) "Validity of responses to survey questions." Public Opinion Q. 14 (Spring): 61-80.

PHILLIPS, D. L. (1971) Knowledge From What? Theories and Methods in Social Research. Chicago: Rand McNally.

——— and K. J. CLANCY (1970) "Response biases in field studies of mental illness." Amer. Soc. Rev. 35 (June): 503-515.

PRICE, J. L. (1969) Social Facts: Introductory Readings. New York: Macmillan.

REDFIELD, R. (1930) Tepoztlan: A Mexican Village. Chicago: Univ. of Chicago Press.

RIESMAN, D. (1950) The Lonely Crowd. New Haven: Yale Univ. Press.

ROBERTS, A. H. and M. ROKEACH (1956) "Anomie, authoritarinaism, and prejudice: a replication." Amer. J. of Sociology 61 (January): 355-358.

ROSENBERG, M. J. (1967) "Attitude change and foreign policy in the cold war era," in J. N. Rosenau (ed.) Domestic Sources of Foreign Policy. New York: Free Press.

——— (1965) "Images in relation to the policy process: American public opinion on cold war issues," in H. C. Kelman (ed.) International Behavior: A Social Psychological Approach. New York: Holt, Rinehart & Winston.

ROSENTHAL, R. (1966) Experimenter Effects in Behavioral Research. New York: Appleton-Century-Crofts.

SEARS, R. (1951) "Social behavior and personality development," in T. Parsons and E. A. Shils (eds). Toward a General Theory of Action. Cambridge, Mass.: Harvard Univ. Press.

SMELSER, N. J. (1969) "The optimum scope of sociology," in R. Bierstedt (ed.) A Design for Sociology: Scope, Objectives, and Methods. Philadelphia: American Academy of Political and Social Sciences.

——— and J. A. DAVIS [eds.] (1969) Sociology. Englewood Cliffs, N.J.: Prentice-Hall.

SROLE, L. (1956) "Social integration and certain corollaries: an exploratory study." Amer. Soc. Rev. 21 (December): 709-716.

STEMBER, C. H. (1961) Education and Attitude Change. New York: Institute of Human Relations Press.

TILLY, C. (1966) "Letter to the editor." Amer. Sociologist 1 (February): 84.

TUMIN, M. M. (1968) "In dispraise of loyalty." Social Problems 15 (May): 267-279.

Webster's (1964) New World Dictionary. New York: World.

WHYTE, W. F. (1969) "The role of the U.S. professor in developing countries." Amer. Sociologist 4 (February): 19-28.

ABOUT THE CONTRIBUTORS

Arlene Kaplan Daniels is a Research Associate at Scientific Analysis Corporation, San Francisco, California.

Gloria V. Engel is Assistant Professor in the Department of Community Medicine of the University of Southern California.

Carolyn Etheridge is Assistant Professor in the Department of Sociology at New York University.

Thomas P. Ference is Associate Director of Executive Programs at the Graduate School of Business at Columbia University.

Eliot Freidson is Professor in the Department of Sociology at New York University.

Fred H. Goldner is Associate Professor and Chairman in the Department of Sociology at Queens College (CUNY).

Richard H. Hall is Professor in the Department of Sociology at University of Minnesota.

Paul Halmos is Professor and Chairman in the Department of Sociology at University College of Cardiff, United Kingdom.

Marie R. Haug is Associate Professor in the Department of Sociology at Case Western Reserve University.

Lionel S. Lewis is Associate Professor in the Department of Sociology at State University of New York, Buffalo.

Philip M. Marcus is Associate Professor in the Department of Sociology at Michigan State University.

Stephen J. Miller is Associate Dean of the Faculty at Harvard Medical School.

Albert L. Mok is Professor of Organizational Sociology at the University of Antwerp, Belgium.

Paul D. Montagna is Associate Professor in the Department of Sociology Brooklyn College (CUNY).

Robert Perrucci is Professor in the Department of Sociology at Purdue University.

Derek L. Phillips is Professor in the Sociologisch Instittut at Universiteit van Amsterdam, Amsterdam, Netherlands.

R. Richard Ritti is Professor in the College of Human Development at Pennsylvania State University.

George Ritzer is Associate Professor in the Department of Sociology at University of Kansas.

Sheryl K. Ruzek is a Research Associate at Scientific Analysis Corporation, San Francisco, California.

Marvin B. Sussman is Professor in the Department of Sociology at Case Western Reserve University.

Irving K. Zola is Professor in the Department of Sociology at Brandeis University.

AUTHOR INDEX